"*Food IQ* is like having a chef buddy with you at all times, whispering suggestions in your ear. Holzman and Rodbard have a unique ability to drill into the psyches of home cooks and answer the questions they didn't even know they should be asking."

—JOSH SCHERER, cookbook author and cohost of *A Hot Dog Is a Sandwich* podcast

"As a casual foodie who has graduated from using kosher salt to craving yuzu kosho, I believe *Food IQ* is the book I didn't know I needed. With good cheer (and advice for good kimchi!), Daniel and Matt have scaled the kitchen walls that separate professional cooks from curious eaters, and the results are inspiring—not to mention delicious."

—ANDY GREENWALD, critic, showrunner, and cohost of *The Watch* podcast

"*Food IQ* answers every culinary question you never thought to ask, stuffed with wisdom one can only glean from having lived decades as a professional cook. The book bridges the gap between the encyclopedic *Flavor Bible* and a culinary school textbook. It's like a homework assignment from that one teacher in fifth grade that you actually wanted to complete."

—JASON STEWART, DJ and cohost of the *How Long Gone* podcast

FOOD IQ

Also by Daniel Holzman
The Meatball Shop Cookbook

Also by Matt Rodbard
Koreatown: A Cookbook

FOOD IQ

100 Questions, Answers, and Recipes to Raise Your Cooking Smarts

Daniel Holzman and Matt Rodbard

PHOTOGRAPHY BY ED ANDERSON
ILLUSTRATION BY MIGUEL VILLALOBOS

HARPER WAVE

An Imprint of HarperCollinsPublishers

HarperCollins books may be purchased for educational, business, or sales promotional use. For information, please email the Special Markets Department at SPsales@harpercollins.com.

FIRST EDITION
Design: Lizzie Allen
Illustration: Miguel Villalobos
Food styling: Katy Watson
Copy editing: Sharon Silva
Editor: Julie Will

Library of Congress Cataloging-in-Publication Data has been applied for.

ISBN 978-0-06-306281-8

22 23 24 25 26   TC   10 9 8 7 6 5 4 3 2 1

For Cheryl & Sherry
THANK YOU
for passing the torch
And for Felicity, Isaac,
Luna & Warren. The future
is yours to take.

contents

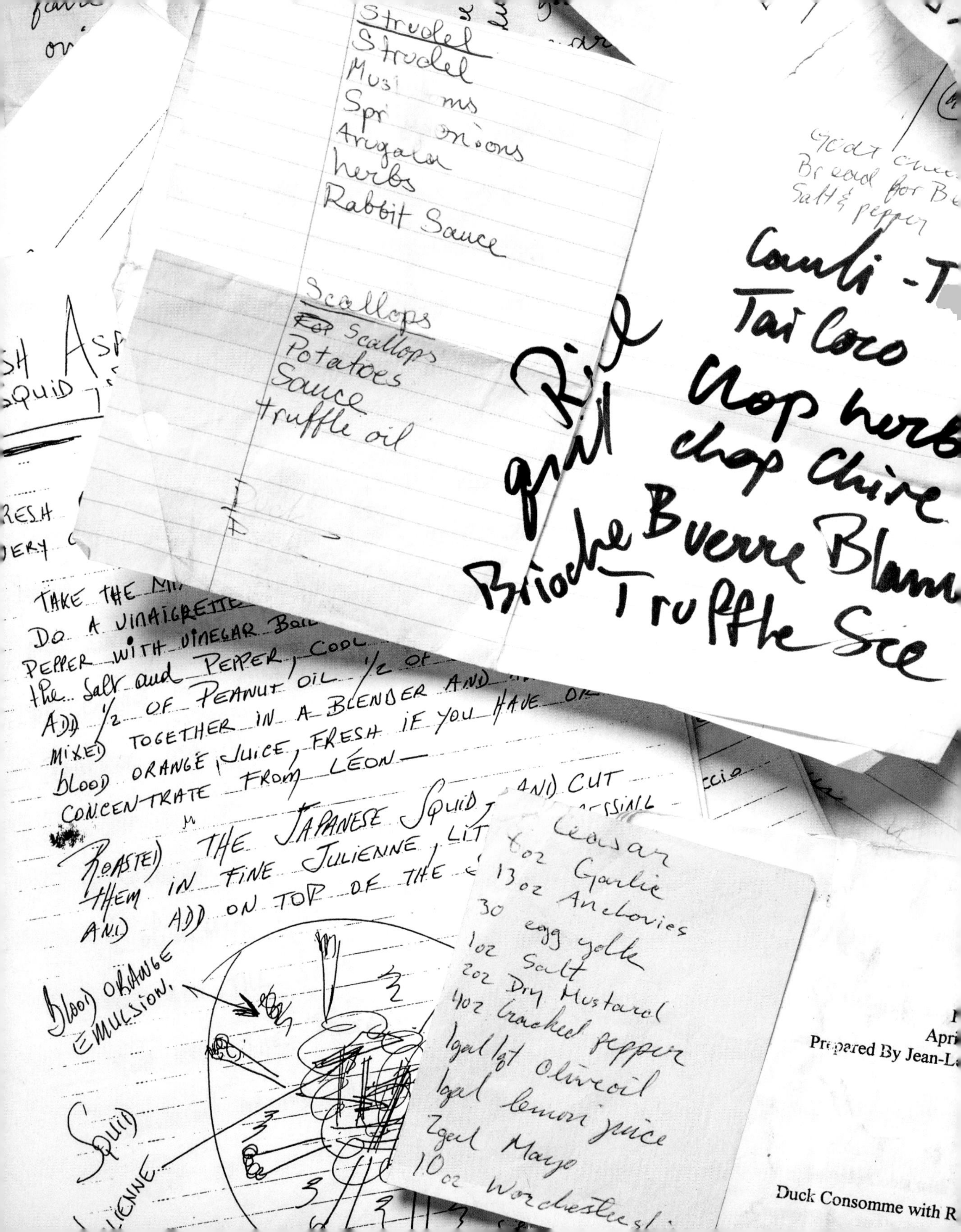

Strudel
Strudel
Mushrooms
Spring onions
Arugula
Herbs
Rabbit Sauce

Scallops
For Scallops
Potatoes
Sauce
truffle oil

Goat cheese
Bread for B
Salt & pepper

Cauli - T
Tai Coco
Chop herb
chop chive
Brioche Buerre Blanc
Truffle Sce

Rice
grill

FRESH ASP
SQUID

FRESH
VERY

TAKE THE MI
DO A VINAIGRETTE
PEPPER WITH VINEGAR B...
the Salt and PEPPER, COOL
ADD ½ OF PEANUT OIL ½ OF
MIXED TOGETHER IN A BLENDER AND
BLOOD ORANGE JUICE, FRESH IF YOU HAVE OF
CONCENTRATE FROM LÉON

ROASTED THE JAPANESE SQUID AND CUT
THEM IN FINE JULIENNE LIT
AND ADD ON TOP OF THE

Caesar
Garlic
4 oz
13 oz Anchovies
30 egg yolks
1 oz Salt
2 oz Dry Mustard
4 oz Cracked Pepper
1 gallqt Olive oil
1 gal lemon juice
2 gal Mayo
10 oz Worchestershi

BLOOD ORANGE
EMULSION

SQUID
JULIENNE

Prepared By Jean-L

Duck Consomme with R

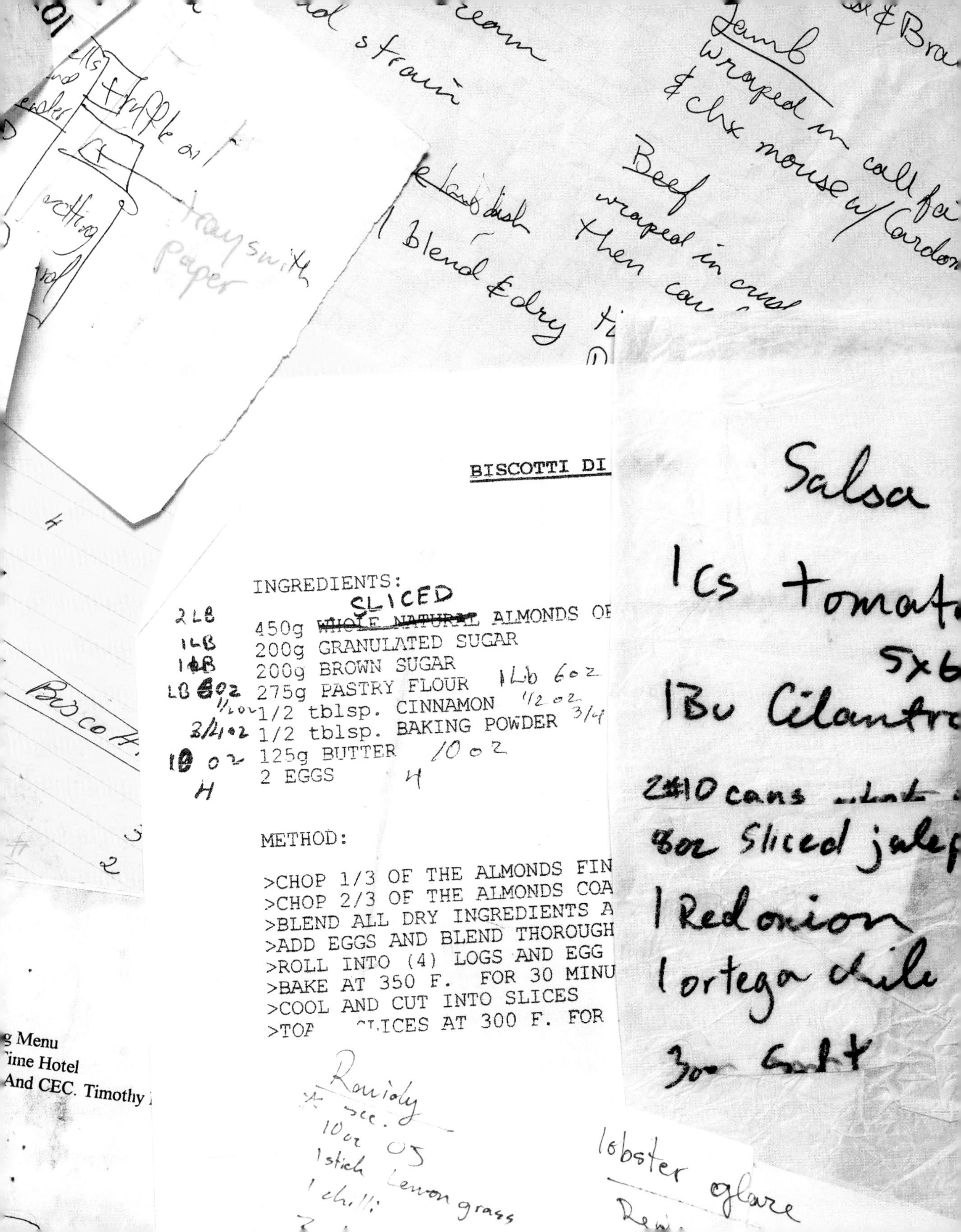

tray with
Paper

strawi

blend & dry ti

Lamb
wrapped in call fai
& chx mousse w/ Cardon

Beef
wrapped in crust
then can

BISCOTTI DI

Salsa

1 cs tomato
5×6
1 Bu Cilantro

2 #10 cans what
8oz sliced jalep
1 Red onion
1 ortega chile
3oz Salt

INGREDIENTS:
SLICED
2 LB   450g WHOLE NATURAL ALMONDS OF
1 LB   200g GRANULATED SUGAR
1 LB   200g BROWN SUGAR
LB 6oz 275g PASTRY FLOUR   1 Lb 6oz
1/2 oz 1/2 tblsp. CINNAMON   1/2 oz
3/4 oz 1/2 tblsp. BAKING POWDER   3/4
10 oz   125g BUTTER   10 oz
  H   2 EGGS   H

METHOD:

>CHOP 1/3 OF THE ALMONDS FIN
>CHOP 2/3 OF THE ALMONDS COA
>BLEND ALL DRY INGREDIENTS A
>ADD EGGS AND BLEND THOROUGH
>ROLL INTO (4) LOGS AND EGG
>BAKE AT 350 F.   FOR 30 MINU
>COOL AND CUT INTO SLICES
>TOP   SLICES AT 300 F. FOR

Biscotti

Ravioly
sce.
10oz   O5
1 stick Lemon grass
1 chili

lobster glaze

Introduction

FOOD WRITER AND EDITOR Matt Rodbard is a confident—though confidently nonprofessional— home cook and tireless asker of questions about food and cooking. As the founder of the James Beard Award–winning food magazine *TASTE*, that's his job, after all. Daniel Holzman is a professional chef, cookbook author, and dedicated home cook—a rare breed of on-the-clock food pro who relishes evenings at home making dinners of clay pot chicken, spaghetti vongole, and mushroom foil yaki for an audience of (sometimes) one. He's a chef who actually makes dinner like a civilian.

Matt and Daniel are very good friends who met when Matt covered the opening of Daniel's Lower East Side restaurant, the Meatball Shop, in 2010 and peppered Daniel with a series of questions about his meatball mix and pork-to-white-bread ratio. It turns out that questions would bring the duo together, and it's questions that continue to cement their friendship. They've written popular columns together for both *Saveur* and *TASTE*, and they talk about food constantly: while texting story ideas to each other, jumping into each other's Instagram feeds, traveling to outer boroughs and far-off continents to taste new foods, and cooking together in their home kitchens in Brooklyn and Los Angeles. Well, in truth, Daniel makes dinner and Matt watches as Daniel grills Akaushi beef and improvises salsa verde to top the roasted Japanese sweet potatoes he pulls out of a rental apartment's aging gas oven. And Matt asks questions along the way—many, many questions.

Food IQ is inspired by Matt and Daniel's constant conversations about food, and it tackles some of the most discussed, though rarely clarified, questions about home cooking and food culture today. In the process, it teaches cooking fundamentals, imparts little-known culinary trivia, and reveals everything you wanted to know about salting meat, cooking in a microwave, making great pizza at home, and acknowledging the Global Pancake Power Rankings™—all in an action-packed format. It is also inspired by Daniel's lived experience as a chef who is constantly asked cooking questions by friends, family, late-night television hosts, random Twitter followers, and anybody who has uttered the line "I was wondering about . . ." in his presence. This is hardly a complaint. Daniel loves talking about food, and he loves educating those willing to listen. Is making your own hummus worth it? Should I cook with MSG? Should I be embarrassed to reach for canned beans? Why is my whole roast chicken always dry? These are a few of his favorite questions. Or more accurately, they are three of the one hundred favorites that are answered in the book.

You might be wondering, how did Daniel and Matt come to the one hundred questions, and how do you actually use this book? The questions were established through the highly scientific process of Daniel and Matt creating a Google Doc, looking at their shelves packed with cookbooks and textbooks, talking, debating, and gently arguing about whether a hamburger is a sandwich (there are no spoilers in this introduction). There was some of that, but the questions are also inspired by those Daniel and Matt are frequently asked on social media and through their work as a cooking educator and food writer, respectively. Early on, they surveyed friends and family (thank you all!), and they tapped into their past writing for some of the greatest hits.

Are there more than one hundred questions to answer? Of course. There are enough questions to fill a hundred books! But this first edition of *Food IQ* covers the one hundred most important and timely topics for today's home cook right now—for everyone looking for food enlightenment in 2022 and beyond. Daniel and Matt see you. They call you the Foodie 2.0. Don't wince—*foodie* is a term to celebrate, and this book marks the coronation of a new generation of foodie.

Are You A Foodie 2.0?

Food IQ has a big promise: to help readers cook better and smarter, and to increase their food knowledge along the way. But what exactly is food knowledge, and why do smarts and intuition matter so much more than simply following a recipe? Foodies 2.0 are people who love cooking, eating, and talking about food, but who aren't necessarily as confident behind the burners as they'd like to be. Matt recognized this growing interest in food beyond recipes after founding *TASTE* in 2017. From day one of running the magazine, he was blown away by the sophisticated and passionate reader emails and social media messages he received. There was a real thirst for information about food beyond recipe aggregation and facilitating "getting dinner on the table" (a tired cliché used when addressing an increasingly large and important audience: you). In his opening editor's letter published on February 7, 2017, Matt wrote, "Fish sauce, za'atar, chipotle, 'nduja, Chinese black vinegar, pomegranate molasses, kimchi—these are some of the new ingredients that are found in the modern American pantry, and *TASTE* will publish stories that clarify and celebrate this exciting evolution." Five years later, that pantry has grown, as have the questions.

Increasing your food knowledge is about more than learning how to braise chicken thighs (though this is addressed herewith as well). Food knowledge is essential cultural currency, cashable at dinner parties with friends, around the water cooler (or in Slack channels), and on the front lines of social media. This is the book that tackles some of the most prescient food topics of these times (as well as "wtf is a gastrique?"). *Food IQ* is your buddy the chef sitting down over a glass of Michter's to talk about investing in a mandoline. It's your buddy the food writer, sitting down over a cup of naturally processed Ethiopian pour-over coffee to talk about why shrimp are not overrated, just frequently overcooked, and leading an exciting discussion on modern culinary anthropology. Daniel and Matt are here for you—as home cooks, as fans of food writing and television, and as human beings. Just as the great game maker Milton Bradley emblazoned it takes "A minute to learn . . . A lifetime to master" on his board game Othello, learning to cook takes time, and you won't master all of the topics and techniques covered in this book overnight. But food is a lifelong journey, and Daniel and Matt are your guides as you read and cook through this book. And hopefully much longer.

How To Use This Book

How do you eat a dinosaur? One bite at a time. This is Daniel's way of saying that learning to cook is a series of incremental steps taken over time. This journey starts with a question, which twists and turns over seven thematic chapters, starting with some of the most important basic information and progressing to more advanced topics. Earlier chapters tackle fundamentals (such as "What is brown butter, and why is everybody cooking with it?" and "Fresh herbs v. dried herbs: When is it okay to reach for McCormick?"). There's a chapter addressing tools and technology (knives, ovens, woks, microwaves, blenders, Chemex, and the Instant Pot are all covered), while later chapters focus on busting myths ("Why is the farmers' market so damn expensive?") and mastering hacks ("My roasted vegetables never get properly crispy. How do I make that happen?"). Finally, the book rounds out with Daniel and Matt's twelve favorite dishes to cook forever (including pizza, scrambled eggs, pancakes, and the chicken cutlet) and some weekend cooking projects that are well worth their time.

Although the book can be read from front to back, each question and its answer stands alone, allowing you to dive into the questions that interest you most. There's an emphatic call to invest in a thirteen-dollar digital scale, and a concise breakdown of how to

make greens at home taste like the greens at your favorite Chinese restaurant. There's straight talk about why it's perfectly okay to cook with frozen fish, and why canned tomatoes from California are a better bet than the prized (and sometimes fraudulent) San Marzanos from Mount Vesuvius. The secret to making guacamole at home taste like it came from your favorite Mexican restaurant? It's not what you would guess in one hundred attempts.

Recipes Enter the Picture

Each question includes an exciting recipe developed by Daniel, stretching from snacks (Five-Minute Rosemary Sourdough Crackers) and vegetable sides (Leeks Gribiche, Whole Salt-Roasted Onions) to fish and meat courses (Salmon Porchetta, Chicken Basquaise, Tamales de Rajas) and the world's greatest hash browns, Pommes Anna. These recipes play a critical role in increasing your food knowledge and learning to cook smarter. Not only are they extremely cookable, but each of the one hundred recipes is also directly related to the question at hand, serving as a mini experiment to help you, the reader, better understand and absorb the concepts addressed in the question. Daniel and Matt promise that, after reading the question and answer and then cooking the recipe through, you will gain a deeper understanding of home cooking.

The Experts

While Daniel and Matt led the conversation, it was very clear from the start that *Food IQ* needed more (many more!) voices than theirs. Fortunately, they have an incredible group of friends and colleagues who were willing to contribute their knowledge and expertise. Daniel and Matt went directly to the source for information on everything from the global influence of curry powder and the disputed origins of adobo to cooking with MSG (it's really, truly okay and amazing) to tracing the twisting path of the natural wine boom. The knowledge from the more than twenty-five cookbook authors, chefs, bakers, journalists, and mothers (two, to be precise) interviewed for the book plays out in the detailed answers as well as the short and extremely fun interviews in the recurring "Friends of Food IQ" sections.

In some instances, these interviews led to even more questions, requiring a complete rethink of the answer. Oh, the editing! In others, Daniel and Matt got to catch up with an old friend about a topic that is near and dear to them. One thousand tons of gratitude to everyone who gave their time, knowledge, and, in a couple of cases, even recipes. 🙌 to (in order of appearance) **Simone Tong**, **Cathy Erway**, **Helen Rosner**, **Shirley Chung**, **Sumi Ali**, **Ina Garten**, **Deb Perelman**, **Cara Nicoletti**, **Sherry Yard**, **Eric Ripert**, **Kyle Itani**, **Skye LaTorre**, **Leela Punyaratabandhu**, **Ligaya Mishan**, **Meherwan Irani**, **José R. Ralat**, **Chantal Martineau**, **Sherry Holzman**, **Claire Saffitz**, **Cheryl Rodbard**, **Thérèse Nelson**, **Priya Krishna**, **Andrea Nguyen**, **Roy Choi**, and **Yotam Ottolenghi**.

Cook, Read, Cook, Read, Ask More Questions . . .

When this book was being written, Daniel and Matt intended for readers not only to flip to the recipes that look interesting to them but also to read through the questions and answers as if they were the latest from Ann Patchett or Viet Thanh Nguyen. You can sit down and metabolize the book cover to cover, or you can pick and choose what most interests you. The hope is that the experience is both educational and fun (and the fact that you've gotten to the end of the book's introduction makes the authors think that you're already on the right track).

After reading about canned beans, dashi, nixtamalization, making yogurt, or faking pit-smoked barbecue, perhaps other questions will come to mind. To close, don't be a stranger. Daniel and Matt are here to answer, discuss, and debate any of the following one hundred questions and any more that pop up for their next book. You can reach out to them (@chefholzman and @mattrodbard). And with that, on to question number one.

FOOD IQ

Misunderstood, Undiscovered, Overlooked, and Underappreciated . . . Ingredients!

Ingredients are the foundation of cooking—the ones and zeros for the software called recipes—and sourcing the proper produce, proteins, acids, and spices is critical to success in the kitchen. But with such a staggering variety of ingredients available everywhere, from big-box grocery stores to fancy specialty food shops and incredible Asian supermarkets, there's much to be confused by. In this chapter, Daniel and Matt explain the misunderstood and uncover the unappreciated.

Which onion should I use: red, white, or yellow?

→ **HAVE YOU EVER WONDERED** why so many recipes call for onions? What's the reason for all that chopping and slicing, and are those tears on the cutting board really worth it? It comes down to one word: sweetness. Onions hold a lot of sugar, and by adding a diced onion to a braise or sauce, you're ramping up the sweet—while amplifying the surrounding flavors—in a way that cannot be replicated by simply adding granulated sugar.

When considering the different types of onions—mainly red, white, and yellow (also called Spanish)—it's important to keep in mind that each serves a specific purpose, though they can be substituted for one another in a pinch. If you were to taste each of them blindfolded, you'd be hard-pressed to tell the difference. That said, each has its strengths.

"Sweet" onions like Maui, Bermuda, Vidalia, and Walla Walla have roughly the same amount of sugar as the common types. The reason they taste sweeter is because they have less sulfur, the compound found in the soil that makes onions taste sharper (and less sweet). This is why raw onions are often cooked over low heat, a process called sweating, which literally sweats the sulfur out of them to produce the milder cooked onion flavor people love.

Now here are the differences. A **red onion** is used primarily for its color, which is why it's favored in pickling, in salads, and as that slice in your burger. If you cook a red onion, the color is lost.

The **white onion** has more tender flesh and is less sharply flavored than the other onions. It's also good for pickling and is prominently used in Latin American cooking (think pico de gallo) and in ceviche. White onions are great raw when used in smaller amounts as an accent. Think of how well the bracing bite of finely diced raw onion works on a Chicago-style hot dog.

The **yellow onion** is the workhorse for both home and restaurant kitchens. Have you ever walked by a restaurant in the morning during a delivery? No matter if it's an Italian, Greek, Mexican, Chinese, or Denny's, you will undoubtedly spot a fifty-pound bag of yellow onions being dropped off. Spanish onions are the foundation of Latin and Mediterranean cooking and the anchor of sofrito and mirepoix. They are what you use for soups, stews, and for making stocks. They're the sautéed onions that go on top of your burger, and the ones you turn to for caramelized onions (see page 160).

When buying an onion at the supermarket, think of it like an apple. It should be firm, with no soft patches or black spots. Yellow onions have the longest shelf life, and in general, onions can last in the crisper of a refrigerator for up to three months.

The question Daniel often receives is: How do I chop an onion without watering eyes? Once again, it all comes back to sulfur. If you use the sharpest knife you own to slice an onion, less sulfur will be released into the surrounding air. With a dull knife, you are crushing the onion, not slicing it, which releases a troublesome vapor that leads to discomfort. As for those chefs asked to chop thirty pounds of onions before service? You get used to it, according to Daniel. "It's like an Everest explorer kvetching about the cold." •

HOW TO SLICE AN ONION

When you slice an onion, you choose between rings and Parisian (French cut), the longitudinal or lengthwise cut from the bolster (the root end that holds the onion layers together) to the flowering end. An onion's fibers run longitudinally, so cutting horizontally will sever the fibers, creating rings, which are great for raw and pickled preparations or quick hard sautés. A Parisian cut will keep the fibers intact, which is great when you want to keep the pieces from falling apart, as when caramelizing onions for French onion soup.

WHOLE SALT-ROASTED ONIONS

Onions play a supporting role so often that they can be taken for granted. By slowly roasting them whole in their skin, the basic yellow onion transforms into anything but basic—deeply caramelized, with soft creamy flesh and insanely concentrated sweetness. Serve them as an appetizer with a drizzle of your best olive oil and a squeeze of lemon, or use them to accompany a roast chicken or steak on a special occasion.

Serves 4

---

4 large, round yellow onions

2 cups kosher salt

6 tablespoons extra-virgin olive oil

1 lemon, quartered

1. Preheat the oven to 350°F.

2. Cut off the top of each onion 1 inch below the flowering tip to expose a small circle of flesh. Divide the salt into four equal piles on a sheet pan and nestle an onion, cut side up, in each pile. Avoid cutting the bolster of an onion unless necessary to keep the onion standing upright, and if you do cut, be careful not to penetrate too deeply. Drizzle each onion with ½ tablespoon of the oil.

3. Place the pan in the oven, being careful not to dislodge the onions from their perch. Roast until the tops are a deep golden brown and a chopstick inserted through the top pierces the flesh without resistance, about 4 hours.

4. Remove the pan from the oven and let the onions rest for 5 minutes before lifting them off the pan. Peel off the three or four dry, burnt outer layers from each onion and then trim off the bolster. Drizzle the remaining 4 tablespoons oil evenly over the onions and serve with the lemon wedges for squeezing on top.

What's my olive oil strategy?

→ **YOU KNOW THAT EXPENSIVE** Thom Browne suit you bought seven years ago and wore only once? And now you're twenty-five pounds heavier and it doesn't fit? (Besides, the custom tailoring is out of style.) Well, the same idea holds true with fancy olive oil. It's got a shelf life, and if you're going to spend the money on it, you better plan to cook with it. This should be your strategy.

Olive oil can be broken into three categories, priced at roughly $10, $20, and $35 or more per liter. Each has a purpose, and we'll call them mild, fancy, and finishing. The mild stuff, most of what you find in your average grocery store under labels like Colavita and California Olive Ranch, is perfect for cooking and using in salad dressings—and that's it. It doesn't have much flavor, and it doesn't cost an arm and a leg, so there's no need to be stingy. When heating olive oil to sauté garlic or fry an egg, the subtle fragrance evaporates off, so using anything other than the mild stuff would be a waste.

Fancy olive oil, usually sold in smaller 500-milliliter bottles, is not for cooking or for making dressings. The strong flavor that distinguishes this category can be bitter and off-putting when mixed with acids like lemon and vinegar. These oils should be used, instead, for marinating—say, in a Spanish tuna conserva, or with roasted peppers. In these instances, a quality olive oil is integral to the final result, though it cannot be too extreme, with overpowering peppery or grassy flavors, or it will clash and overpower.

Intensity is reserved for finishing oils, where a small bottle sells for as much as fifty dollars. Sold in specialty stores (look for the Italian brand Laudemio to start), they should be reserved strictly for drizzling over finished bowls of cacio e pepe, seasoning your flat minestrone, or sprinkling over freshly baked focaccia. Finishing oils are intense, often spicy, and pungent, and they have the shortest shelf life of them all. Any good olive oil has a packed-on date printed on the label, so check for it before you buy to make sure you're getting the current vintage to maximize shelf life.

All olive oils, no matter the quality, should be stored in a cool, dark place. The worst spot to keep your olive oil is in the cabinet above your stove. Excessive heat and even sunlight will turn a good olive oil bad—and fast—transforming the golden liquid with notes of sunshine and spice into something closer to a box of crayons or old motor oil. Daniel keeps his best olive oils in the refrigerator, where they will last for up to a year. ●

SPAGHETTI AGLIO, OLIO, E PEPERONCINO
TOASTED GARLIC AND OLIVE OIL

Serves 2

Kosher salt

8 ounces dried spaghetti

½ cup mild extra-virgin olive oil

6 cloves garlic, thinly sliced

1 tablespoon crushed Calabrian chiles in oil, or 1 teaspoon red chile flakes soaked in 1 teaspoon white wine vinegar

½ cup fresh flat-leaf parsley, roughly chopped

¼ cup freshly grated pecorino romano cheese

This recipe, for one of the great Roman pasta dishes, is as simple as they come. But simple doesn't mean boring. Talk about garlic, olive oil (the mild variety), aged pecorino, and crushed Calabrian chiles in oil (the authors favor Tutto Calabria brand). And if you don't like spice, feel free to use less or skip the chiles completely.

1. Bring a large pot of heavily salted water (⅓ cup salt per 4 quarts water) to a rolling boil over high heat. Add the pasta and cook, stirring occasionally, for 1 minute less than the package instructions suggest for al dente. Drain, reserving 1 cup of the cooking water.

2. While the pasta is cooking, heat the oil and garlic in a large frying pan over medium-low heat and cook, stirring frequently, until the garlic just begins to color, about 3 minutes. You don't want the garlic to brown intensely, so add a few tablespoons of water to cool the pan if necessary. (Beware, as the oil may splatter a bit.)

3. Add the chiles and half of the parsley and cook, stirring continuously, for 1 more minute. Then add a few tablespoons of the pasta cooking water to arrest the cooking and set the pan aside off the heat until the pasta is ready.

4. Add the drained pasta and half of the reserved cooking water to the pan with the garlic mixture and finish cooking over medium-high heat, stirring constantly, just until the water evaporates, about 1 minute. (You can add the rest of the reserved water if you prefer your pasta less al dente.) The sauce should coat the pasta evenly.

5. Toss the pasta with the remaining parsley and serve immediately, garnished with the remaining pecorino.

How should I think about salt, and is there a big difference between Diamond Crystal and Morton kosher salt?

→ **UNDERSTANDING HOW TO USE** salt is important. No, scratch that. Understanding salt is critical. It's foundational. It can be the key to whether your roasted vegetables, pasta sauces, chicken soup, and vinaigrettes end up outstanding or just meh. This is because your tongue can taste only a few flavors (95 percent of what you taste comes from what you smell), and salt is one of them.

Kosher salt is widely evangelized as the ideal salt for home cooking, and for good reason. Its coarse texture makes it easy to measure, and its larger crystal structure makes each pinch less salty (compared to the finely granulated iodized stuff you find in the shakers on the tables of your favorite diner). Plus, kosher salt has a grit to it that feels right in the hand and offers a satisfying crunch in the mouth. Yet not all kosher salt is created equal.

The two most popular brands of kosher salt are Diamond Crystal, which made a major marketing push with chefs in the mid-1990s, becoming an industry standard, and Morton, a traditional home-kitchen favorite. Their textures are very different, and they work differently in all recipes, from meat cures to your weekend batch of brownies. Diamond Crystal is fluffier and pyramid shaped, while Morton is rolled flat and more condensed. If you weigh out a pound of each, they contain the same amount of saltiness. But when scooped in a teaspoon (the most common method for home cooks), Morton granules pack much tighter, effectively delivering double the saltiness!

The difference is so great that Carla Lalli Music, former food director at *Bon Appétit*, implemented a Diamond-Crystal-or-die edict for her test-kitchen workers. Carla knows things. The key, with whatever salt you end up using, is to stay consistent with the type and even the brand. For those pressured moments when your beurre blanc needs a kiss of salinity, you have to know exactly what each pinch of salt will deliver.

Another thing to keep in mind: home cooks often misuse exotic and expensive salts. Contrary to the persuasive advertising, there's absolutely zero discernible difference in flavor among salts. Whether pulled from crevices in lava rocks in Hawaii's coastal waters or chiseled from a Himalayan mine in Pakistan, all salt tastes the same, regardless of its color or cost. But there's no need to ban them from your shelves, as a little texture and a pop of color go a long way when finishing a dish. So continue using your fleur de sel and your Maldon, but be sure they're served intact, delivering their intended textural crunch. ●

FLAVORED SALTS

Flavored salts, whether blends or a single type, are a perfect way to correct or enhance a finished dish quickly, making them a good thing to have on hand. For example, Daniel likes to use a pinch of lemon salt made with citrus zest, coriander seeds, and rosemary to add subtle nuance to roast chicken or fish, or he will deploy a smoked salt to inject an intense burst of wood fire to anything grilled or seared. The downside of cooking prolifically with any one mix is, well, everything will start to taste like that great mix, so choose your battles wisely, and when in doubt, opt on the side of subtlety.

DILL PICKLES

2 hearty side portions

---

28 grams (1 ounce) kosher salt

4 cups water

6 unwaxed Kirby cucumbers, halved lengthwise

A few dill sprigs

2 or 3 cloves garlic

½ teaspoon red chile flakes, or more if you like your pickles extra spicy

Brine pickles are vegetables preserved through wild yeast fermentation. They are a little less sour than your traditional store-bought pickle, allowing the vegetables' flavor to shine through. The process sounds fancy, but it couldn't be any easier, and this recipe works well with not only cucumbers but also most vegetables that you'd think to pickle, such as carrots, turnips, sunchokes, garlic, and onions. You can play around with the flavoring ingredients, but the salt-to-water ratio, which yields a 3 percent salt-brine solution, must be followed for the best results. (You'll need to get out your scale for this recipe.) To preserve their freshness, many commercially sold cucumbers are coated with an edible wax, which interferes with the pickling process. So make sure you buy unwaxed cucumbers at a farmers' market or from an organic grocer.

1. In a saucepan, combine the salt and water over high heat and bring just to a boil, stirring to dissolve the salt. Remove from the heat and let cool completely. This is your 3 percent salt-brine solution.

2. Pack the cucumbers, dill, garlic, and chile flakes into a clean, widemouthed quart jar. The cucumbers should fit snugly, as you don't want them to float once the brine is added.

3. Pour in the cool brine solution. The cucumbers should be completely submerged. If necessary, wedge them down so they don't float above the liquid (a lid from a to-go plastic pint container, trimmed to fit, works perfectly for this).

4. Cover the jar with a loose lid (do not tighten it down, as gas needs to escape) and leave it in a cool, dark place, such as your pantry cabinet. (If the jar is filled to the brim, the liquid may bubble out, so it's best to set the jar on a tray or in a bowl.)

5. After 48 hours, there should be some bubbling action. If there's none, you will need an extra day. Fermentation is temperature dependent; the hotter your kitchen, the faster the process. Once you see some bubbles forming, tighten the lid and transfer the jar to the refrigerator to slow the process. Your pickles will be ready to eat 3 to 4 days from the time you put them in the refrigerator. Be aware that these pickles will keep fermenting, becoming more sour with time. But after a few weeks, they will turn soft and mushy, so eat them when they're good and ready, around 7 to 10 days.

Is it okay to cook with frozen seafood?

→ **IT'S A FACT OF** life and of culinary consequence: the smaller the animal, the faster its meat goes bad. Let's take the scallop. Fresh off the day boat (the day the mollusk has been pulled from the water and lands on your plate), the scallop is sweet and smacking of the sea. On day two it is still delicious, just a little less sweet. But by day six, nobody wants to sear that sucker.

The point is, we enjoy the hell out of seared scallops. And we want scallop nigiri at the sushi bar all the time (Sundays included—sorry, Bourdain). So how does this work if you don't live near a dock in Portland, Maine? We've got good news: Unless you were dining at Le Bernardin, the restaurant scallops you ate were very likely previously frozen. That's the case with most of the seafood we eat. And this is okay!

A quick FYI: The whole snapper, halibut, monkfish, tilapia, and turbot resting on beds of crushed ice at Whole Foods were frozen, too. Technology has come a long way over the past decade, and that iPhone sitting in your pocket isn't the only example. These days, fish is being cleaned, portioned, and frozen right on the freaking boat! The faster and colder you freeze something, the better the outcome, and the IQF technology (short for individual quick freezing) is close to perfect. So even if you haven't realized it, you love frozen fish, too. Then what's the stigma around frozen fish all about? A lot of it is left over from a bygone era, but you still need to pay attention to the sourcing of fish.

So, how do you cook frozen seafood, specifically the kind you pull directly from the freezer, as opposed to the previously frozen fish from the market counter? Fishmongers are professionals, but you're paying a premium for them to defrost, display, and discard any old product. Big-box sellers like Costco and Walmart sell large bags of mahi-mahi, halibut, and salmon fillets, and much of it is excellent. But you need to know how to handle it.

When cooking with these icy fish bricks, the most important thing is to defrost them slowly, ideally in the refrigerator overnight, for a gradual thaw. We've all run frozen meat under the tap in an act of desperation, but fish is way more fragile than meat, and the rapid thaw can lead to soggy results. Next, pick frozen seafood that has a neutral flavor, like shrimp, scallops, and tuna. More flavorful fatty fish, like salmon, is often hit or miss—and the quality can vary greatly from bag to bag, even when buying the same brand. Last, and most important, choose a recipe that lends itself to the product on hand. Instead of searing with a simple burst of lemon juice, which you would reserve for fresh fish, think about cooking with bolder sauces that will complement your catch. Consider recipes with a tomato base, like bouillabaisse, or marinades like lemony salmoriglio and the all-purpose misoyaki, which complement the qualities of the fish while masking its imperfections ●

GINDARA MISOYAKI
MISO COD

Serves 2

¼ cup white miso

⅓ cup mirin

¼ cup sake

⅓ cup packed light brown sugar

2 (6-ounce) frozen cod fillets

Miso black cod is a dish traditional to Japan but popularized by the celebrity chef Nobu Matsuhisa in New York City in the early 2000s. Now you see this recipe everywhere, from traditional omakase counters to high-end Japanese fusion restaurants. The reason is the flexibility and practicality of the preparation. When you freeze fish, it breaks the cell structure, making the fish slightly mushy once defrosted. So the idea here is to apply a pronounced marinade—made with miso, mirin, sake, and brown sugar—that will mask some of the imperfections of the frozen fish while firming up the flaky flesh.

1. In a shallow bowl just large enough to hold the fish, stir together the miso, mirin, sake, and brown sugar, mixing well. Coat the frozen fish completely with the miso mixture, cover, and refrigerate for at least 12 hours or up to 3 days. Alternatively, a plastic freezer bag works perfectly for marinating the fish.

2. When ready to cook, position an oven rack in the middle of the oven and preheat the broiler. Line a sheet pan with parchment paper. Transfer the fish to the prepared pan. Spoon a few teaspoons of the marinade over the top of each fillet, discarding the rest.

3. Broil the fish until just cooked through, about 5 minutes. A metal skewer or chopstick should pass through the center with little or no force. Note that the sugars will caramelize, and the fish will blacken but won't be burned. Serve warm.

I love the greens at my favorite Chinese restaurant. Can I make those at home?

→ **MATT AND DANIEL SPENT** many, many nights (and mornings and early afternoons) driving and taking the train to Chinatown in New York, San Francisco, and Los Angeles—and, well, visiting China too. Yes, there were some exhilarating grocery shopping adventures, but those trips were mainly spent eating lacquered ducks plucked from roast-house windows and bowls of hand-pulled noodles, or smoothing out hangovers with morning dim sum feasts or late-night cauldrons of Chengdu-style hot pot. Looking back across all the meals, one dish that consistently stands out is the ubiquitous platter of delicately cooked greens. Tender and sweet, sometimes crunchy, and always with a slap of salt, a plate of yu choy ("oil vegetable"; bok choy's tender cousin), ong choy (morning glory or water spinach), or dou miao (pea shoots) is the perfect accompaniment to any meal.

Shopping for produce at a Chinese grocery store can be intimidating for the uninitiated. The sheer variety of greens, piled high for inspection, is daunting. Cooking them can also be intimidating, which Daniel admits he felt until spending the time to learn about the ingredients. What he observed was that the greens are actually quite easygoing and somewhat interchangeable, lending themselves to quick cooking techniques, most notably blanching or sautéing. The next time you find yourself at an Asian market shopping for freshly pressed sesame oil, fermented Sichuan peppers, or Choco Pies, pick a bunch of greens at random and cook away. You won't be disappointed. ●

Born in Chengdu, China, SIMONE TONG has lived and studied in Hong Kong, Beijing, Macau, Singapore, and Australia. Simone, who holds degrees in economics and psychology, is currently the chef-owner of Little Tong Noodle Shop in New York City.

What's your favorite greens and sauce combination?

I love gai lan (Chinese broccoli) with oyster sauce, but my favorite is a stir-fry of pea shoots with garlic. Chinese pea shoots are always more tender. I'm not sure whether it's a different variety of pea—maybe it's the snow peas that they use? I also love morning glory with shrimp paste, but that's more of a Southeast Asian take.

How do I know which oyster sauce to buy? Which one is the best?

Lee Kum Kee invented oyster sauce—that one is the best. The company was founded by Cantonese from Hong Kong, which is by the ocean.

Why are vegetables so inexpensive in Chinese supermarkets, and should I be suspicious of their quality?

No. Chinatown is cheap because of their short supply chain. The markets have direct connections to their farmers; it's a different system that pulls out the middlemen.

GAI LAN (CHINESE BROCCOLI) WITH OYSTER SAUCE, FRIED GARLIC, AND SESAME

Often overlooked amid plates of dan dan noodles and crispy duck, simply prepared greens are a true highlight of Chinese restaurant menus. Whether stir-fried, stewed in broth, or blanched, greens often steal the show. We are calling for gai lan (Chinese broccoli) here, but this dish can be made with any of the soft greens found in your local Asian market. The trick to sweet and crispy fried garlic is blanching the slices, which hydrates the flesh so it cooks evenly before browning. This is a great recipe on which to test–carefully!– your mandoline skills (see page 60).

Serves 4

Kosher salt

2 large bunches gain lan, tough stem ends trimmed and discarded (about 1 pound total)

¼ cup oyster sauce

1 tablespoon toasted sesame seeds

Garlic Chips for garnish (recipe follows)

1. Bring a large pot of heavily salted water to a boil. Add the gai lan and blanch until just tender, about 3 minutes. Drain, rinse under cold water, then drain again and dry, gently squeezing out any excess water.

2. Put the gai lan into a large bowl, drizzle with the oyster sauce, and toss to coat, then plate. Garnish with the sesame seeds and garlic chips just before serving.

Garlic Chips

Makes about ½ cup

8 cloves garlic, thinly sliced lengthwise on a mandoline

1 teaspoon kosher salt

2 cups vegetable oil

1. In a small pot, combine the garlic with cold water to cover and bring to a rolling boil over high heat. Remove from the heat, drain immediately, and dry the slices on a paper towel. While the water heats, pound the salt in a mortar with a pestle or grind in a spice grinder until reduced to dusty flecks that will stick to the hot crispy garlic.

2. In the same small pot, combine the oil and blanched garlic and heat slowly over medium heat. Meanwhile, ready a small plate with a paper towel (called a landing pad in restaurants). Cook the garlic until it just begins to brown, about 5 minutes. Then, using a small fine-mesh strainer, lift the garlic from the oil and transfer it to the towel-lined plate. Season the garlic with the salt while it is still hot. Let the garlic-scented oil cool, then transfer it to an airtight container and use to bring a subtle roasted garlic flavor to anything cooked with it, such as the rib eye on page 114.

What is brown butter, and why is everybody cooking with it?

→ **OVER THE PAST DECADE** or so, Big Brown Butter has quietly infiltrated our home kitchens and our bodies, systematically moving from house to house and overtaking our central nervous systems—forcing our fingers to type "brown butter baking recipe" into search bars on phones and computers. Or so it would seem. Brown butter is everywhere, and to this day, the food-media industrial complex loves a great brown butter yarn—and it makes sense: brown butter adds an intoxicating nutty flavor that is captivating, mysterious, and intensely delicious. But how did we get here? Allow the authors to clear things up a little.

Butter consists of three components: fat, milk solids, and water. If you were to melt a stick of butter slowly on the stove, pour it into a clear-glass tumbler, and let it cool off, you would have a thick layer of cloudy butterfat at the top and a thin layer of dissolved milk solids at the bottom. Clarified butter, or ghee, is the pure butterfat that can be poured off the top, and it is used in all sorts of cool things (see below). But it's the thin layer of dissolved milk solids that we're here to discuss.

When you heat butter in a pan to more than 175°F, these milk solids—which have a deep sweetness and sharp acidity—start to caramelize and will eventually burn if you aren't careful. We've all left butter on the stove for too long and returned to a black, bubbling, bitter pool of yuck. To make brown butter is to find the exact moment when the solids have caramelized to a shade of, you guessed it, brown. Thank you, Mr. Maillard, for discovering this beautiful browning reaction. The fat is left scented with the sweet and nutty flavor. This takes a little patience and around fifteen minutes of low-heat cooking, but it lasts for a month in the fridge, so feel free to make a big batch when you do. But why do we love it so much?

Take a sugar cookie, for example, and swap out the regular butter with brown butter. The cookie's crunch, shape, and frosting are all the same. But with brown butter, it has a toasted nuttiness that adds another layer of intrigue and a deliciousness that kills at the company cookie swap. You can compare it to cooking a rib eye. It's perfectly okay when done over a low and slow flame, but cooking it over high heat gives the steak a brown crust that improves both texture and flavor development.

Classic applications of brown butter can be found across the sweet and savory spectrum, from France's famous tarte Tatin, an upside-down apple tart baked with brown butter caramel, to the puckeringly sour trout Grenobloise.

Brown butter can be used as a condiment as well. Charlie Bird, a restaurant in New York City, famously serves a scallop crudo with lemon, brown butter, and salt. The result is an astonishingly complex dish from four simple ingredients. Other classic applications include the early 2000s trattoria fixture: butternut squash topped with brown butter and fried sage.

Le Bernardin founding chef Gilbert Le Coze, whose exemplary and progressive fish cooking in the late 1980s was legend, elevated the classic bistro dish of poached skate with capers and brown butter by adding reduced fish stock and using the protein to emulsify the sauce into a silky blanket for the fish. So you can thank M. Le Coze, who died too young of a heart attack in 1994, for bringing skate back into the limelight.

Brown butter is one of few true panacea ingredients. It's comforting, interesting, accessible, and affordable, and it makes already good things great. It's easy to implement and difficult to mess up (just watch the pan!). So while we may collectively cringe at the brown butter–scented candles, we will always hold it near and dear in the pan and on the plate. ●

HOW DO I COOK WITH CLARIFIED BUTTER?

Remember that thick layer of clear fat that rises to the top when butter is heated? Pour that off and you've got yourself bona fide clarified butter, also widely known by its Indian name, ghee. It is a versatile ingredient that can be used to fry, sauté, or grill with the flavor of butter up to an incredibly high 465°F without burning. It's also lactose-free, and it meshes with popular paleo and Whole30 diet plans.

You can purchase ghee in shelf-stable tubs at health food stores, international supermarkets, and Whole Foods. (You can also make it yourself—quickly and for a lot less money.) In Indian cooking, ghee is used to unlock freshly ground and toasted spices in a process called tempering. Start with a dal or sambar from one of your favorite Indian cookbook authors. Daniel and Matt love *Indian-ish* by Priya Krishna and *My Two Souths* by Asha Gomez. Or try replacing oil with clarified butter the next time you roast fingerling potatoes.

TROUT GRENOBLOISE

Serves 2

2 (5-ounce) skin-on trout fillets

Kosher salt and freshly ground black pepper

8 tablespoons (1 stick) unsalted butter

2 slices white sandwich bread, crusts removed and cut into ⅛-inch cubes

2 tablespoons vegetable oil

½ cup all-purpose flour

2 tablespoons capers, drained

2 tablespoons chopped fresh flat-leaf parsley

2 lemons, supreme segmented and cut into ¼-inch triangles, juice reserved

This is the first classic French dish Eric Ripert taught Daniel when Daniel went to work at Le Bernardin, and it remains one of his favorites. Crispy trout skin and crunchy croutons are bathed in warm brown butter and balanced by bright acidity from lemon segments. A couple of key techniques are used here that are important to master. The first is to supreme a lemon into segments–a tricky cutting technique that works with any citrus to remove all of the bitter rind and fibrous pith, yielding only the tender flesh for presentation. Check out YouTube for a quick tutorial. The second is the use of cold and/or wet ingredients to arrest the cooking of dry ingredients in fat. Butter can quickly turn from brown to burnt black if the capers aren't added at just the right moment to instantly cool the pan.

1. Season the trout fillets on both sides with salt and pepper and set aside.

2. In a sauté pan, heat 4 tablespoons of the butter over medium-high heat. While the butter heats, set a fine-mesh strainer over a small heatproof bowl and line a small plate with a folded paper towel. When the butter is foaming hot, add the bread cubes and toast, stirring constantly, until golden brown, about 3 minutes. Remove from the heat and immediately pour the contents of the pan into the strainer to drain off any excess butter. Sprinkle the croutons with salt and transfer to the towel-lined plate to absorb any excess fat.

3. In a sauté pan large enough to lay the fillets flat and side by side without crowding, heat the oil over medium-high heat until just smoking. (Alternatively, cook the fillets in two batches, and hold the first one in a low oven until both are cooked.) While the oil is heating, pat the fish dry with a paper towel, then dredge the skin side in the flour and shake off the excess. When the oil is ready, add the fillets, skin side down, and cook until crispy and golden brown on the first side, about 4 minutes. Then flip the fillets and cook the underside for an additional minute. Remove from the pan, pat the fillets with a paper towel, and then arrange them, skin side up, on warmed individual plates.

4. Wipe the pan clean and return it to medium-high heat. Add the remaining 4 tablespoons butter and cook, swirling the pan until the butter begins to foam and brown, about 3 minutes. As soon as the butter is golden brown, add the capers and cook by swirling for 30 seconds, then add the parsley and lemon triangles and juice. Bring to a boil and immediately pour over the fish. Garnish with the croutons and serve immediately.

Fresh herbs v. dried herbs: When is it okay to reach for McCormick?

→ **ALL HERBS ARE GOOD** when they're fresh. *Some* herbs are good dried; most of them are not. This poses a bit of confusion. The rule of thumb is, if you're cooking a recipe that calls for a fresh herb, you're better off leaving it out than substituting its dried equivalent. And if the herb is central to the dish, then choose another dish to cook until you can source the fresh herbs you need. For example, you aren't going to make pesto with dried basil—really, please don't.

The two widely available herbs that dry well are oregano and bay leaves. (What does a bay leaf do exactly? The answer follows.) When substituting dried for fresh oregano, it's important to note that the leaves shrink and shrivel as they dehydrate, yielding a smaller volume and considerably more concentrated flavor, so use only one-third of what's called for fresh. But resist the urge to use dried basil, tarragon, chives, and thyme. You can find those ingredients fresh at almost all decent grocery stores, and unlike oregano, they lose their nuanced flavor when dried.

So, you've committed to using fresh herbs whenever possible (thank you), but you don't want to waste that big bunch of cilantro or thyme that undoubtedly goes bad before you can use it all? Freezing is the answer. Wrap the herbs tightly in plastic wrap and toss them into the freezer. They will be soft, wilted, and, honestly, look terrible when you thaw them, but the flavor will stay locked in for up to a month, and they will work perfectly for recipes where their presentation and texture isn't key, like cilantro in guacamole or thyme in chicken soup. •

WTF IS A BAY LEAF? LET'S FIND OUT.

There are bay-leaf truthers in this world who believe that a massive conspiracy is afoot. They will tell you that adding bay leaf to a chicken stock or pasta sauce is an act of heresy—a pointless gesture and a moment of (*cough*) culinary fake news that has been foisted upon us by a cabal of cookbook editors and food writers in cahoots with the big spice conglomerates. But before you take up arms in protest of Julia Child, Rachael Ray, and Wolfgang Puck, let us suggest a little experiment.

Fish a bay leaf or two out of the jar, bring it to a boil in ½ cup water, turn off the heat, and let it steep for 15 minutes or so. Give it a taste, and you can lay the argument to rest once and for all. Bay leaves add a subtle vegetal base layer. They won't slap you in the face with flavor, but they do offer a delicate herbal quality and elusive sweetness akin to a mild chamomile tea. You may not be able to pick their flavor out of a lineup, but they are one of the fundamental building blocks of complex flavor.

GHORMEH SABZI
PERSIAN STEW WITH LAMB SHANK, PARSLEY, AND DRIED LIMES

Serves 4

⅔ cup dried kidney beans

4 (1-pound) lamb shanks, or 2 pounds boneless lamb shoulder, cut into 2-inch pieces

Kosher salt

2 teaspoons ground turmeric

⅓ cup extra-virgin olive oil

2 leeks, white and pale green parts only, sliced

2 bunches green onions, white and green parts, chopped

1 pound flat-leaf parsley, tough stems discarded, then minced

1 pound cilantro, stems and leaves, minced

¼ cup dried fenugreek leaves

4 cups water

4 dried Persian (Omani) limes, pierced with a fork

1 to 2 lemons, halved, for seasoning

Ghormeh sabzi is the intensely herbaceous and deeply flavorful stew that has been called Iran's national dish. And like all widely made dishes ingrained in a culture (Sunday gravy, Passover kugel), there's plenty of nuance: a tablespoon of tomato paste here, a pinto bean or black-eyed pea there. Strong words have been exchanged over when to add the herbs and whether to use yellow onions or leeks. Alternatively, beef stew meat is exceptionally delicious as well. A food processor works well for chopping the herbs. Serve this classic dish with steamed basmati rice.

1. The night before cooking, in a bowl, soak the kidney beans in triple their volume of water (you can leave the bowl out, covered, at room temperature). Season the lamb generously with salt (aim for 1.5 percent by weight, or about 1½ teaspoons per pound) and the turmeric.

2. The next day, heat the oil in a Dutch oven or other large, heavy-bottomed pot over medium-high heat until just beginning to smoke. Add the lamb and sear, turning as needed, until well browned on all sides, about 15 minutes. (Sear the lamb in batches if needed to avoid crowding.) Transfer the lamb to a plate.

3. Turn down the heat to medium, add the leeks and green onions, and cook, stirring frequently, until soft, about 10 minutes. Add the parsley, cilantro, fenugreek, and 2 teaspoons salt and continue cooking, stirring constantly, until the moisture has evaporated and the herbs are dark, dry, and fully combined. This process can take 20 minutes or longer. Avoid the temptation to quit early, as cooking the herbs thoroughly is important to building complex flavor.

4. Return the lamb to the pot and add the water. Drain the beans and stir them in, along with 2 more teaspoons salt. Bring the mixture to a boil, lower the heat to a simmer, cover, and cook for 1½ hours.

5. Add the dried limes, folding them into the stew, then re-cover and continue cooking until the meat is tender, about 1 hour. If using shanks, the meat should be falling off the bone, and if using shoulder, the meat should show no resistance when pierced with a fork. If the stew is watery, remove the lid for the last 30 minutes or so of cooking. It should be thick when ready.

6. Scoop out the limes, give them a squeeze to season the stew with their juice, and then discard. Taste and adjust the seasoning with salt and lemon juice as needed before serving.

How do I get the most out of my bottle of soy sauce?

→ **DANIEL WAS ONCE DINING** at a backcountry ski lodge in a small Canadian town. Rice pilaf was on the menu that evening, and one of his companions asked the server for some soy sauce to go with it. Interested, Daniel surveyed the group and was surprised by the consensus from the table (albeit a table of mostly older white dudes) that soy sauce should be made available whenever rice was served. Now, objectively, from a culinary point of view, there was no reason for soy sauce to be anywhere near that rice, but the association was still there. Many Americans assume the primary function of a bottle of soy sauce is to season rice. Typically, and a little regretfully, that's where the conversation ends. We're here to talk.

Soy sauce is a gift to the world made by fermenting soybeans, sometimes along with wheat or other grains, then aging the resulting liquid over a long period of time. There are many nuanced variations of soy sauce, depending on the country of origin and prescribed usage. It's also commonly cooked down with sugar, yielding a sweet and salty viscous condiment (the foundation of teriyaki sauce) that is quite delicious, setting aside any 1990s associations you might have.

Most soy sauce can be broken down into light and dark types (aka thin and black, respectively), with the light used as a condiment (the stuff you get in a sushi restaurant to, well, season the rice) and the dark used as a seasoning for cooking and marinating (shout-out to the soy sauce egg).

More understated than its dark companion, the flavor of light soy sauce is often delicately smoky, with acidic undertones and sharp biting salinity. Using it to cook would be a waste for two reasons: many of the volatile flavor compounds would be lost and you would need to add so much of it for its subtle flavor to shine through that you would risk overseasoning the dish. Also, "less-sodium" soy sauce is not the same as light soy sauce. It's best to stick with the fully loaded stuff and use it wisely if salt intake is an issue. Dark soy sauce, on the other hand, is much thicker and deeply flavorful, with a concentrated inky, mineral-rich flavor often bordering on bitter. It can be less salty than its lighter sibling, allowing home cooks to add more to soups, stews, and braises without fear of oversalting.

Dark soy sauces are more like utility sauces used in cooking, including for sauces in the wok, in braises, and as the base for soups. Light soy sauce is more refreshing, with higher acidity. It's used mostly as a dipping sauce and is served with nigiri at sushi bars. You would avoid light soy sauce in cooking because a larger amount of the stuff (required for high-heat cooking) would overpower with saltiness.

Traditionally, some of the finer soy sauces made in China and Korea are produced from 100 percent soybeans, whereas Japanese soy sauce often mixes wheat in with the legumes to add complexity to the finished product. Japanese tamari, made from 100 percent soybeans, is often referred to as "gluten-free" soy sauce. While similar in flavor to soy sauce, it is actually made through a different process, as a by-product of miso production.

As with all of the world's favorite fermented seasonings, soy sauce is rich in free glutamates, which naturally intensify flavors when combined with salt (like naturally occurring MSG; see page 32). Adding a little soy sauce to soups, stews, salad dressings, and marinades helps brighten the flavors. MSG, after all, makes everything just a little bit more delicious.

Where does Bragg Liquid Aminos fit in this discussion? It's basically hippie soy sauce (made from soybeans and purified water), and it's closest to tamari. We like it, too. Our mothers were hippies, so Paul and Patricia Bragg played a role in raising us. ●

CATHY ERWAY **is a cook-book author, podcast host, and James Beard Award-winning writer. Her love of soy sauce runs deep.**

Can you describe the flavor of soy sauce?

Salty, umami, savory, intense. A little goes a long way. And it's just really, really delicious.

How do you approach cooking with soy sauce?

Both light and dark soy sauce can be used as a seasoning component, just like salt and pepper, or as a condiment. And like salt, I think of soy sauce as an essential cooking ingredient. Light soy sauce is for dipping dumplings or for adding a splash to noodles. Dark soy sauce is used more at the beginning of long-cooked dishes to infuse color and flavor.

In a 2017 article in *TASTE*, you had a bone to pick with food writers calling soy sauce "soy," which you found strange, given how many different foods are made from a base of soybeans. Have things improved?

Not really. It's a shorthand that maybe grew out of restaurant kitchens; I can see that. But for restaurant critics and food writers, it's odd.

FOOD IQ

KAKUNI
JAPANESE BRAISED PORK BELLY

Serves 2

---

1 pound skinless pork belly, cut into 2-inch cubes

2-inch knob fresh ginger, smashed with a rolling pin

1 green onion, root end trimmed and left whole

1 cup dashi (see page 196) or water

¼ cup sake

¼ cup light soy sauce

3 tablespoons mirin

¼ cup sugar

1 tablespoon kosher salt

For Serving

Karashi (spicy Japanese mustard), optional

4 green onions, white and green parts, thinly sliced

Cooked short-grain white rice

Similar to pork chashu (braised pork shoulder popularized as a ramen topping), kakuni (literally, "square simmered") is a soy sauce-braised pork belly dish popular in Japan. Gently simmering the rich belly meat in a bath of sweet soy sauce breaks down the collagen and melts the fat, rendering the meat unbelievably moist and tender. Cooking low and slow and cooling the meat in the cooking liquid are the keys to retaining moisture. Fish can also be braised in the style of kakuni—fillets of mackerel, tuna, and bonito are popular options. Simply cut the cooking time to 15 minutes for perfect, pescatarian-friendly, results.

1. Select a heavy pot large enough to accommodate the pork in a single layer on the bottom. Add the pork, ginger, whole green onion, dashi, sake, soy sauce, mirin, sugar, and salt to the pot. If the pork is not covered by liquid, add water as needed until it is submerged.

2. Bring the liquid to a gentle boil over high heat, then immediately lower the heat to a simmer and cover the pot. Simmer the pork until fork-tender, about 2 hours.

3. Transfer the pork to a plate and reserve. Skim and discard the fat, then strain the cooking liquid through a fine-mesh strainer, discard the solids, and return the liquid to the pot. Bring to a boil over medium-high heat and boil until reduced by half.

4. When ready to serve, preheat the broiler. Position an oven rack about 8 inches from the heat source. Arrange the pork belly cubes on a sheet pan and broil, basting every minute with a spoonful of the reduced braising liquid, until sizzling brown, about 5 minutes.

5. Divide the pork between individual bowls and add 1 inch of braising liquid. Garnish each with a spoonful of karashi and the green onions. Serve with a side of rice. Save the remaining braising liquid for braising more pork, seasoning rice, or using as a soup base.

What's the difference between Parmigiano Reggiano and pecorino romano?

→ **PARMIGIANO REGGIANO AND PECORINO** romano, two iconic aged Italian cheeses, are often mistakenly presented as interchangeable, especially when viewed as a cheese to grate over a bowl of pasta. This couldn't be further from the truth. In fact, their similarity ends with their firm texture and country of origin.

Parmigiano Reggiano, a raw cow's milk cheese produced in Italy's Emilia-Romagna region, is nicknamed the "king of cheese"—and regal it is. Real Parmigiano Reggiano, produced at 299 dairies surrounding the towns of Parma and Reggio Emilia, follows a strict set of guidelines under DOP protection (short for "protected designation of origin" in Italian). The cows must eat only grass and be milked twice a day, and the milk must be processed within two hours of milking. Preservatives are strictly forbidden, and the cheese must age for a minimum of one year—and often twenty-four to thirty-six months. It's one of the most delicious foods on earth: rich and nutty, smacking with umami, and deeply satisfying to eat by the chunk.

Pecorino romano is a completely different animal—literally. It's made from the milk of sheep (pecore) and is much younger—aged between five and eight months, with a sharper, gamier flavor and extremely high salt content. Pecorino romano was traditionally produced in Lazio, the region surrounding Rome, but the cheese can be produced on the island of Sardinia as well. Because of the sharp, salty bite of pecorino romano, the cheese is almost never enjoyed on its own, but rather as a seasoning and accompaniment grated over pasta or broken into small pieces and served with vegetables.

What should you keep in mind when cooking with these cheeses? First things first, Parmigiano Reggiano shouldn't be grated on pasta! We said it. Enter grana padano, Parmiginao Reggiano's more affordable little brother, designed for grating. True Parmigiano Reggiano is too refined and too expensive to be grated over pasta; it deserves to be savored on its own, with a glass of Lambrusco and maybe a drizzle of good balsamic vinegar—all the children of Emilia-Romagna. Grana padano is similar to Parmigiano Reggiano but has slightly looser production restrictions and is way less expensive. It's produced in a larger section of northern Italy (in and around the Po Valley), and at a higher volume per year. The cheese can be sold younger, allowing for grater-worthy pricing.

Daniel compares cooking with Parmigiano Reggiano to using a hunk of beautiful Jasper Hill Cabot Clothbound Cheddar in a batch of mac and cheese. That said, if you cannot resist the Microplane with that thirty-five-euro hunk you brought back from Modena, that's okay. It's your life, your cheese.

As for when to choose between grana padano and pecorino romano, GP is great on dishes from Italy's north, like a Bolognese or a risotto alla milanese. It adds a buttery, nutty richness to a Sunday lasagna and when grated on the Caesar, Mexico's most famous salad (that story is for another day).

Pecorino romano should be reserved for cooking from central and southern Italy, where simpler preparations with fewer ingredients are more common. Break a few chunks into a bowl of freshly blanched fava beans or grate a healthy portion over any of Rome's four iconic pastas: spaghetti alla carbonara, cacio e pepe, bucatini all'amatriciana, or pasta alla gricia.

And a word about that green shaker of "Parmesan cheese" that you may have grown up with: that ain't the Italian cheese we are talking about. It's mostly ground-up cheese trimmings (sometimes white Cheddar, Havarti, and mozzarella) along with cellulose powder that serves as a filler. It's great for a walk down memory lane, but that's about it. •

BABY SHELLS IN PARMESAN BROTH

Serves 2

2 cups Parmesan Broth (recipe follows)

Kosher salt

8 ounces baby shell pasta

1 carrot, peeled and thinly sliced

Fried chile oil (see step 1 of Smoky, Spicy Southern Italian Crudo, page 164) for drizzling

2 small handfuls arugula

Grana padano cheese for grating

Freshly ground black pepper

The star here is the cheese broth, a flavor-packed and highly versatile broth worth saving your hard, unwaxed cheese rinds for. Keep a sealable container in the freezer and add the rinds as you accumulate them. You'll be surprised how quickly you've saved up enough to make a batch of broth. Or if you don't have rinds, or you're in a hurry, most cheesemongers who sell grated cheese have saved their rinds and will sell you some. As the broth cooks, make sure to be prudent and stir it regularly, scraping the bottom; otherwise, the cheese will stick and burn.

1. In a saucepan, heat the broth over medium heat until hot. Season with salt if needed, then adjust the heat to keep the broth at a bare simmer.

2. Bring a medium-large pot of heavily salted water (⅓ cup salt per 4 quarts water) to a rolling boil over high heat. Set a timer for 2 minutes less than the package instructions suggest for al dente, add the pasta, and cook, stirring occasionally. When the timer sounds, add the carrot to the boiling pasta water and cook for 1 more minute, then drain and divide into two bowls for serving.

3. Divide the hot broth between the bowls. Drizzle with chile oil, then top with a handful of arugula, a generous grating of grana padano, and a few grinds of pepper. Serve at once.

Parmesan Broth

6 cups water

1 yellow onion, thinly sliced

4 ounces Parmesan cheese rinds

2 bay leaves

1. In a heavy pot, bring the water to a rolling boil over high heat. Add the onion, cheese rinds, and bay leaves and stir continuously until the broth comes back up to a boil. Turn down the heat to low and simmer gently, stirring frequently, for 1 hour. If the cheese begins sticking to the pot bottom before the broth is ready, switch the contents to a second pot, being careful not to scrape any burnt pieces into the clean pot, and continue to simmer.

2. Strain the broth through a fine-mesh strainer. You should have about 4 cups. Measure out 2 cups for the pasta and set aside. Let the remaining broth cool, then transfer to an airtight container and refrigerate for up to 2 weeks or freeze for up to 3 months for another use.

Why do chefs like pork so much?

→ **YOU MAY NOT REALIZE** it, but when you are eating bacon—crumbled on a salad, lounging on your BLT, or served alongside your scrambled eggs—you are eating cold pork. And cold pork, it turns out, is a really good thing. Pork fat has the unique innate quality of melting at a low temperature, which gives it an especially moist mouthfeel, even when it's cold. This may not seem like a big deal, but it's the main reason you love prosciutto, mortadella, salami, and all those other bites that tempt you on the charcuterie board. Other animal fats have higher melting points, so they leave you with a waxy mouthfeel, which is why you rarely see lamb or beef served cold.

Fat plays an important role in nearly every recipe, as it lubricates the tongue and makes food taste moist. And many ingredients dissolve in fat, not water, so without adequate fat, you can't properly taste them. Red chile flakes offer a good example: Drop a pinch of chile flakes into a little water, bring the mixture to a boil, and then let it cool. The chile water won't taste like much. Take that same pinch and simmer it in melted pork fat or olive oil? The heat will immediately jump out at you.

Chefs love pork fat for all of these reasons. It also has a relatively neutral flavor (compared with beef, chicken, and especially lamb fat), which makes it extremely versatile. Pork fat plays a central role in piecrust and Mexican tamales, and in biscuits and Calabrian 'nduja. Home cooks should view pork fat, and its less PR-friendly name, "lard," as an opportunity instead of a surgeon general's warning. Now that you know the virtues of pork fat, you understand why the pig is king among chefs. ●

SPICY PORK MEATBALLS

Makes 24 golf-ball-size meatballs

---

2 pounds ground pork (preferably from a fatty cut like shoulder)

2 teaspoons kosher salt

2 to 3 pickled hot cherry peppers, minced

¼ cup pickling liquid from hot cherry peppers

4 slices white sandwich bread with crust, minced (about 3½ cups)

3 eggs, lightly beaten

This is Daniel's favorite meatball recipe—of many meatball recipes. He is a cofounder of the popular Meatball Shop, after all, so he knows his way around orbs of meat. This recipe showcases the quality of the pork, and it's a prime example of applying the theory that less is more when working with the products you love—in this case, pork fat.

1. Preheat the oven to 450°F.

2. In a large bowl, combine all the ingredients and hand mix until thoroughly incorporated.

3. Roll the mixture into golf-ball-size meatballs, making sure to pack the meat firmly. As they are shaped, arrange them in a 9-by-13-inch baking dish (it's okay if they touch).

4. Roast until firm and cooked through, about 17 minutes (or until an instant-read thermometer inserted into the center of a ball registers 165°F). Allow the meatballs to cool in the baking dish for 5 minutes before serving.

Should I cook with MSG?

→ **FOR YEARS, DANIEL AND** Matt have been fans, and vocal supporters, of cooking with MSG—short for monosodium glutamate. The white, flaky substance, sold in bags and shakers under the brand names Accent and Ajinomoto, enhances and intensifies flavors and helps activate your taste buds so you can better taste your food. It's that simple.

What isn't as simple is the fifty-year xenophobic attack on its safety. This dates back to a 1968 letter published in the *New England Journal of Medicine* that erroneously linked MSG to headaches and musculature pain. The letter catalyzed a public health scare coined "Chinese restaurant syndrome" that still persists today. (Bear in mind that MSG—hiding behind names like "autolyzed yeast"—is present in a great many processed foods that are widely consumed without any concern for their safety, including canned soups, cold cuts, instant ramen, and Doritos.) But years after its scientific exoneration, the court of public opinion is still deliberating over the ingredient's place in a home kitchen—with little information on how to actually cook with it effectively. This needs to change.

When placed on the tongue by itself, MSG tastes like a mild salt. This is because MSG doesn't have any distinct flavor. Instead, it adds a round and rich mouthfeel known as umami, or the fifth taste. Because it doesn't hold a specific flavor, save saltiness, the easiest way to cook with it is to create a blend: make a 10-to-1 mix of kosher salt to MSG, or roughly 1 tablespoon MSG for every ⅔ cup salt, and then season as you regularly would throughout your cooking process. Adding more MSG than the 10-to-1 ratio can overwhelm your taste buds. (A note of caution: adding a few too many pinches of ground allspice to your autumn roast of root vegetables usually isn't an issue, but when spiked with MSG, it could turn your mildly unpleasant misstep into a pumpkin-spice Hindenburg.)

This is why it's imperative to know how, and how much, MSG to use in various cooking techniques. "It's like the contrast slider in Photoshop," says food writer Helen Rosner. "If you boost the contrast a little bit, it makes everything look a little sharper and really nice, but if you boost it too much, it looks like garbage."

MSG works well at the beginning of cooking when added to dressings and marinades, but for dry and fried foods like French fries, popcorn, and potato chips, add MSG at the very end to wake up your taste buds on first contact. Or use it along with Maldon salt as a finishing seasoning for roasted meats. ●

friend of
FOOD IQ

HELEN ROSNER has served as the *New Yorker***'s roving food correspondent since 2018, when she wrote a colorful article about her visit to the "high church of umami" outside Tokyo.**

MSG gets a bad rap, no?

It's so bizarre because it's really just the representation of a fundamental building block of cuisine. You take a high-glutamate food and set it out in the right conditions and flakes will appear. Boom, homemade MSG. The stuff in the shaker is the chemical salt version of that. But it doesn't taste like salt; it tastes like a savory flavor. To me, it just tastes like chicken bouillon. But for somebody who is new to MSG, thinking about it as a booster for your salt is a really wonderful on-ramp to understanding it as an ingredient.

After writing the story, you've become a bit of an MSG ambassador, it seems.

Unwittingly an ambassador, and I just want to say that when people who are opposed to MSG talk about it, that requires a bit of linguistic slipperiness. Sometimes I think that's intentional, sometimes I think it's not. But I think it's really important to distinguish between MSG, which are little pearlescent white flakes that come in a jar, and glutamates, which provide the savoriness in foods.

You call your trip a visit to the "high church of umami." What did you see?

I took a series of commuter trains to get out to the museum, which has its own dedicated stop, and I followed these Ajinomoto panda footprints to this massive complex to start the tour. It was just delightful. And while it is typical corporate propaganda about the glories of the company as a whole, the museum, which is more like a science museum, was really cool. There was a glass vial of the first extracted MSG. It was fucking cool as hell.

CEVICHE WITH A SECRET

Serves 2 to 4

---

12 ounces sushi-grade firm white fish fillet (such as fluke, black bass, or hamachi), diced into ¼-inch pieces

1 tablespoon kosher salt

¼ teaspoon MSG

½ small red onion, minced

Juice of 3 limes

1 jalapeño chile, stemmed, seeded, and beaten to a pulp with a mortar and pestle

¼ cup finely chopped cilantro stems and leaves, kept separate

2 cups tortilla chips

Daniel learned the secrets of a truly great ceviche while working with the famous Peruvian chef Flavio Solorzano. There are two secrets that help unlock the dish's full potential. First, you must smash the chiles to break their cell structure and help release their juices to flavor the dish, and second, using MSG is a must. There's no greater challenge than simplicity: the best ingredients, carefully selected and simply prepared, yield the greatest results. And here's a great example.

1. In a bowl, season the fish with the salt and MSG, then cover and refrigerate.

2. In a small bowl, stir together the onion, lime juice, and chile and let them marinate for 10 minutes.

3. Add the chile-lime mixture and cilantro stems to the seasoned fish, re-cover, and let sit until the fish begins to cure, at least 20 minutes at room temperature and up to 2 hours in the fridge. The fish will firm up and take on an opaque-white cooked appearance.

4. Just before serving, toss in the cilantro leaves, then adjust the seasoning with additional lime juice and salt if needed. Serve with the tortilla chips.

How do I get the most out of a can of tuna?

→ **AMERICANS ARE MYOPIC WHEN** they view cans of tuna. The conversation begins and ends with that childhood tuna sandwich. But not all tuna sandwiches are created equally (ever try adding a hard-boiled egg?), and cans of tuna have a whole lot more to offer. Your first step is accepting the fact that a mayonnaise-rich tuna salad on salty Ritz crackers is perhaps the greatest pairing on earth.

Outside of the United States, where canned fish is considered a second-rate product, cans of tuna have range. In Italy, Spain, Portugal, and many other parts of the world, canned fish is a prized specialty and can be quite expensive—with colorful cans advertising premium seafood in a grand tradition called "conserva." So, how do you get the most out of those cans?

First, you should recognize that tuna is packed in two different ways: with water or with oil. Water-packed tuna is what you likely encountered in your middle-school lunchroom. It's lighter and lower in calories, but it's dry and lacks flavor, requiring ridiculous amounts of mayonnaise or other fats to moisten it sufficiently. Most high-quality tuna is packed in extra-virgin olive oil, which is sold in cans and jars in many grocery stores. Genova and Tonnino are two widely available Italian brands, and we also really like the Spanish brand Ortiz. The latter's white tuna is caught with a pole and line in the Cantabrian Sea . . . and it's delicious.

When cooking with high-quality canned tuna, the goal should be to highlight the fish. The obvious first move is Niçoise salad. Along with blanched haricots verts and hard-boiled eggs, chunks of olive oil–rich tuna are served with boiled potatoes and, of course, Niçoise olives. Good canned tuna is delicious when served simply with freshly cooked pasta and a splash of lemon juice and olive oil, or with grilled peppers and red wine vinegar on toast.

Avoid using the good stuff for dishes like Daniel's favorite, the tuna melt, an open-face tuna salad sandwich served warm with a crown of melted Cheddar cheese. Matt's Grandma T made a killer cold tuna mac salad with shell macaroni, chopped celery, pickles, sweet onion, and cups of Hellmann's. Because canned tuna lasts for more than a year, a good tuna conserva is a staple pantry item. You can serve it straight with crackers and lemon, or whip up a delicious meal with a minute's notice, provided you have the good stuff on hand. ●

TUNA CONSERVA WITH CHICKPEAS AND GRILLED RAPINI

Serves 2

_____

8 ounces rapini, tough ends trimmed

1 (7-ounce) jar good-quality olive oil-packed tuna, drained with oil reserved

3 tablespoons extra-virgin olive oil

2 cloves garlic, smashed

Pinch of red chile flakes

Kosher salt

1 (15-ounce) can chickpeas, drained

1 small shallot, minced

1 tablespoon red wine vinegar

Grated zest of 2 lemons and juice of 1 lemon

This is a quick and hearty summer meal utilizing what you have around the house: vegetables, a pantry of oils and spices, and hopefully some really good cans or jars of olive oil-packed tuna. Almost any vegetable will work well, so if you don't have rapini (broccoli rabe), feel free to substitute zucchini, cabbage, cauliflower, or summer squash. If you don't have a grill, use a grill pan on the stove, or a quick sauté with a little garlic and olive oil in a frying pan will work just fine, too.

1. Heat your grill to high to burn off any old stuck-on food before giving the grill rack a good scrub with a grill brush. Wiping the grill with a paper towel drizzled with oil will help clean the soot left after brushing.

2. In a large bowl, toss the rapini with the reserved tuna packing oil, 1 tablespoon of the olive oil, the garlic, chile flakes, and a healthy pinch of salt, coating it evenly.

3. Pile the rapini on the grill rack, close the lid, and grill, tossing with tongs every so often, until cooked through and evenly charred, about 7 minutes.

4. While the rapini cooks, in a bowl, combine the tuna, chickpeas, shallot, the remaining 2 tablespoons olive oil, the vinegar, and lemon zest and juice and mix well.

5. When the rapini is ready, add to the tuna mixture and toss to mix well. Adjust the seasoning with a few drops of lemon juice and with salt if needed.

TINNED FISH IS HAVING A MOMENT

Canned fish is big these days, with a new generation of home cooks embracing the tinned treasures. A blogger named Drew Mellon reviews sardines from all over the world, including cans from Tunisia, France, and Vietnam. Anchovies have ventured beyond paste to become focal points of their own, with fillets being highlighted as more than a flavoring agent. Don't be afraid of the cans of fish in your local supermarket. Chances are those preserved clams are better than you think. Matt's *TASTE* colleague Anna Hezel has written an extremely fun cookbook on the subject, *Tin to Table*, and you should seek it out.

Mashed, roasted, fried: How do I know which potato to use?

→ **THERE'S A LOT TO** consider when confronting the bins of grocery-store potatoes. And, honestly, how many times have you winged it completely with that choice—grabbing that bag from Idaho and hoping for the best, with the evening's picnic salad or holiday mash hanging in the balance? Potatoes are pretty user-friendly, but they have specific qualities worth learning about if you want to prepare the perfect roast.

One type of potato works better with deep-frying, while another should be avoided at all costs when making latkes. And then there's the most flexible potato of all. And then there are those purple ones! What's up with those?

At the supermarket, you will undoubtedly find three main types of potato: Russet, Red Bliss, and Yukon Gold. And each falls (mostly) into one of two categories: starchy or waxy. There are, of course, other types of specialty potatoes to think about: fingerlings (semi-waxy and great for roasting), German butterballs (starchy and perfect for a creamy and particularly sweet mash), and peewees (great for soup). But most of our cooking revolves around the big three, and if you master these, the others will all make sense.

The starchy potato is what it sounds like. When baked and cracked open, the flesh tastes chalky and dry, but it absorbs incredibly well. What this means is that the starchy potato can take on a lot of fat. Enter the russet potato, your go-to spud for mashed potatoes at Thanksgiving, for your late-night French fries cravings, and for potato gnocchi, potato pancakes, and extra-crispy hash browns. Be mindful, however, that the russet will fall apart when cooked through—and dissolve completely into a starchy mush when cooked beyond that—so it makes a lousy addition to brothy soups where chunks are the goal.

Waxy potatoes are lower in starch and higher in moisture, and the waxier the potato, the less likely it is going to fall apart when cooked. Red Bliss potatoes are waxy, and while they're a little bit of a throwback to the 1970s and 1980s, they are really great to roast and braise. They also make a welcome addition to soups and stews, where they keep their form during the long cooking time.

Yukon Golds are somewhere in between waxy and starchy, and sometimes they're called an all-purpose potato (at least that's what Martha Stewart calls them, and nobody wants to argue with Martha). They are the great utility player in the potato game, with a sweet flesh and tender skin, great for roasting, boiling, and even mashing. In fact, Daniel often uses YGs for his mashes. They are sweeter and offer a little more flavor than their starchy kin, and you can mash the skin right in there should you wish (unlike the russets, which need to be peeled). In restaurants, cooks use a stand mixer with the paddle attachment to mash potatoes, and you can do the same with your countertop KitchenAid, with the added bonus that the paddle will catch most of the skins and save you some time on peeling if you choose to go with Yukon Golds. •

POMMES ANNA

Serves 6

¾ cup (1½ sticks) high-quality unsalted European-style butter

3 pounds russet potatoes

Kosher salt

Pommes Anna is as impressive today as it undoubtedly was on Auguste Escoffier's table more than a hundred years ago. Nothing quite highlights the versatility of a humble tuber more poignantly than this classic three-ingredient beauty that is rich, fancy, and perfect for your next dinner party. The trick to a successful Pommes Anna flip (the moment the brown and bubbly crown comes into view) is patience. Cook the potatoes on one side until the natural starches "glue" the layers together and a shake of the pan doesn't jiggle or dislodge any of the slices. That's when you flip, and it's the moment of truth.

1. Preheat the oven to 425°F.

2. Select a 10-inch heavy-bottomed sauté or cast-iron pan with a tight-fitting lid. Place over medium heat and add the butter, and heat until the butter melts and just begins to bubble. Pour off nearly all of the melted butter into a small bowl, leaving just a thin layer on the pan bottom. Reserve the melted butter.

3. Using a mandoline (see page 60) ideally, or a chef's knife, slice the unpeeled potatoes into thin (about ⅛₆-inch-thick) rounds. Starting from the edge of the pan, arrange a layer of the potato rounds, overlapping them slightly and moving toward the center in a spiral pattern, until the entire surface is covered. When the layer is complete, brush it with a

healthy wash of the melted butter and sprinkle with ¾ teaspoon salt. Continue adding layers of potato slices, topping each with butter and salt, until you've exhausted your supply of potatoes. Depending on how tightly you've spiraled each layer, you will end up with between three and five layers. Finish with a final brushing of butter and sprinkle of salt.

4. Heat the pan over medium-high heat, gently shaking it from time to time, until the juices start to bubble through to the top, about 10 minutes. A telltale aroma of toasting potatoes will start to blanket your kitchen.

5. Cover the pan and bake for 20 minutes. Transfer the pan to the stove top, remove the lid, and give the pan a shake while looking for movement between the slices. The potatoes are ready to flip when the slices have glued themselves together, forming a loaf. Ideally, the entire loaf has come unstuck on its own. If it hasn't, using a small, flexible spatula, gently loosen the sides and bottom from the pan.

6. Invert a large, flat plate over the pan and, holding the plate and pan firmly, invert the pan and plate together, then lift off the pan. Slide the potatoes back into the pan, place over medium-high heat, and cook until the underside is beautifully golden brown, about 10 minutes.

7. Depending on which side is more beautiful, slide the potatoes from the pan onto a serving plate or invert the potatoes onto the plate. Cut into wedges to serve.

What do I do with all these ugly squashes in the supermarket?

→ **HOME COOKS JUST DON'T** know what to do with all these gnarly-looking gourds, their skins banged up with bumps and boils. They're hard as a rock and can be scary to negotiate with even the sharpest knife. But with a little knowledge, squash is a pretty amazing ingredient to focus on. First things first, we all know about butternut squash, which is consistently sweet and perfect for the namesake (and perhaps a little dated) soup you might have last eaten at your uncle's retirement dinner. But there's also kabocha, delicata, crookneck, and acorn squash to consider—all worth exploring, and for their different qualities.

In the case of the kabocha squash, the skin is tender and delicious, so you don't have to peel it. The sweet, meaty flesh can be chalky when roasted, so braising is a good cooking technique to look to. Acorn squash has a beautifully firm texture and sweet, nutty flavor. It can be easily portioned—sliced along the riblets—and roasted with olive oil and a few drops of honey. Delicata is another tender squash with an edible skin. For best results, cut it in half or into rings, remove the seeds, and roast with olive oil. The rings are perfect for a salad. Spaghetti squash—split, roasted, and coaxed out with the tines of a fork—has a great crunchy texture and works, well, as a spaghetti substitute, tossed with your favorite red sauce. Please note that contrary to what the Internet tells you, it does *not* taste like spaghetti.

The key to manipulating these squashes and their rhinoceros-like skin is either to blanch them or microwave them for a minute to soften their skin for easier cutting. It's a great tip that Daniel learned from his friend Kyle Itani's Japanese grandmother.

Although some of these hard-skinned squashes are available year-round in the United States, their season traditionally begins in the fall and lasts through the winter months. Summer squashes (sometimes lumped into a category known as zucchini) are from the same family, but they are soft-skinned and faster cooking and, despite their name, are typically in the market all year long. Each of the summer squashes has its own unique properties and flavor, but they can all be cooked similarly and can be swapped into any recipe that calls for zucchini. This includes the deep green, round Eight Ball squash, a favorite of Daniel's that is meaty and can be grilled or stuffed with fragrant beef and rice. ●

DELICATA SQUASH SALAD WITH ARUGULA, RICOTTA SALATA, AND TOASTED PUMPKIN SEEDS

Serves 4

---

2 delicata squashes, halved lengthwise and seeded, or 1 medium butternut squash, halved lengthwise, peeled, and seeded

4 tablespoons extra-virgin olive oil

4 thyme sprigs

Kosher salt

4 ounces baby arugula

¼ cup toasted pumpkin seeds

½ cup freshly grated ricotta salata or other aged sheep's milk cheese (such as Manchego or pecorino)

2 tablespoons red wine vinegar

Freshly ground black peepper

Delicata squash has silky smooth flesh and skin so tender you don't need to peel it. When sliced and roasted, the concentrated sweetness intensifies, emitting a toasted-honey aroma and a rich, nutty flavor. The versatile squash works as well on its own as a side dish as it does as the starring vegetable in a winter lasagna or stew. Here, it's paired with crunchy toasted pumpkin seeds, peppery arugula, and ricotta salata, a semihard, pleasantly salty ricotta cheese popular in southern and central Italy that adds a creamy texture.

1. Preheat the oven to 450°F. Line a sheet pan with parchment paper.

2. Cut the squash halves into ½-inch-thick half-moons and transfer to a large bowl. Drizzle with 2 tablespoons of the oil, add the thyme and a big pinch of salt, and toss to mix well. Arrange the squash slices on the prepared pan.

3. Roast the squash slices until tender when pierced with a knife, about 20 minutes. Let cool completely.

4. In a large bowl, combine the cooled squash slices, arugula, pumpkin seeds, and all but a few teaspoons of the cheese. Drizzle with the remaining 2 tablespoons oil and the vinegar, add an additional pinch of salt, and toss to mix well. Garnish with the reserved cheese, grind some pepper over the top, and serve.

Tools and Technology

Smart cooking starts with investing in a proper collection of pots, pans, knives, pokers, prongs, and other sharp objects– plus a few things you can plug into the socket. In this chapter, Daniel and Matt don't tell you all the things you need to buy; you can go online for that. Instead, they answer pressing questions about the gear and technology you read about in your favorite food publications.

Should I feel guilty for loving my microwave?

→ **NO KITCHEN APPLIANCE IS** a panacea, but the microwave may come the closest. What a great tool for the active and ambitious home cook, and how greatly misunderstood and misused a tool it is. Daniel was once cooking for his young niece and nephew and needed to make a quick beurre manié, an uncooked roux that is equal parts butter and flour used for thickening. Without time to allow the butter to soften at room temperature, and unable to use the heat of a flame lest he melt the butter, the microwave was the only way to go. It heats both the outside and inside of the butter at the same time, creating a uniform temperature throughout, ideal for other common kitchen endeavors like baking.

Daniel didn't feel guilty that he used the microwave because he knows it comes in handy to speed up a hundred simple tasks: need to boil a cup of water, soften a kabocha squash for cutting, crisp bacon perfectly in four minutes, or bake a potato before the first commercial break? The downside of the microwave is that when it's used with the wrong ingredient, or when you nuke too long, it can tighten proteins until they're as tough as a tennis ball. Daniel and Matt got together to sort out what is okay and what is forbidden—like a frozen Lender's bagel. (Matt has PTSD about this.)

Here's what is okay to use a microwave for: baked potatoes, nachos, quesadillas, melting chocolate, defrosting, reheating, softening ice cream (but only if you are going to eat the full pint; refreezing is no good), popcorn (just don't forget about it, lest your entire office get extremely mad at you). Cookbook author Priya Krishna cooks basmati rice in the microwave: 1 cup basmati to 2½ cups water, 16 minutes on high power, and it's done. Let's examine nachos. Conventional wisdom would say that the oven is the best place to make them. Wrong. Layer chips, beans, cheese, and meat all in a pile, and a one-minute zap later, you have perfect nachos. The oven burns chips, and even if you build and bake the nachos in stages, the bottom gets burnt.

Here's what is not okay to use a microwave for: pizza, steak, mostly anything made of ground meat (like meatballs), frozen bagels. Matt, born in the Midwest and not raised with proper bagel etiquette, has deep-seated trauma from over-defrosting Lender's bagels to a puck-like consistency in middle school.

When Daniel was working at Le Bernardin on the hot-appetizer station, he was responsible for a pretty avant-garde, and delicious, monkfish appetizer. The fillet was layered with truffles and foie gras, then wrapped in a blanched Savoy cabbage leaf. The dish was an expensive supplemental item, an addition to the already pricey tasting menu, and a real pain in the ass to make. As one of the first courses to arrive, it needed to be fired immediately when the guest was seated, and it took exactly twelve minutes to cook, steamed to order. Any undue delay in cooking, and the guests would have to sit and wait. Just lifting the lid to take a peek at the progress would release the steam and ruin the timing of a perfectly timed meal.

The difficulty was that you couldn't check on the fish until cutting it open to serve. Some pieces would be perfect, but others needed more time. Alas, once cut, you couldn't steam it further or you'd have a soggy mess on your hands. So it's fair to say that on certain occasions, when Daniel sliced into the monkfish fillet to plate, the monkfish was raw and starting over wasn't an option. Twelve more minutes of waiting for your second course during a $300 tasting menu is a deadly sin. *But . . .* pop the fish into the microwave for ninety seconds, and it's perfect every time. So after the fiftieth time undercooking it, microwaving it, and being berated by his boss, Daniel convinced the chef that they'd be better off just microwaving the fish in the first place. It wasn't an easy sell, but sometimes the microwave really is the best option—even at a three-star Michelin restaurant. ●

SIX-MINUTE MICROWAVE-POACHED COD WITH MUSHROOMS

Serves 2

---

1 large portobello mushroom, stemmed and cap cut into bite-size wedges

2 tablespoons dry white wine or water

2 (5-ounce) frozen cod fillets

½ lemon

½ teaspoon kosher salt

1 tablespoon unsalted butter

2 tablespoons chopped fresh flat-leaf parsley

Poaching fish in a microwave isn't something chefs generally boast about—or really ever do, for that matter. But it's time for Daniel to brag. This works perfectly every single time. The microwave works by emitting energy waves that jostle water molecules, heating them up and cooking the fish evenly with its own moisture. Covering your plate with plastic wrap locks in all the flavor and makes this a no-cleanup recipe. This recipe works just as well with fresh fish—simply reduce the cooking time by a minute or two.

1. Arrange the mushroom wedges on the plate on which you intend to serve the fish (make sure it is microwave-safe) and add 1 tablespoon of the wine to each plate. Place the fish on top, squeeze the lemon half evenly over the fish, and then season each fillet with ¼ teaspoon of the salt. Top each fillet with a ½-tablespoon pat of the butter. Cover the dish tightly with plastic wrap.

2. Microwave on high power for 6 minutes, stopping to rearrange the plate halfway through.

3. Let the fish rest for 1 minute before opening the microwave. To test if the fish is ready, uncover and gently insert a metal skewer, chopstick, or thermometer probe through the center, feeling for resistance. If the implement plunges through with no resistance, the fish is ready. If it is difficult to insert, re-cover the plate with plastic wrap and cook for an additional minute. When ready, uncover the fish, garnish with the parsley, and serve immediately.

What's the difference between a $30 knife and a $150 knife?

→ **THE FIRST KNIFE DANIEL** received was a gift from his mother. He was fourteen years old and working at Candle Cafe, a vegan restaurant located on the Upper East Side of Manhattan. His mother bought him an American version of a curved and thin-bladed Japanese usuba knife, which was a popular choice among hippie food professionals at the time. It worked wonders on all those mushrooms, cabbages, sweet potatoes, and turnips. His next knife was a pricey (and thick) Sabatier vegetable cleaver, another gift from his mom. But this one was absolutely useless, and it would serve as a wall ornament for the next twenty-five years. His next and most important knife was a nine-inch Wüsthof chef's knife, acquired from a fellow cook at Le Bernardin to settle a debt. It's the perfect size and blade for a professional chef of his stature, and it has followed him from job to job ever since (thanks Jeff O'Neill).

The point here is that love for a knife, no matter the price, material, structure, or fancy European name, is mostly in the eye of the dicer, with usefulness defined by the owner's needs. But there are some things to keep in mind, particularly when it comes to spending a lot of money on one.

Thinking about the knife's steel is important, and it comes down to hardness and softness. The harder the steel (measured on something called the Rockwell scale), the sharper you can make it, and the longer it will keep its edge. But there's a downside as well: the harder the steel, the more difficult it is to sharpen, and the more brittle and prone to chipping it becomes. The truth, however, is that most people are never going to sharpen their knives. Henckels makes

a great knife for a home cook because it's hard and holds its edge longer. Wüsthof is slightly softer and wins over the professional chef who sharpens his or her knives often.

As for the rest of a knife's structure—the shape, the style of the bolster, the scales, rivets, and butt—it comes down to a matter of preference. And keep in mind that a knife is an object we often make visible in our kitchens, whether it's laid across a cutting board, resting in a block, or hung from a magnetic strip (but hopefully never tossed in a drawer to jostle and dull itself, lying in wait to bite an unsuspecting hand reaching blindly for its blade).

The home cook is going to look at, and likely handle, his or her knives every single day. So buying a knife that meshes with your preferences is critical. It should feel nice in your hand, and the balance and look of the blade should get you excited. Then think about functionality: is it thin and elegant and good for slicing, or is it thick and heavy and strong enough for chopping? And maybe don't pay a fortune for it.

You can buy a quality Dexter-Russell or Victorinox plastic-handled cook's knife for $26. This is what most professional butchers use, and you can replace it every year or two. With its thinner blade and softer steel, it dulls quickly, so you'll need to sharpen it more often. In addition to his $500 Nenohi Nenox Corian-handled chef's knife from Korin in New York City (the best place to buy fancy Japanese knives in America), Daniel uses a Victorinox paring knife, which he loves for its thin, flexible blade that can skillfully whittle fragile vegetables—plus, a good paring knife seconds as an excellent steak knife. Matt loves his $40 plastic-handled Seki Magoroku chef's knives that he bought at Tokyu Hands in Shibuya. The answer is to spend $100 on a single knife (if you have the scratch), but less is okay. Also, avoid investing in a set of knives. They are great for kitting out an Airbnb, but ultimately, you will use a single knife more than the sum of the set. ●

CLASSIC ITALIAN CHOPPED SALAD

Daniel and Matt grew up eating Italian-style chopped salads from local pizzerias and red-sauce Italian joints in Manhattan and Kalamazoo, Michigan, and they'll continue eating them into the sunset of their lives. Classics never go out of style, and this is the tribute. The best part about this dish is its versatility as a catchall for leftover vegetables, lunch meats, and cheeses. Feel free to substitute, add, and subtract ingredients based on what looks good in your local market and whatever you have on hand to use up in the fridge.

Serves 4 to 6

½ sweet red onion, sliced thin

1 tablespoon red wine vinegar

Kosher salt

1 head crunchy green lettuce (such as romaine or iceberg), diced

2 Belgian endives, diced

½ cup pitted black olives, roughly chopped

1 cucumber, peeled, halved, seeded, and diced

1 large beefsteak tomato, halved through the equator, each half gently squeezed to release seeds, and flesh diced

3 celery stalks, diced

8 ounces mild Provolone cheese, diced

4 ounces salami, diced

1 (15-ounce) can chickpeas, drained

¼ cup Italian Vinaigrette (recipe follows)

Freshly ground black pepper

1. In a small bowl, toss the onion with the vinegar and a pinch of salt and set aside to macerate while you cut the remaining vegetables.

2. In a large bowl, combine the lettuce, endives, olives, cucumber, tomato, celery, cheese, salami, and chickpeas. Drizzle with the vinaigrette, sprinkle with a healthy pinch of salt, and grind pepper over to taste. Toss to mix well, then taste and adjust with more vinaigrette if needed. Top with the marinated onion and serve.

Italian Vinaigrette

Makes ½ cup

2 teaspoons Dijon mustard

3 tablespoons red wine vinegar

1 teaspoon kosher salt

1 teaspoon sugar

2 teaspoons chopped fresh oregano leaves

1 small clove garlic, minced

⅓ cup extra-virgin olive oil

1. in a small bowl, whisk together the mustard, vinegar, salt, sugar, oregano, and garlic. Slowly add the oil while whisking vigorously to emulsify. Alternatively, combine all of the ingredients in a small jar with a tight-fitting lid, cap tightly, and shake the ever-living heck out of it.

2. You will need ¼ cup for the salad. The remainder will keep in an airtight container in your fridge for up to 1 month.

I talk the talk, but should I buy a wok?

→ **THE SHORT ANSWER IS,** yes, you should buy a wok. It's one of the most versatile cooking surfaces around, and it can be used for making dishes within and outside of the Asian vernacular. A wok is amazing for one-pot meals, and it has the ability to perform multiple cooking techniques in the same pan at the same time. You can blister green beans around the rim while frying minced garlic and building a sauce in the center.

Woks are shaped from either thin carbon steel, so they heat up extremely quickly (and also cool down fast), or heavy cast iron, which heats slowly and retains its heat. With thin woks, the stove is cranked to high, and the cooking is fast and often intense. But unlike other cooking surfaces, the heat is most intense at the outer rim of the pan, as the flames lick up the sides while the center remains significantly cooler. This allows the home cook to sear meat and vegetables on the smoking edges while simultaneously cooking a sauce in the center. A quick flick of the wrist and the charred pork belly or blistered beans drop into the simmering center. Stir, plate, and you're on to the next dish. Peek into the kitchen of a busy Cantonese restaurant and you'll see lines of cooks clanging away with great focus and pageantry. It's a beautiful sight. Thicker cast-iron woks are used like Dutch ovens for searing, braising, and boiling.

You can pick up a wok online or at your local restaurant supply store, and it need not be an expensive purchase. Both Daniel and Matt have been cooking with carbon-steel woks that they picked up in New York's Chinatown for twenty dollars. There

are a couple of other things to keep in mind before you buy. Woks are sold with flat and round bottoms. For electric stoves, the flat bottom is necessary, but otherwise, buying a round model is ideal because it gives the most depth for cooking with wet ingredients without minimizing the dry cooking area along the sides. Make sure to buy a wok with a single wooden handle so you can use it like any other pot or pan in your kitchen. The loop handles might look cooler, but then you'll need a thick cloth or pot holder to avoid burning your hand. ●

friend of FOOD IQ

After she emigrated from Beijing and worked her way up through the kitchens of Thomas Keller, Guy Savoy, and José Andrés, SHIRLEY CHUNG was a finalist on season 14 of _Top Chef_. She is the author of _Chinese Heritage Cooking from My American Kitchen,_ and she owns and operates a Chinese American restaurant, Ms Chi Cafe, in Los Angeles.

What are the challenges you face when using a wok at home, versus in your commercial restaurant kitchen?

In the restaurant, flames shoot out of the burner, giving the wok energy, allowing for a final stage of caramelization to finish a stir-fry. Wok energy preserves freshness and locks in flavor. At home, my stove isn't hot enough, so I like to use a charcoal grill to fire my wok. I also deglaze with alcohol, like Shaoxing rice wine, and flambé the ingredients to give them a final lick of fire.

Do you need to season a wok, and how do you keep it from rusting?

Treat your wok just like you would a cast-iron pan. Keep it dry and oil it with either vegetable oil or lard. You can clean it out over the fire with salt, then burn the oil onto it to give it a nonstick-like coating. If your wok gets rusty, an old Chinese trick is to heat your wok with a slice of raw onion over the rust spot until the onion is completely charred. Rub the charred onion over the rust, and the rust will disappear. I don't know how it works, but you'll be amazed by how well it does.

What's your favorite dish to cook in a wok?

I have been making fried rice since I was six years old. It's the simplest dish but one of the hardest to do well. You need to work in stages, first blanching your veggies and protein in oil, then sautéing your aromatics and cooking your egg, before adding your rice and cooking it in a single layer so that each kernel is toasted. If your rice is too greasy, add more egg, and the egg will soak up the oil.

WOK-BLISTERED GREEN BEANS WITH BLACK BEAN SAUCE

Serves 3 or 4

¼ cup vegetable oil

1 pound green beans, stem ends removed and well dried

3 cloves garlic, finely chopped

1½-inch knob fresh ginger, peeled and minced

2 green onions, white and green parts, thinly sliced

½ teaspoon red chile flakes

4 teaspoons Chinese black bean sauce (the Juan Cheng Pixian Douban brand available online is best)

2 teaspoons sugar

2 teaspoons light soy sauce

3 tablespoons Shaoxing rice wine

Kosher salt

We love cooking green beans in a wok because you can properly blister them on the outer edge of the pan while building the sauce in the middle. This cooking technique, and the sauce, works for many other vegetables (broccoli, cauliflower, and zucchini come to mind), so feel free to play with whatever's in the fridge. You can also add chicken, pork, shrimp, or beef, too. Just dice the meat into bite-size pieces and toss it with a little cornstarch before frying to the proper temperature.

1. Heat the oil in a wok over high heat until it begins to smoke.

2. Add the green beans and cook, stirring frequently, for 3 minutes, then push them to the outer edges of the wok to blister.

3. Add the garlic, ginger, green onions, and chile flakes to the center of the wok and cook, stirring constantly, just until they begin to brown, about 2 minutes.

4. Add the black bean sauce, sugar, and soy sauce to the ginger mixture, then deglaze the pan with the wine, adding it along the rim and then stir to incorporate, folding the green beans into the sauce. Continue cooking, stirring frequently, for 2 more minutes. Taste and adjust the seasoning with salt if needed, and serve warm.

I'm not a street pharmacist. Do I really need a digital scale?

→ **TEN YEARS AGO, DANIEL** bought a used Edlund-brand digital scale for eleven dollars at a restaurant supply store on the Bowery in New York City and has used it every day since. Three years ago, Matt bought a bright orange Escali Primo scale for thirty dollars off Amazon, and he uses it every day too. Let's start by saying that there is no downside to owning a digital scale. It's cheap, and it doesn't take up a lot of space. It's also essential for making great coffee (see page 68). So there's that.

But what's more important is that all good restaurant kitchens work more by weight (pounds, grams) and less by volume (spoons, cups). This is for a very good reason: cooking with a scale is both faster and more accurate. When it comes to measuring anything solid, from spices to all-purpose flour to cups of chopped parsley, it's really tough to stay consistent by volume. Take that parsley, for instance. How much parsley would it take to fill a cup using the *least* amount of leaves possible, and how much could you pack in if you really wanted to get the *most* in there? The amount would vary greatly. A teaspoon of finely ground garlic powder may be easier to codify, but with kosher salt, the difference is extreme: Morton's packs nearly twice the volume of Diamond Crystal (see page 8). When using weight, the variability is removed, so you can follow a recipe much more accurately. A hundred grams of parsley is always the same amount, whether you pack it into a small ramekin or scatter it across a large bowl.

With baking, measuring in weight is even more important, particularly when you're batching recipes up and down (called scaling a recipe—for a reason), and it's especially useful when baking by percentage weight (called baker's math; see page 124). A loosely packed cup of flour can weigh a third less than a tightly packed cup. And exactly how many pounds per square inch register a tight pack? A half cup of flour can mean the difference between chocolate chip cookies coming out gooey and chewy as advertised or closer to a muffin in consistency. We've all visited cookie muffin land. It's a sad place.

And even when taking accuracy out of the equation, cooking by weight is faster and cleaner because you can quickly add and subtract amounts. For example, if you need twenty-five grams kosher salt, you can place your salt cellar on the scale, hit tare (clocking to zero), and then remove the salt directly from the container (it will read twenty-five grams lighter when you've removed the proper amount), saving yourself the need to dirty a measuring container. A scale is also essential for figuring out how much seasoning to use for meat, which can generally be calculated as a percentage of the weight of the meat (1 to 1.5 percent of the total weight is a good beginning range). Place your Berkshire pork chops on the gram scale, multiply its weight by .015, and you have the ideal amount of salt for seasoning your cuts.

Spoons are great. Cups are even better. We aren't telling you to throw them out. The fact of the matter is that the modern American way of writing recipes is by volume—including most of the recipes in this book. And with a deeply rooted home-cooking style, it's unlikely this will change outside of baking books (any good baking book will offer both measurements). But for anybody who has squeezed a half cup of honey from that little bear for spiced cookies or a pecan pie, and then attempted to get that entire half cup into the recipe from a measuring cup, you know how much of a pain in the ass it is. The scale is your savior. ●

GERMAN PRETZELS

Homemade pretzels are one thousand times better than anything you've ever had dried, at the mall, or peddled from an NYC hot dog cart. They are sweet, soft, tangy, and crunchy all at the same time—true carbohydrate nirvana. Making pretzels is a serious endeavor worth taking on, and this recipe requires special ingredients like lye (or baking soda in a pinch), barley malt syrup, and pretzel salt (although Maldon works well as a substitute), so some planning and extra time is needed. If you want to bake like a pro, get used to weighing everything. The three columns below represent baker's percentages (to help you scale the recipe easily), gram weight (for consistently accurate results), and approximate volumetric measures (for the folks who just want to make delicious pretzels without getting a math headache).

Makes 6 large pretzels

Unsalted butter 5%	15 grams	1 tablespoon
Flour 100%	300 grams	2½ cups
Water 56%	168 grams	⅔ cup
Kosher salt 1.8%	6 grams	1 teaspoon
Active dry yeast 2%	6 grams	1 teaspoon
Malt 2%	6 grams	1 teaspoon

Food-grade lye or baking soda for the water bath

Pretzel salt or Maldon salt for topping

1. In a small pot, melt the butter over low heat.

2. Put the flour, water, salt, yeast, malt, and melted butter into the bowl of a stand mixer fitted with a dough hook or a large bowl. In the mixer on low speed or with a wooden spoon, mix together until all the ingredients are thoroughly incorporated and a thick dough forms. Turn the dough out onto a lightly floured work surface and knead until soft and smooth, at least 8 minutes. Transfer the dough to a large, lightly greased bowl (use butter, shortening, or vegetable oil spray), cover the bowl with plastic wrap, and let rest at room temperature for 30 minutes.

3. Transfer the dough to a lightly floured surface and divide into six equal pieces, then let rest, uncovered, for another 10 minutes. Meanwhile, preheat the oven to 450°F. Line a large sheet pan (18 by 13 inches) with parchment paper and lightly grease the parchment with butter, shortening, or vegetable oil spray.

4. One at a time, roll each dough piece into a 24-inch-long cylinder, then gently twist the cylinder into a pretzel shape: make a big loop, cross one end over the other, and then bring the ends back up to form two small loops with the ends joining the lower body of the large loop, pressing the ends in firmly. As each pretzel is shaped, transfer it to the prepared pan. Let rest for 30 minutes to rise.

5. While the pretzels are rising, make the lye water bath. Wearing rubber gloves and eye protection, make a 4 percent lye solution by gently mixing 40 grams (about 3 tablespoons) lye into 4 cups water in a deep bowl. You can use baking soda in place of the lye, but you won't get the true dark pretzel color and taste: in a small pot, bring 4 cups water to a boil, add ¼ cup baking soda, stir just until dissolved, then remove from the heat and let cool completely. One at a time, dip each pretzel into the lye or baking soda solution for 15 seconds, turning it once, then return it to the sheet pan and sprinkle it with pretzel salt.

6. Bake the pretzels until deeply browned, about 15 minutes. Cool on a wire rack for at least 5 minutes before serving.

Warning: Cooking with lye can be dangerous business, so read the safety instructions, and wear gloves and eye protection.

Should I invest in that heavy mortar and pestle?

→ **MORE THAN FOUR THOUSAND** years of tradition, from Moses to Sandy Koufax, is incredible. But for thirty-five thousand years, people have been pounding away in their kitchens, and caves, with impressive results. And it's without a doubt that the mortar and pestle will last for another thirty-five thousand years because this ancient combo really is one of the most versatile pieces of kitchen equipment around, functioning as a garlic press, spice grinder, mixing bowl, and blender all in one.

The mortar and pestle was built for smashing and mashing. Take garlic, for example. The problem with chopping garlic is that everything it touches will taste like garlic! Good luck washing the garlic flavor out of your cutting board or off of your knife. The garlic from three days ago will show up in your mango slices today. Second, in a classic vinaigrette recipe, you need raw garlic, but you don't want an errant chunk showing up with a mouthful of endive. The mortar and pestle easily pulverizes the garlic into a paste and keeps it isolated from the rest of your cooking.

With herbs, there are moments when you want to finely chop them for a beautiful presentation, and there are times when you want to release their flavors. When Daniel makes porchetta, he smashes together lemon zest, garlic, rosemary, black pepper, and salt. The result is a deeply intense flavor that chopping won't achieve.

In the United States, the mortar and pestle is widely known for its use in French and Italian cuisine, but really, it's found in every country around the world. That tableside guacamole service is not just for a flare of showmanship—it's an ideal way to transform ripe avocados, cilantro, and limes into something pretty remarkable. In Thai cuisine, the mortar and pestle is the ultimate tool for making fiery

curry pastes. You can buy a rough stone one, which Daniel likes the best for grinding. A smooth marble or porcelain one is better for sauces, like a silky smooth aioli. Or buy a deep wooden set and the incredible *Pok Pok* cookbook for a recipe to use it with.

Daniel loves his oversize, unglazed set from Milton Brook, but whatever your pleasure, you don't have to spend a ton of money on one. Just make sure your mortar is big enough so you can give your ingredients a good smash without fear of exploding spices scattering all over your kitchen. •

SALMON PORCHETTA

Serves 2

---

2 tablespoons extra-virgin olive oil, plus more for drizzling

2 (5-ounce) skin-on salmon fillets

Kosher salt

¼ teaspoon black peppercorns

¼ teaspoon fennel seeds

1 clove garlic

1 small rosemary sprig, chopped (about 1 teaspoon)

Grated zest of 1 lemon

Porchetta is an iconic slow-roasted pork recipe with roots dating back to fifteenth-century central Italy. Traditionally, a young pig is stuffed with rosemary, garlic, black pepper, lemon zest, and fennel seeds and cooked slowy over a wood fire until its flesh is tender and juicy and its skin is shatteringly crispy. Preparing salmon in the same style is one of Daniel's signature dishes, and it's a great way to share the incredible flavors with pescatarian friends. The simple preparation takes only a few minutes, but the rich fish, paired with the intensely flavorful, citrus-forward spice rub, may become a weeknight favorite for years to come.

1. Preheat the broiler. Position an oven rack about 8 inches from the heat source. Drizzle a little oil on a baking pan just large enough to hold the salmon.

2. Season each salmon fillet all over with ½ teaspoon salt.

3. In a mortar with a pestle, crush the peppercorns and fennel seeds. Add the garlic, rosemary, and a pinch of salt and continue smashing to a fine paste. Add the lemon zest and oil and mix to incorporate.

4. Place the salmon, skin side down, on the oiled pan and spoon the seasoning mix over the top, being careful to distribute the mixture evenly so it forms a nice even crust during cooking.

5. Broil the salmon until the top is crispy and browned and the flesh is juicy and just cooked through, about 6 minutes. To test if the fish is ready, gently insert a metal skewer, chopstick, or thermometer probe through the center, feeling for resistance. If the implement plunges through with no resistance, the fish is ready. If it is difficult to insert, return the fish to the broiler for an additional minute or as needed.

What is a mandoline, and is it really worth a possible trip to the emergency room?

→ **SOME PEOPLE ARE SCARED** of the mandoline, and to be honest, this razor-sharp slicer can be pretty scary. One false move and two of your knuckles can end up as part of your tarte Tatin. Or, as Daniel says, it's like poker: an expensive lesson to learn. But if you weather the possibility of an evening at the ER and view the slicer's exposed blade as a razor blade—that is, don't play around with it—you will reap the benefits of one of the most useful pieces of cooking gear under thirty bucks.

Mandolines aren't a necessity, and you can do most things without one. But they will save a *lot* of time and improve your presentation. And let's face it, you'll be a lot more inclined to tackle that potato gratin knowing the slicing will take you only five minutes: simply adjust the blade to the proper thickness and slice (carefully) with abandon. There's nothing more satisfying than watching uniform slices peel off the underside effortlessly. Thinly slicing radishes and celery for a salad won't be a chore but a pleasure with the help of a thirty-nine-dollar plastic Benriner slicer. Garlic cloves for garlic chips, cucumbers for a large salad, onions for a backyard barbecue's worth of burgers—all are handled in record time.

When Daniel was a young cook at Le Bernardin, one of his first daily jobs was to put a large bag of shallots and two cases of fennel through a mandoline fitted with the vicious teeth attachment to yield the tricky julienne cut with a single glide. The final dish was an oyster escabeche, the mollusks gently poached in olive oil with a hit of vinegar added at the end; nobody in the dining room would have known the danger he endured. Naturally, after inevitably nicking himself each time he tackled a shallot, his next task was to slice three hundred lemon wedges. The moral of the story is to use the provided safety shield until you're well acquainted with your new toy.

And here is one additional piece of advice: just because you can slice something paper-thin doesn't mean you should. Sometimes a little toothsome bite is needed so your celery slices don't disappear. Paper-thin onion slices on a burger may look good on Instagram, but they don't deliver the crunch necessary to cut through the rich grilled beef (and cheese and bacon and mayonnaise), so turn the screw to the left and give those slices some gumption. Simply put, always be mindful of thickness. That adjustment screw is there for a reason. ●

RAW CAULIFLOWER SALAD WITH TOASTED SUNFLOWER SEEDS

Serves 4

Anchovy Vinaigrette
3 olive oil-packed anchovy fillets

½ clove garlic

2 tablespoons drained capers

Pinch of kosher salt

1 tablespoon Dijon mustard

2 tablespoons red wine vinegar

1 tablespoon liquid from jarred capers

5 tablespoons extra-virgin olive oil

1 cauliflower

Kosher salt

½ cup chopped fresh flat-leaf parsley

½ cup sliced green onions, white and green parts

¼ cup dried currants or raisins

¼ cup toasted sunflower seeds

Freshly ground black pepper

The first time Daniel tried a raw cauliflower salad was at chef Jonathan Waxman's iconic Barbuto restaurant in New York's Meatpacking District. As with so many of Waxman's dishes that highlight simple, often underappreciated ingredients, the raw cauliflower salad was a masterpiece of restraint. And it helped catalyze the cauliflower renaissance that recently rescued the underappreciated vegetable from the supermarket freezer section, placing it on Michelin-starred menus around the world. When thinly sliced, the crunchy, cruciferous vegetable is the perfect building block for a hearty salad tossed with toasted sunflower seeds and dressed with a tangy anchovy vinaigrette. Feel free to experiment with other dried fruits and nuts or to substitute your favorite dressing.

1. To make the vinaigrette, in a mortar with a pestle or in a small food processor, combine the anchovies, garlic, capers, and salt and puree. Add the mustard, vinegar, and caper liquid and continue pureeing. Slowly drizzle in the oil while continuing to mix until the vinaigrette emulsifies.

2. Cut the cauliflower into quarters, remove any leaves, and trim away half of the stem, being careful to leave enough to hold the florets together. Adjust your mandoline for medium-thin slices (about ⅛ inch or 3 mm thick), then slice all of the cauliflower quarters into a large bowl. Add 1 teaspoon salt and toss to coat evenly.

3. Add the parsley, green onions, currants, and sunflower seeds to the cauliflower, then drizzle the vinaigrette over the top and stir and toss to mix well. Season to taste with salt and pepper. Serve immediately.

Should I buy a donabe, a tagine, a Dutch oven, a clay cooker, or all of them?

→ **THE ALLURE OF A** one-pot meal is hard to deny. We lust after the simplicity of the cooking (set it and forget it), and the beauty of the cooking vessel itself is part of the attraction. There's no better feeling than lifting the lid of a cauldron tableside, revealing the fruits (or stone-fruit tagine) of your labor with a burst of steam and gentle applause from the group. A little showmanship goes a long way toward acing your dinner-party exam (remember, the guests are always grading).

When thinking about buying a fancy cooker, you have many options. Some are designed for a specific dish and must be used to cook that dish properly, while others are more versatile and forgiving. Many make useful additions to your home kitchen, while others aren't worth the overweight baggage fee to get them home from your vacation. And there's one that every kitchen should house—more on that later.

Among the most recognizable is the **tagine**, a portable ceramic oven from North Africa used to cook hearty, one-pot stews that, like the vessel itself, are called tagines. A tagine has a distinctly tall, conical lid that is designed to funnel the condensing steam down the sides and back into the wide and shallow bottom. The design maximizes the conservation of moisture, a handy feature for traveling across the arid desert sands. The delicious namesake stews are a layered mix of spiced meats and vegetables braised with minimal water and often incorporating a sweet component of fresh or dried fruits.

The **clay cooker** is a throwback to the 1970s, when German company Römertopf started widely distributing an Etruscan-inspired earthenware cooker. Daniel's mom used one in New York City to make chicken and rice. Matt's mom used a small one for roasting garlic. The clay cooker also utilizes a steam-roasting technique that rewards you with incredibly moist and tender results. Daniel cooks lamb necks for hours in a clay cooker, and he uses one for bread baking. The important thing to remember with clay, which is porous, is that it needs to be soaked ahead of cooking, and that the oven temperature needs to start low—too hot and it will crack.

The **donabe** is a Japanese-style clay cooker that can be thick enough to be placed directly over a fire. It's a versatile earthenware vessel often used to cook rice, but it works perfectly well for braising meats and fish, and for soups. Donabes often incorporate a third piece: a glazed clay strainer that allows you to steam fish or vegetables while simultaneously cooking rice below.

But of all the world's pots, if Daniel and Matt had to choose only one, it would be the heavy-sided, enameled cast-iron **Dutch oven**. With a tight lid and a sturdy build, a Dutch oven can be used for basically any style of cooking: on the stove top for searing stew meat, shallow frying chicken, boiling dumplings, or finishing pasta, and in the oven for long wet or dry braises, baking sourdough, or cooking a classic pot roast. These heavy cookers are sold in every size and at every price point (except cheap). Le Creuset and Staub are two popular French brands that sell their pots in a swath of trendy colors (plus red). If buying a new Dutch oven is out of your financial reach, visit a local swap meet, garage sale, or flea market, where good-quality vintage pieces can be acquired for much less. ●

DJEJ MCHERMEL

CHICKEN TAGINE WITH CHERMOULA AND GREEN OLIVES

Serves 4

---

3 pounds chicken drumsticks and thighs

Kosher salt

1 cup chopped fresh cilantro

½ cup chopped fresh flat-leaf parsley

3 cloves garlic, finely chopped

1 tablespoon sweet paprika

1 teaspoon ground cumin

½ teaspoon ground turmeric

4 tablespoons extra-virgin olive oil

½ preserved lemon, pulp removed and chopped, seeds discarded, and rind sliced

Small pinch of saffron threads (optional)

1 yellow onion, thinly sliced

½ cup green olives, pitted

Juice of 1 fresh lemon

Daniel had his first tagine at Cafe Mogador, a beloved neighborhood restaurant in Manhattan's East Village. The busy café has been serving traditional Moroccan food for close to forty years, and it's still one of Daniel's favorite places to visit, particularly for tagine. This version, chicken mchermel, is served with green olives and preserved lemons, and it utilizes a robust marinade style called chermoula, which has many variations (this one is with fresh herbs, preserved lemon pulp, garlic, and spices). If you don't have a tagine, you can make the recipe in a Dutch oven or any clay pot. But there's something special about the look of the tagine when you raise the lid tableside and the fragrant steam pours out, so here's your excuse to buy one.

1. The night before cooking, season the chicken with about 1 tablespoon salt (about 1 percent by weight) and set aside. In a large bowl, combine the cilantro, parsley, garlic, paprika, cumin, turmeric, 3 tablespoons of the oil, the preserved lemon pulp, and the saffron, if using. Add the chicken to the bowl and rub the marinade all over the pieces, coating well. Cover and refrigerate overnight.

2. Two hours before you're ready to eat, line the bottom of your tagine with the onion slices, drizzle with the remaining 1 tablespoon oil, and sprinkle with a pinch of salt. Add the chicken, making sure to include all of the marinade. Using a diffuser to ensure your tagine doesn't crack, place the tagine over medium heat, cover, and heat until the marinade begins to boil, about 10 minutes. Lower the heat to a gentle simmer and cook for 1 hour.

3. Add the olives and preserved lemon rind slices, re-cover, and continue cooking for 15 minutes longer. The chicken should be falling off the bone tender. Season with the lemon juice before serving.

PRESERVED LEMONS ARE HAVING A MOMENT

A lot has been written about preserved lemons and the Cooking Internet has gone nuts as of late (and rightly so). They add the energy of tangy citrus to many dishes, such as bean salad, poached salmon, fried rice, and salad dressing, to name only a few. They have a deep flavor that can't be replicated by any other ingredient. Making them is extremely easy, but it takes time. There are some recipes for "quick" preserved lemons in which you cook the fruit with sugar and extremely salty water, but they won't give you the flavor of a true preserved lemon. For the real deal, cut some lemons in half lengthwise, pack them into a jar or Tupperware container, and cover them completely with a mixture of four parts kosher salt to one part sugar. For half a dozen lemons, that's 2 cups sugar and 8 cups kosher salt. Cover tightly and refrigerate for 3 months. Yes, it really takes that long. But it's worth it.

Check on them from time to time, adding more salt as necessary to keep them covered. They will last for up to a year under the salt, so dig them out one at a time and give them a rinse before using them. So the next time you have a few too many lemons lying around, preserve a batch. You can start by doing a few at a time in a small jar.

How do I make great coffee, and do I need to spend $300 on beans and gear?

→ **THERE IS SOMETHING TO** be said for paying attention, and possibly very close attention, to anything that you consume daily, or as much as four times every *day*. But the truth is that coffee is often an afterthought for people who care a great deal about everything else they put into their bodies. For many who think deeply about food, coffee is a great blind spot. It's a means to an end, and that's about it. Morning lubrication to get the gears moving. A cortado at four o'clock with coworkers to talk about the pitch deck. Sanka at grandma's house. That bag of Dunkin' Donuts French vanilla that sits in your freezer. Matt shivers at that last thought. Sorry.

Daniel and Matt have talked a lot about coffee over the past couple of years, with Daniel, an admitted dilettante, slowly coming around to Matt's point of view. One thing they agree on is that there is a lot to be said about why coffee is underappreciated and what everybody should be doing to change that. Here, they each take a crack at answering the question.

Daniel: There is no reason you shouldn't make the best coffee you can make, but for nearly a decade, for whatever reason, coffee has exploded within hipster culture. I don't wear a bow tie and a monocle to make a cocktail, so why do I need to be a chemist to make a cup of coffee? I can make a great cup of coffee without breaking the bank if I focus on the areas that make the most difference. It's all about busting through the bullshit and being honest about what makes good coffee good and what's standing on pretense.

First things first, I understand that when you go to a coffee shop, the shop is selling you more than a cup of coffee. It is selling its culture, the theater of it, and you should feel free to bring that home if it tickles your fancy. But don't pretend any of that makes a [insert expletive] bit of difference to the way your coffee actually tastes. Ultimately, the fanciest pour over is nothing more than what is made in your nineteen-dollar drip coffee machine, and those do the work for you! So do spend a little more money on high-quality, freshly roasted whole beans; do get a decent burr grinder that will grind your beans evenly, fresh every day; and do portion your coffee-to-water ratio consistently. Those are the things that make a huge, tangible difference. The rest is just snake oil for the suckers.

Matt: I've written about coffee for years, and I've gotten to know some really passionate and hyperaware folks working in progressive coffee circles. Trust me, these are your people, Daniel! I was also lucky enough to travel to several Ethiopian coffee farms with Geoff Watts, the head of coffee at Intelligentsia Coffee. Visiting "origin" was a life-changing experience for me, both as a journalist and a coffee geek, and it showed me what goes into growing, buying, and evaluating coffee in the field. It's an extraordinary process, and the farmers around the world, like many forms of agribusiness, just aren't paid enough. We, as a culture, need to think more about the coffee we drink. Nobody at the bar questions paying $7 for an industrial Miller Lite that costs pennies to brew, so why do we complain about paying more than $10 per pound for coffee that's grown and cultivated halfway around the world? To be fairly priced, coffee needs to start at $20 a pound, or around 50 cents per cup at home.

I personally buy coffees from all over the world, including through online retailers and at my favorite café roasters in New York. At home, I hand brew using a Chemex and a gooseneck kettle (that Daniel rolled his eyes about until his brother bought him one for his birthday!), and I uniformly weigh out my water and coffee, hitting a 15:1 ratio each time. The point of keeping the method consistent is not only to brew the most enjoyable cup each time, but to be able to grade the coffee consistently each time—tasting for sweetness and acidity, which can

friend of
FOOD IQ

SUMI ALI is the cofounder and head roaster of mail-order coffee company and budding media empire Yes Plz, based in Los Angeles.

swing wildly from country to country and from roast to roast.

Sparkling wine drinkers might think of it as the difference between drinking a wild Montlouis-sur-Loire pét-nat and Veuve Clicquot Yellow Label Brut. Each is high quality, though they are strikingly different. A naturally processed coffee from the Guji zone in Ethiopia drinks very differently from a blend of Brazilian and Colombian washed coffees. But to taste this difference, each cup needs to be brewed in a uniform way—same weight, same water every time.

I agree with some of Daniel's points, mostly that there is a real mythos of the coffee bar these days, and that these public spaces have become more than a place to grab some cold brew and a scone. And I agree that coffee snobbery, like meat snobbery and balsamic vinegar snobbery, has no place in food. But, bro, automatic drip versus pour over? There is a difference. That said, I am fully in support of using an automatic drip machine. They can be programmed to brew ahead of time and to keep coffee warm for hours. When buying one, the key is to find a machine that brews evenly and doesn't scorch the coffee sitting in the carafe. The market offers many quality brands like OXO and Bonavita, to name just two. But in the end, the most important element is measuring your coffee and water and hitting that exact ratio. ●

Why will people pay twelve dollars for a Coors Light, and then complain that a cup of freshly roasted, perfectly extracted coffee costs more than three dollars?

Craft beer has done a really good job of bringing everyone along for the ride and getting customers to pay more. But there's also a cultural barrier. I've never heard of somebody getting made fun of for paying eight dollars for a PBR, but every day I hear, "You spent three dollars for a cup of coffee?!" For coffee, as an industry, we've done a pretty good job of trying to get the price up, given that the cost of producing coffee in a responsible way is ridiculous. We're focused on getting people from drinking grocery-store, non-specialty coffee to a highly curated and super-fresh experience. But we still have a ways to go.

Freshness is key. Coffee goes bad! People aren't seeing that.

Coffee is more of an ingredient than a food product, and ingredients go bad. Coffee is like lettuce—you want it to be fresh, but it's up to you to prepare it.

What's the most important tip for figuring out what kind (variety or region or roast style) of coffee you like?

It's not as concrete, and coffee has a more ephemeral nature than wine. It comes down to the question we ask our customers: Do you like this coffee of ours better than what you had yesterday? And are you looking forward to next week? That's all we can ask.

A PERFECT CUP OF COFFEE

8 fl ounce serving:
290 grams water, 16
grams coffee

12 fl ounce serving:
415 grams water, 23
grams coffee

16 fl ounce serving:
525 grams water, 29
grams coffee

24 fl ounce serving:
800 grams water, 45
grams coffee

This coffee recipe comes from the fine folks at Intelligentsia, a pioneering specialty coffee company founded in 1995. Along with running some of the finest cafés in Chicago and Los Angeles, the founders virtually invented a direct-trade model that places an emphasis on equitable payment to their partners in Africa and Central and South America. Pour over is a precise way to brew that utilizes drippers, including the Chemex and Hario V60. Pour-over fans enjoy the ritual of grinding, blooming, and pouring hot water over the grinds from a slow-pour gooseneck kettle. Does it make a superior cup? It's debatable, but the methodical approach to a pour over has appealed to coffee drinkers for decades. Don't have a Chemex or a digital scale to weigh your coffee? No worries. Use these same coffee and water amounts in your automatic drip machine. For conversion, 5 grams equals 1 tablespoon ground coffee.

1. Fill your kettle and set it to boil. If you have a digital kettle, set to between 205° and 210°F.

2. Take a paper filter, open it up, set it in the brewing device, and rinse it thoroughly with hot water. This will ensure that no papery taste resides in the brew, and it will heat the brewer. If you are using a Chemex, position the filter so that the side of the filter with the three folds is against the spout.

3. Weigh the coffee beans and grind on a medium-to-fine setting.

4. Place the brewer with its filter on the scale, add the ground beans, and hit tare to reset the weight to zero. (See page 56 for more about buying and working with a digital scale.)

5. Once the water reaches the correct temperature, start your timer and pour three times as much water as coffee (e.g., 23 grams coffee x 3 = 69 grams water) over the grounds. The goal is to moisten the grounds with an even saturation, so pour slowly. This essential step allows the coffee to degas, enabling the water to absorb the full potential of the coffee. This is called the bloom.

6. After about 1 minute, add the rest of water in stages (100 to 250 g at a time) until reaching the desired final brew weight. Pour the water slowly (8 to 10 g per second) in a spiral pattern that goes from the center out to the perimeter and back to the center again. Avoid pouring directly onto the paper filter above the coffee.

7. Once the liquid disappears from above the grounds, the brew is finished.

So I bought the sous vide machine. Now what?

→ **IN THE LATE 2010S,** there was a great wave of sous vide hype, with companies like Anova and Joule selling hundreds of thousands of units to eager home cooks with the promise of simplifying their lives and giving them an edge in their meat and vegetable cooking. Think flawlessly cooked steaks every time with no more effort than if you were tossing them on the grill—or so the pitch went. And while the excitement about the hundred-dollar gadget has cooled a little as of late, there's still a really good reason to dust it off (if you own one), and even to buy one in the first place.

Sous vide cooking applies hot water set at a precise temperature for even heating that cannot be achieved with any conventional kitchen tool. Think about roasting a pork loin in an oven set to 350°F. In order for the center of the loin to reach 140°F, the outside receives greater exposure to the heat, and it will inevitably be overcooked by the time the inside comes up to the desired temperature. With the sous vide machine, you can set it to reach the target temperature evenly throughout, from edge to edge, then sear the outside quickly for color and caramelized flavor.

But let's get real: unless you're Grant Achatz, you're not cooking with your sous vide machine every day. For a few strategic meals throughout the year, though, it comes in handy big-time, and it's worth the investment. Daniel invariably uses it every year for his Thanksgiving turkey. (Talk about a little pressure—the chef handling the spotlight dish during America's annual cooking holiday.) After removing the legs (which he braises), he cooks the breast using a sous vide machine. Why? It's the only way to keep the tender meat from overcooking. Know why the thinly sliced turkey breast at your favorite deli is always so moist? You guessed it—they turned to sous vide to cook that sucker at just the right temperature. For a holiday like Thanksgiving, sous vide cooking offers the added benefit of freeing up the oven, so you don't have to argue with Aunt Mary about when she can cook her pecan and pumpkin pies. "The failure rate with a sous vide recipe is really, really low," says chef and cookbook author Hugh Acheson who, unsurprisingly, wrote a book about sous vide that Matt likes to call Hugh Vide (it's a great book). "You just need to know the optimum temperature, and you will really nail the recipes."

Another great time to whip out the sous vide machine is for those backyard barbecues. Grilling steaks for a large group can be intimidating if you're not an experienced cook, but with the "reverse-sear" technique, you can use sous vide to bring it to the proper, perfectly medium-rare temperature, then throw it on the grill for a couple of minutes for a crusty outer layer. The result is a tender and juicy New York strip with a perfectly crusted exterior.

Daniel likes to bring out the sous vide machine for vegetables, too. He learned to poach endives with kosher salt, lemon juice, chicken stock, and thyme from chef Laurent Manrique, who seals them in a vacuum-sealed bag before immersing them in the sous vide bath. The technique concentrates the sweetness, yielding an intensely flavorful result. The endives are tender, yet they retain their crunchy snap and are delicious as a side dish, quickly seared in butter; chilled in salad; or on their own. And by the way, it's a common myth furthered by the sous vide companies that you need to use one of their proprietary fancy-pants bags to cook in. This is wrong—a ziplock plastic freezer bag will work just fine.

With a sous vide machine, you can geek out like *The Food Lab*'s J. Kenji López-Alt and soft-poach eggs directly in their shells, or long-braise short ribs for twenty-seven hours to medium-rare perfection. But for most people, it's more about cooking a great steak than about channeling your inner molecular gastronomer. And another pro tip: a sous vide machine will heat up a kiddie pool in no time. ●

THE BEST CHICKEN BREAST

Serves 4

---

4 (5-ounce) boneless, skinless chicken breasts

Kosher salt

2 thyme sprigs

¼ lemon

Ask any chef how they feel about boneless, skinless chicken breast, and your question will be met with disdain. If you're looking for flavor, throw a dart at basically any other part of the chicken and it would best the breast. But if you're eating with your overall health in mind, then boneless, skinless chicken breast offers the best protein bang for your buck. The problem is that the chicken breast is very lean, and the proteins are fragile and easily overcooked. You have to cook them perfectly, low and slow, to retain their moisture. But when you do, there's something really wonderful about the tender, cut-with-a-fork chicken nirvana of a textbook breast. Once you go sous vide with these, there really is no going back.

1. Set your sous vide machine to 145°F.

2. Place the chicken in an airtight plastic freezer bag and season with salt (aim for 1.5 percent by weight, or 2 teaspoons). Add the thyme, squeeze the juice from the lemon quarter into the bag, and add the spent lemon. Push as much air out of the bag as possible and seal it.

3. Poach the chicken in the water bath for 1 hour. For the best results, cool the chicken in the bag in the refrigerator before opening it.

4. Serve cold, sliced on a sandwich or salad, or reheat gently in the microwave or oven.

What's the difference between nonstick, cast iron, stainless steel, and carbon steel pans?

→ **THERE ARE MANY TYPES** of cookware and cooking surfaces on the market, and Daniel is often asked which one is the *best* . . . without much else to inform his answer. The truth is, the best cookware is the pan you feel most comfortable searing, sizzling, and sautéing with. Yes, that seems like an attempt to duck the question, but it is actually a setup of sorts to help explain the different types of pans available and how they work for the different jobs in the kitchen. However, one thing is absolutely true for Daniel, who has more than two decades of experience using different cookware: the most expensive is most certainly *not* the best. Here are some thoughts on each.

Nonstick: Frankly, it's a pan that shit doesn't stick to, and it's widely suggested as the go-to choice for frying eggs. But "nonstick" doesn't necessarily speak to the characteristics of the actual pan. There are incredibly thin nonstick pans that don't hold heat and sturdier ones that retain heat and cook evenly. In general, a nonstick pan has a coating that prevents food from sticking when it's cooking. Most high-quality pans are sold free of PFOA, short for the scary sounding perfluorooctanoic acid. Although cancer links have been rumored, the American Cancer Society has not categorized the substance as a carcinogen. In general, nonstick pans should be thought of as disposable and should be replaced whenever stuff starts sticking to them or when their surface starts to scrape away. So investing big bucks in a nonstick pan isn't the best move. And using nonstick for everything is a lazy cook's crutch and not something Daniel supports. Nonstick pans are good for certain tasks, like grilled cheese and fried eggs, but they aren't for everyday cooking.

Cast iron: This is a heavy pan that holds heat extremely well, meaning that when you crank the burner up to high, the heat will be absorbed by the metal, and the pan will maintain its temperature much better than other materials. This is why cast iron is great for cooking meat at a high temperature or for pan-frying chicken in oil. You want the temperature to remain consistently high for a longer period of time, even when dropping in cold meat. Cast iron is also good for baking corn bread because the intense heat gives it that nice crispy crust. The only drawback to cast-iron pans is that they rust if they're not cleaned and cared for properly.

Stainless steel: This is the most common cookware material because of its even heat distribution, durability, cleanability, and low weight. In the 1970s, engineers at All-Clad Metalcrafters, based in Canonsburg, Pennsylvania, discovered the technique for bonding stainless steel to aluminum, and with that the stainless-steel pan was born. Matt long had a hang-up with stainless steel because of the idea that stuff sticks to it, but Daniel was emphatic that the problem comes down to user error, and that with proper technique, nothing will stick to the surface. The key to cooking with stainless steel is to make sure the pan is properly heated before adding your ingredients and to be patient when things are sticking—with time, they will inevitably cook themselves free. Daniel compares frying an egg in stainless steel to driving a car with manual transmission. Part of the romance of cooking is mastering the different tools of the trade. Knowing how to cook confidently with stainless steel is a skill that bears fruit for a lifetime. By the end of writing this book, Matt had thrown out most of his nonstick pans and was on the stainless-steel express train.

Carbon steel: The more you cook with carbon steel, the more it becomes like a nonstick surface. You can think of it as a portable griddle, or as a lighter-weight version of cast iron, as it holds heat longer than stainless steel but heats up (and cools down) faster than cast iron. Carbon-steel pans are specialty cookware, and they require special care to maintain their surface (you can use the same technique for seasoning cast-iron vessels to keep them in proper working order). They work well for specific jobs, like getting extra-crispy skin on fish (see page 122), searing vegetables like Brussels sprouts and zucchini for a perfect golden brown crust, and griddling pancakes or English muffins.

Matt wondered if **copper pots** were just for assholes. But Daniel assured him that while they're heavy and expensive, they also hold amazing cooking properties, as long as it's a proper copper pan and not just copper plated. Copper holds heat like cast iron, but it has a stainless-steel laminate surface. It's the best of both worlds, and there is nothing like cooking a steak in a copper pan. Just be aware that it takes a really long time to heat up, and once it's hot, it will stay ripping hot. So mind the heat, as once you get copper hot, it can be tough to control. ●

HOW DO I CARE FOR A CAST-IRON PAN EXACTLY?

It might be a family heirloom, or something you just ordered on Amazon, but your cast-iron pan deserves your love and attention. Keeping the pan seasoned (the thin black layer that coats the surface is the season) is important for maintaining its performance. You can think of it like taking your car in for an oil change or a tune-up. One way to keep your pan seasoned is to cook with it all the time. This will naturally maintain the layer (which is also why washing it with soap is shunned, as it degrades the natural season).

But the truth is, most people aren't bringing out their heavy metal pan all the time, so the next best thing is to season it manually. It's quite simple: Preheat the oven to 500°F. Next, coat the cast iron with a thin layer of vegetable oil, making sure to rub it all over with a paper towel. Heat the pan in the oven for at least 1 hour. Repeat this process every couple of months.

Rusting can also be an issue with cast-iron pans, which is why it's super important to dry them completely after washing. Heating your pan over an open flame for 3 to 4 minutes is the best way to dry it out, then rub in a little oil with a paper towel to protect it. If you don't, rust spots will eventually arrive.

THE CAST-IRON QUESADILLA THAT WILL CHANGE THE WAY YOU QUESADILLA

Serves 1

———————————

1 teaspoon
vegetable oil

2 (8-inch) flour
tortillas

⅓ cup freshly grated
mozzarella cheese

⅓ cup freshly grated
Monterey Jack
cheese

⅓ cup freshly grated
Cheddar cheese

¼ cup salsa of choice
(optional)

¼ cup sour cream
(optional)

¼ cup guacamole
(optional)

Hot sauce for serving

A perfect quesadilla is hard to beat, unless, of course, there's a better quesadilla reality out there. Anyone who's made an overfilled quesadilla knows that the best part is the crispy fried cheese that oozes out of the fold, sticking to the pan along the edge. Here's a technique borrowed from a Mexico City taco stand that Daniel stumbled upon. He watched what he thought was a disastrous mistake as the taquero put the cheese down on the griddle first, then the tortilla on top. But to his amazement, the crispy fried cheese stuck to the tortilla, not to the grill, creating a perfect layer of golden brown, crunchy ambrosia that changed the way he looked at quesadillas ever after.

1. Coat a well-seasoned cast-iron pan (you can use a nonstick pan if you're feeling timid) with the oil, wiping out the excess with a paper towel, and warm the pan over medium-high heat.

2. Add a tortilla to the pan and toast until just beginning to brown, about 2 minutes, then remove and reserve.

3. Add half of the cheese to the pan, sprinkling it evenly to make a circle just slightly larger in diameter than the tortilla. Carefully place the toasted tortilla on top of the cheese toasted side down, centering it. Spread the remaining cheese over the tortilla, then place the second tortilla on top of the cheese.

4. When the cheese has browned, after about 4 minutes, using a small metal spatula, carefully peel up an edge to get underneath. Once you have lifted up an edge, it should be easy to peel up the entire crispy mass with the spatula. Then, working carefully, flip the whole thing over to toast the second tortilla and melt the cheese in the interior. This should take about 3 minutes.

5. Serve the quesadilla piping hot with whatever accompaniments— salsa, sour cream, guacamole, hot sauce—you like.

F, Marry, Kill: stand mixer, food processor, blender?

→ **LET'S PLAY THAT FUN** and highly subjective game called F, Marry, Kill with three of the most popular small appliances: the blender, the food processor, and the stand mixer. All three play an integral role in the kitchen and are essential in preparing many classic dishes. That said, in the *Food IQ* universe, some stay and some go. Daniel and Matt's full responses are revealed at the end. But first, how does each appliance work?

A **stand** or **planetary mixer** whisks, mixes, and kneads, turning baking a cake from a chore into a one-bowl miracle. Can you make bagels without a stand mixer? Yes. But you also get a free bicep workout. Whisking egg whites into a stiff peak for meringue? The mixer can do this for you. For "spiralizing" daikon radish and grinding meat for meatballs, the attachments of a stand mixer are feats of engineering, though some are less successful than others.

A **food processor**, on the other hand, is most useful for chopping dry ingredients—chopping as if with a knife thousands of times over—with slicing and grating attachments that work well for most ingredients. Because of their wide, flat bowls and fast-moving blades, food processors are also ideal for making emulsified mixtures. You can whip up a big batch of pesto or mustard vinaigrette in no time.

A **blender** spins much faster than a food processor, with a pitcher-shaped bowl that's specifically designed for liquids and purees. Some blenders tout other features, but the reality is that they are really good at one thing, and one thing only—blending.

Each piece of equipment has a specific strength. A stand mixer whips cream perfectly, but good luck crushing ice. If you tried to make whipped cream in a food processor, it would turn to butter, but throw some ice in there, and you've got yourself a perfect bed for that shrimp cocktail. If you tried to make pesto in a blender, it wouldn't spin because there isn't enough liquid to keep the solids in contact with the blade. If you tried to blend a soup in a food processor, it would push everything around and make a terrible mess. You get the picture.

So where do Daniel and Matt shake out with F, Marry, Kill?

Daniel: F—Stand Mixer **Marry**—Blender **Kill**—Food Processor

The logic: The food processor is a convenience, not a necessity. Get better knife skills; it's that simple. The blender provides the only thing that I cannot do by hand. Matt, go make me a frozen margarita with your hands. It ain't gonna happen. As for the stand mixer, I do a lot of baking, and while I could knead all that dough without one, it wouldn't be a pretty picture.

Matt: F—Blender **Marry**—Food Processor **Kill**—Stand Mixer

The logic: The blender does its job so well, but it does only one thing really well. A stand mixer is used mostly for baking, and the joy of baking hasn't quite hit me like all those sourdough bros out there. But a Ninja food processor saves my ass more than many appliances. It's great for chopping vegetables and herbs for sauces and meat marinades, bread crumbs for chicken cutlets, and the occasional pesto. ●

BITTERSWEET WATERMELON AGUA FRESCA

Makes 4 cups

4 cups peeled, seeded, and diced watermelon

1 lime, quartered

3 tablespoons sugar

2 cups water

1 cup ice cubes, plus more for serving

Small pinch of kosher salt

On a late-August day, a professional kitchen can be a hot place to work, apropos of the old saying, "If you can't stand the heat, get out of the kitchen." Well, most working cooks can't get out of the kitchen, so the next best thing is making a giant pitcher of bittersweet agua fresca to keep the trains running. Blending whole limes rather than juicing them adds a subtle bitter element to this recipe that will refresh your palate and keep you wanting more. But beware, this drink has a shelf life, and the juice will continue to grow bitter over time, rendering the drink unpalatable after a few hours. So make what you can drink, and drink what you make.

1. In a blender, combine all of the ingredients, cover tightly, and blend on high speed until liquefied.

2. Strain the mixture through a fine-mesh strainer into a pitcher, then serve immediately over ice.

Note: This recipe works well with oranges, pineapple, cantaloupe, and almost any other fruit and with cucumber and mint. You can add a knob of ginger for extra spice and flavor, and if you're done with your work in the kitchen, feel free to add a splash of vodka or rum.

What's the difference between a regular, convection, and steam oven? And when do I turn on the fan?

→ **THE MOST COMMON OVEN** used in the United States is powered by electricity, with large coils located at the top (for broiling) and the bottom (for roasting). Electric (radiant) ovens have come a long way since their rise in popularity in the 1930s, and while a gas range is still best for sautéing up top, electricity is absolutely king down below. Electric ovens are more consistent and efficient than gas, and electric heat is drier, making it ideal for baking and roasting (gas contains water molecules, which turn to steam when the gas is burned).

Convection ovens are a step up on the oven food chain. While you don't need to turn on the fan to use one, when you do, a high-powered blast of circulating hot air intensifies the heat and creates an ideal cooking habitat. The convection setting does come with a lot of confusion, however. For example, when exactly do you turn the fan on?

Roasting with the convection fan running is like supercharging your engine; the more intense, drier heat will caramelize your roast chicken, yielding beautifully golden, crispy skin. Just like the air fryer, your convection fan will toast your vegetables, browning them evenly. This is why convection is ideal for roasting meat and vegetables, and why it's not great for recipes that require gentle radiant heat, such as breads, cookies, and custards. As for that Thanksgiving turkey? You wouldn't want to roast it on the convection setting for fear of drying and burning the skin over the course of the long cooking process. That said, a last-minute hit with the fan can crisp up the skin before serving.

Steam ovens, popular throughout Europe, have drawn more fans stateside as of late. They are expensive and a little finicky, but they come with serious benefits. Adding steam can speed up the cooking process (when steam condenses, it deposits a great deal of energy, which is why steam burns are so much worse than hot-water burns). Steam roasting is the secret behind Peking duck's ethereal, crispy skin and the crackling of Chinese roast pork. Steam is essential for baking breads, which is why the famous Jim Lahey no-knead bread recipe uses a cast-iron pot, trapping the bread's natural moisture, softening the crust, and allowing it to break open and rise. High-end appliance companies like Miele and Wolf sell steam ovens for several thousand dollars, so if you're going to shell out that kinda dough, you'd be well served to learn how to use it. ●

ROASTED SWEET POTATOES WITH TOASTED PUMPKIN SEEDS AND GREEN ONION

Serves 4

---

3 large sweet potatoes, cut into ¾-inch-thick disks

5 tablespoons extra-virgin olive oil

Kosher salt

¼ cup toasted pumpkin seeds

Juice of 1 lemon

3 green onions, white and green parts, thinly sliced

Daniel grew up eating his mom's oven-roasted sweet potatoes, which she stabbed with a fork and wrapped in foil. The flesh was sweet and delicious, but the skin was wet, chewy, and unappealing, and he can still hear his mom telling him to "eat the skin—it's the healthiest part." Nevertheless, he's got love for the tubers, and tossing them with a healthy amount of oil helps crisp the skin, while spacing the slices out flat on a pan helps caramelize the sweet flesh to a deep golden brown.

1. Preheat the oven to 425°F. Have ready two large sheet pans (18 by 13 inches).

2. In a large bowl, toss the sweet potatoes with 3 tablespoons of the oil and 1 tablespoon salt, coating evenly. Arrange the potato disks on the sheet pans, laying them flat with ample space around each slice for good air circulation. Use a rubber spatula to collect any oil remaining in the bowl and drizzle it over the potatoes.

3. Roast the potatoes until the bottoms are crispy and deep golden brown, about 20 minutes. Remove the pans from the oven and flip each potato disk over. Return the pans to the oven and roast the potatoes until well browned on both sides and soft through when tested with a fork, about 15 minutes longer.

4. When the potatoes are ready to serve, toss the pumpkin seeds with the remaining 2 tablespoons oil, the lemon juice, and 1 teaspoon salt. Arrange the sweet potatoes on a serving dish and top with the toasted pumpkin seeds and green onions.

I bought an Instant Pot on Black Friday two years ago. Now what the hell am I supposed to cook with it?

→ **DANIEL CAN BE A** pretty cynical dude when it comes to fly-by-night cooking gadgets. It's sort of the chef way. The air fryer? Don't get him started. The yolk separator? A waste of kitchen drawer space. The Ron Popeil Showtime Rotisserie? Maybe that one's got some merit—at least it does what it promises. So when he received an Instant Pot for free as part of a promotional gig with a cookware company, he was slightly dubious, to say the least. But soon he realized that the Instant Pot is really just a digital pressure cooker, and it operates in the same way as the clunky (and rumored unfairly to be terrifyingly unsafe) analog one his mom used to make beans on the stove (and Al-Qaeda used to make bombs).

Turns out the Instant Pot is a modern mechanical marvel and can be extremely useful for all types of home cooks, as long as you know what to do—and not to do—with it. Does it cook things instantly? Not really. But an instant is merely a social construct, like a New York second—which Daniel's Grandpa Morton defined as the time it takes for the guy behind you to honk his horn after the light turns green. Cooking is all about patience, and just like the microwave (see page 46), an Instant Pot can be a useful cooking tool. At the end of the day, the Instant Pot saves time—and that is a very good thing.

First, let's look at how a pressure cooker works. When you heat things up to 212°F in a regular pot, the water inside starts to boil. The boiling releases a great amount of energy and drastically slows the cooking process, which is why it can take hours and hours to braise a tough cut of meat or cook dried beans from hard to creamy. Plus, boiling water agitates the ingredients, breaking them down, which can be a bad thing when you're cooking fragile things like beans, potatoes, or rice.

The solution for faster, gentler cooking is sealing the container and allowing the pressure to build, increasing the boiling temperature in the process. This is how you can go from hard, unsoaked dried beans to creamy perfection in just under an hour. Rich and robust chicken soup in forty-five minutes? Soft and creamy polenta in less than two hours? Done and done. The pressure cooker is your answer, and with its digital readout and simplicity (it plugs into an electrical socket, so there's no stove required), the Instant Pot is legit. This isn't a sales pitch, but Daniel and Matt call it like they see it. With all of this said, should you actually buy one? If you have the space and a little extra dough, it comes in handy. But you could always just buy yourself an old-school analog pressure cooker and spend the savings on Rancho Gordo heirloom beans. ●

BONE BROTH? YEAH, WE CALL THAT STUFF STOCK.

Isn't this whole bone broth thing just a gimmicky way to sell stock? Daniel and Matt certainly think so. But mom's chicken soup really did make you feel better, so who cares what the label calls it as long as it tastes good, right? Well, as long as it tastes good and you're not getting poorer by the pint. Bone broth sounds sexy and rolls off the tongue, but you can't take sounding good to the bank, so you might as well save yourself some dough and grab a box of Swanson Natural Goodness—or, better yet, save those roasted chicken carcasses and make a batch of bone broth on your own. The bones from a roast chicken make a quart of good-quality broth that stays well frozen for up to a month, so you've got no excuses.

friend of FOOD IQ

INA GARTEN is a best-selling cookbook author, a television food personality, and a steady hand that guides millions in the kitchen every single day.

The Instant Pot craze—we've given it some space. We've given it some time. What's your take on that device?

I have one! It's just still in the box [laughing], so I don't know. But I actually started working on a cassoulet in an Instant Pot, so I'll let you know.

What is some kitchen equipment that people may be surprised that you reach for often?

I have very simple kitchen equipment. I don't have a lot of fancy gadgets. I mean, I basically just have All-Clad pots, Le Creuset, Wüsthof knives, and stacks of sheet pans. I think those are really important. I probably have six or seven sheet pans, and because I'm always roasting something, baking something, I use them a lot.

What's a great recipe hack you've discovered recently?

If you take a pint of vanilla Häagen-Dazs and leave it in the refrigerator, it melts, and then you can pour some—it's crème anglaise basically that has been frozen; you've just defrosted it. Pour it on a plate and put a piece of chocolate cake on it and you've got a great dessert.

PRESSURE COOKER POLENTA WITH BUTTER-BRAISED MUSHROOMS

Serves 4 to 6

7 cups chicken stock (or substitute bouillon)

2 cups coarse-ground cornmeal or grits (not instant polenta)

Kosher salt

1 tablespoon extra-virgin olive oil

8 ounces button mushrooms, halved

8 ounces oyster mushrooms, stem ends trimmed and broken into bite-size pieces

8 ounces portobello mushrooms, stemmed, then caps peeled and cut into bite-sized wedges

2 tablespoons minced shallot

2 thyme sprigs

¼ cup dry white wine

4 tablespoons unsalted butter

½ cup heavy cream

½ cup freshly grated grana padano cheese

Freshly ground black pepper

Making polenta is a labor of love, and to cook it properly takes hours of stirring over low heat. In the end, the time spent is worth it, and you're rewarded with an unparalleled silky-smooth texture and deeply satisfying richness. That is, of course, unless you have a pressure cooker, in which case you don't have to wait, so you can have your polenta posthaste. There is literally nothing lost in the pressure cooker over the stove. Mushrooms in cream sauce are a classic accompaniment. And you can add a few Spicy Pork Meatballs (page 31) for the ultimate comfort-food meal.

1. In a pressure cooker or Instant Pot, stir together the stock, cornmeal, and 1 teaspoon salt. Seal the lid and bring to a boil over medium-high heat or the high temperature setting on your Instant Pot. Lower the heat to medium and cook for 45 minutes, then turn off the heat and let cool with the lid closed for 1 hour.

2. While the polenta is cooling, heat the oil in a large frying pan over high heat until it begins to smoke. Add all of the mushrooms and cook, stirring frequently, until they begin to stew in their own liquid, about 4 minutes. Add the shallot, thyme, and ½ teaspoon salt and continue cooking, stirring frequently, until all of the liquid evaporates, about 6 minutes. Add the wine and continue cooking, stirring frequently, until the wine evaporates, about 1 minute. Add 2 tablespoons of the butter, stir to incorporate, and set aside off the heat. Remove and discard the thyme stems.

3. When the polenta is ready, follow the manufacturer's safety instructions to release the steam and carefully remove the lid. Stir in the cream, half of the cheese, and the remaining 2 tablespoons butter and adjust the seasoning with more salt if needed. If the polenta has a soupy texture, wait for 10 minutes before serving, as polenta thickens as it cools.

4. Serve the polenta with the mushrooms spooned over the top. Garnish with the remaining cheese and a few grinds of pepper.

Hacks, Technique, and Really Good Advice

Home cooking is all about linking together a string of right moves while avoiding that single wrong one that can scuttle a promising batch of fresh cavatelli or olive oil-poached cod. And the anxiety of avoiding that wrong move can make even the most seasoned home cooks second-guess themselves. In this chapter, Daniel and Matt answer several commonly asked questions that pop up in everyday cooking, with explanations that will help you avoid the Siren's song and crashing onto the rocks of burnt fish skin and rock-hard gnocchi.

How do you build the perfect sandwich?

→ **SANDWICHES ARE BEAUTIFUL, SANDWICHES** are fine; we eat sandwiches, but where do we draw the line? There's a lot to unpack before deciding your position on what is and isn't a sandwich. Is a taco a sandwich? And if so, does it stand to reason that a hot dog is one, too? Is a hot dog therefore not a taco as well? Certainly, at least, all can agree that a taco isn't a hot dog. And there's the question of whether or not you prefer to disqualify the hamburger for its unfair advantage (in the court of popular opinion, it has already been crowned the world's greatest work of art between two bun halves). Ask any two Americans to argue the merits of their favorite sandwich, and you'll get about as much agreement as you would discussing Lebron v. Jordan for NBA G.O.A.T. But here are three truths we *can* all agree are self-evident.

1. If the fillings spill out, the sandwich ceases to be a sandwich at all.

2. Sandwiches purchased in transportation hubs (airports, train and bus stations) are sandwiches at their worst possible incarnation. While the corned beef wrapped in plastic at the LaGuardia kiosk seems like a logical choice for the famished traveler, please, just don't go there—unless you're in Italy or Japan, where the sandwich bill of rights is alive and strong, and all sandwiches are respected equally.

3. While not governed by any universally respected legislative body, sandwiches bearing a recognizable name (Reuben, Cuban, croque madame, or otherwise) should be constructed to reflect their widely accepted design. Nobody wants to order a Philly cheesesteak and find themselves presented with chicken and barbecue sauce.

And no matter what your sandwich of choice may be, there are a few critical things to consider when building one. First and foremost, take timing and durability into consideration. Are you eating the sandwich right away, or are you packing a lunch for later? A soggy sandwich is a nonstarter (Chicago Italian beef being one of the few exceptions), so how long it's going to sit will weigh heavily on material choice and design. One way Daniel prevents moisture migration from increasing the sog quotient is by building a fat-based barrier between the bread and the rest of the sandwich (translation: spread butter or mayonnaise on the bun).

Fat and water don't mix, so a thin coating prevents the moisture (in the crisp lettuce, pickles, and tomatoes) from soaking into the bread. Speaking of the bread—perhaps the most overlooked and underappreciated component—it is often taken for granted as simply a meat-and-cheese delivery mechanism. In actuality, bread makes the sandwich and executes the ratio. The ratio is everything: the magic proportion of bread to ingredients that ensures proper balance, an inverse relationship between width and mass. The ideal bread could be anything from dense and thin Danish dark rye (rugbrød) to thick and fluffy Texas toast. Large holes in your bread are another land mine to avoid. Although a hallmark of a good artisanal loaf, bread with too many (or too large) holes can spray condiments like Old Faithful when pressure is applied and should be avoided by the most astute sandwich artists. Daniel and Matt have debated the merits of using a crusty baguette. Plenty of classics, including the jambon-beurre, have been constructed on the king of breads, but beware. A hard baguette, akin to broken glass–like Cap'n Crunch, threatens the sanctity of the roof of one's mouth.

As for the condiments and fillings, here are some thoughts. Tomatoes should always be placed near the center, or they will juice up the outer layers of the sandwich. Also, it's a great idea to treat your tomatoes to a light sprinkle of salt and vinegar before placing them. Vinaigrette plays a starring role in many of the world's classic sandwiches, from the muffuletta to Subway's Cold Cut Combo. The last piece of advice is the most important: when in doubt, leave it out. Maybe those barbecue potato chips don't actually need to be added to your already perfect turkey and Muenster. Maybe those pickled jalapeño slices should be reserved for next week's nachos, not shoehorned into your roast beef on rye. Use restraint, trust your instincts, edit wisely, and have some faith. As was said earlier, sandwiches are beautiful, sandwiches are fine. •

DANIEL AND MATT'S TOP FIVE SANDWICHES

DANIEL: From fast food to gourmet and everything in between, the **Hamburger** is the undisputed champion of sandwich history. The semi-obscure **Muffuletta**, an import from Sicily and virtually unheard of outside of New Orleans, is made with Italian cold cuts (salami, ham, mortadella), Swiss cheese, and a slathering of olive salad and giardiniera (pickled vegetables). The **Chicken Parmesan Hero** is my childhood favorite, my first love, my prom date of sandwiches, and it still has my heart. When I'm sad or depressed or missing my pop, I crave the wit of a **Philly Cheesesteak**. It includes grilled onions and paper-thin slices of griddled beef tangled in creamy, melted American cheese on a soft hoagie bun. The **Jambon-Beurre** is elegant in its simplicity. The Parisian classic is nothing without the bread it's built upon. A slender baguette, an ample spread of the highest-quality butter, a few thick slices of jambon (cooked ham), and the crisp refreshment of crunchy cornichons (pickled baby cucumbers) make for simple perfection.

MATT: The **Bánh Mì**, a product of French colonization of Vietnam, takes the best of French cuisine (bread, pâté) and Vietnamese culinary traditions (fish sauce, pickled vegetables like carrots and daikon radishes, an abundance of herbs like cilantro, basil, and mint) and mashes them up in the most beautiful way. A **NYC Deli Egg and Cheese** is made on a seeded kaiser or light yeast roll that conceals a soft, folded omelet, sweet Heinz ketchup, melty American cheese, and black pepper. **Japanese Convenience Store Egg Salad** sandwiches, made with Kewpie mayonnaise and the softest milk bread, are why you stop at a Lawson or 7-Eleven several times a day while visiting Japan. **PBJ** (peanut butter and jelly) is the fuel for cookbook writers and star NBA point guards, and it will be my ride or die until my final days. **Grilled Cheese**—see the recipe.

THE BEST GRILLED CHEESE

Makes 1 sandwich

---

1 tablespoon unsalted butter

2 slices white sandwich bread

2 slices American cheese, or 2½ ounces Cheddar, Monterey Jack, mozzarella, or Swiss cheese, grated

The trick to a great grilled cheese sandwich is toasting both sides of the bread in butter in the pan. Starting with the inside first gets the bread extra warm and crispy, which helps melt the cheese, and the buttered inside protects the bread from getting soggy. This recipe calls for classic American cheese, but feel free to experiment with other cheeses and with other types of bread.

1. Melt ½ tablespoon of the butter in a large heavy-bottomed frying pan over medium-high heat. Add both slices of bread and toast on the first side until golden brown, about 4 minutes.

2. Flip the bread, add the remaining ½ tablespoon butter to the pan, and top each piece of bread with a slice of cheese or half of the grated cheese. Cook until the cheese begins to melt and the bread begins to toast on the underside, about 2 minutes. Flip one bread slice, cheese side down, atop the other slice to close the sandwich and continue cooking, flipping the sandwich as needed to toast both sides, until the cheese is oozing out and the sandwich is toasted golden brown, about 3 minutes.

How do I cook pasta, and why does it always taste better in a restaurant?

→ **THERE'S A STEP MANY** home cooks skip when cooking pasta at home, and this missing step is the difference between the rich, creamy, and toothsome bowls of rigatoni Bolognese you love from your favorite Italian trattoria and the watery, flavorless bowls of limp noodles doused in sauce on your dinner table.

To start, the instructions for cooking pasta properly may sound familiar. Use a lot of salty water in a large pot (simple rule: 4 quarts water plus ¼ cup kosher salt for every pound of pasta). The salt both seasons the pasta and raises the boiling temperature. You want a higher temperature so the water remains boiling when the cool pasta is added, or the pasta will become gummy. Cook the pasta for a minute or two less than the instructions suggest for al dente (always the right choice), and reserve some of that pasta water to finish. Meanwhile, prepare your sauce in a different pan or pot.

Next, drain your pasta and dump it right into the pan with the sauce. It should be a little wet, but absolutely no rinsing of the pasta with tap water is allowed. Matt's midwestern parents "taught" him this rinsing technique, which works wonders for cold pasta used in pasta salad but leaves the noodles waterlogged and strips them of their starch—starch that is essential for emulsifying the sauce (see page 91) so it will stick to the pasta. Once in the pan, cook the pasta in the sauce for the last minute and a half or two, adding a little hot water at a time as needed. This can be hot water from the tap or reserved pasta water.

It turns out that both work equally well (see below for more on this!).

This is when the magic happens: the critical ninety seconds during which the starch helps the oil and water on its journey to emulsification, creating a rich, creamy coating that will stick to the noodles rather than pooling at the bottom of the bowl. You are reducing the water with heat until a perfect starch ratio essentially glues the oily fats from the sauce to the watery liquid, binding them together and marrying them, along with any of the vegetables or herbs in the sauce itself (canned tomatoes, pesto, aged cheese, butter, and all that good stuff), to the pasta.

The trick is to time this moment to coincide with the pasta being perfectly cooked. For this reason, you add a little water at a time, tasting as you go, until you're a moment away from the perfect al dente texture, then you quickly cook off the remaining liquid binding the sauce. Cook too much of the water out and the pasta will start to fry, breaking the emulsification. If this occurs, though, don't worry. Adding a few tablespoons of water to the pan should bring it back together.

This emulsification step is both very, very important and often forgotten. And the magic it creates is fragile and fleeting, which is why it is imperative to serve pasta immediately after the emulsification has happened. Hell hath no fury like a passionate pasta cook watching her noodles go limp. You will know you've timed it just right with a cursory inspection of your bowl after eating. If all your sauce has been consumed with the noodles, you've nailed the dismount. A pool of sad-face marinara, however, reveals that it's time to head back to pasta school. ●

BUT THE LEGEND OF PASTA WATER IS KINDA BULLSHIT

There's this idea that pasta water has a sort of superpower—that the cloudy liquid in which your dried rigatoni has been bubbling for several minutes will ultimately improve the flavor of your sauce and help to emulsify the fat, giving you a creamy sauce that will cling to your pasta. Perhaps Mario Batali should be held responsible for furthering this idea, as he was known for fetishizing pasta water to his dedicated fans (when he had fans). For Daniel, this is a bit of tomfoolery. In real life, and as a frequent pasta home cook, he's never seen pasta water offer enough starch to make any noticeable difference. In restaurants, perhaps, the pasta cooker, having cooked dozens of orders of pasta all night, has a consistency that is near milky, so it's going to add something.

What is imperative is adding water to a pasta sauce, as described above. And that water must be hot. Cold water will slow the process, cooling your noodles and yielding gummy results. Using pasta water solves the temperature problem—but beware that it's incredibly salty. Add too much pasta water to the sauce, and you will instantly overseason it. So be mindful of how much you use, and should you forget to reserve some, hot tap water will work perfectly fine, too. Daniel calls this "pipe stock."

SHELL PASTA WITH BRAISED LEEKS, TINNED SARDINES, AND FRIED BREAD CRUMBS

This pasta was born high in the mountains of Utah. Daniel was visiting a friend at a ski resort when he was put on the spot to cook a meal for some important restaurant-industry people. With limited fresh ingredients available at the local market, he turned to the canned fish aisle—and ended up with a memorable pasta that he still makes to this day. Be careful to mix the pasta gently. Otherwise, the sardines will break down completely, and you'll lose their beautifully soft texture.

Serves 4

Kosher salt

12 ounces shell pasta

3 tablespoons unsalted butter

2 large leeks, white and pale green parts only, diced

⅔ cup dry white wine

2 (3¾-ounce) cans olive oil-packed sardines, undrained

Leaves from ½ bunch flat-leaf parsley, chopped

Grated zest and juice of 1 lemon

1 cup Fried Bread Crumbs (recipe follows)

Freshly ground black pepper

1. Bring a large pot of heavily salted water (⅓ cup salt per 4 quarts water) to a rolling boil over high heat. Set a timer for 1 minute less than the package instructions suggest for al dente and add the pasta, stirring occasionally. When the timer sounds, drain the pasta, reserving 1 cup of the cooking water.

2. While the pasta cooks, melt the butter in a large sauté pan over medium-high heat. Add the leeks and 2 teaspoons salt and cook, stirring frequently, until soft, about 6 minutes. Add the wine and continue cooking, stirring frequently, until evaporated, about 4 minutes.

3. Add the cooked pasta to the leeks along with a few tablespoons of the pasta cooking water (or hot tap water) and the sardines and their oil. Turn down the heat to medium and cook, stirring gently to break up the sardines and adding more water as needed to keep the pasta moist, until the pasta is al dente, about 2 minutes. Add the parsley and lemon zest and juice, season with salt as needed, and stir to mix.

4. Top with the bread crumbs and a few grinds of pepper.

Fried Bread Crumbs

Makes about 1 cup

2 slices stale rustic French country bread or baguette, broken into small pieces

1 cup extra-virgin olive oil

Pinch of kosher salt

1. Set a fine-mesh strainer over a small heatproof bowl. Line a plate with a paper towel. Heat the bread and oil together in a small pot over low heat, stirring frequently. When the bread begins to brown, immediately remove from the heat and pour into the strainer. Turn the bread out onto the towel-lined plate. Let the oil cool, then store in an airtight container in a cupboard and use for future sautéing.

2. Season the bread with the salt, then crush into crumbs with a rolling pin or the bottom of a small pot. Reserve for garnishing the pasta.

How do I strategize a "clean out the fridge" meal?

→ **KITCHEN-SINK COOKING IS THE** jazz of home cooking, and professional chefs are the Lee Morgans and Lester Youngs of the improvisational cooking scene. Matt was once bunking with a chef buddy in Aspen during a food festival, and one morning, the chef, while still probably drunk from the night before (blame the altitude), somehow made the most incredible Egg McMuffin from the rental condo fridge. Daniel believes this inherent ability to improvise isn't just flashing some knife skills. It's because of the difference between the way the chef thinks and the way the home cook thinks. When home cooks make a meal, they usually set out with something in mind—either a dish they are quite familiar with (their dad's chicken soup recipe committed to memory) or a recipe pulled from a cookbook or Epicurious or the back of a box. Chances are, they have shopped specifically for that recipe. The chef, on the other hand, surveys the pantry and refrigerator, looking for familiar patterns to emerge—ingredients that will work in concert to build something delicious. The ability to see these patterns requires an open mind and a fundamental understanding of what goes well together.

When Daniel is presented with this challenge, be it on a ski vacation or while cooking for family, he will first look for foundational ingredients. Potatoes, onions, and garlic can go in any direction. He will also look for sauces and condiments: chile crisp, hot sauce, preserved lemons, sambal, soy sauce. He will pull everything he thinks he might use from the fridge and pantry and place it on the table. At this point, the most important thing to keep in mind is that you don't need to use *everything*. Too many home cooks think they need to cram all of the leftovers into one main. The soy-marinated chicken with tomatoes, spinach, and eggs might work together beautifully. But add in that half jar of marinara sauce and the leftover feta cheese, and your delicious frittata just turned into a circus disaster with you starring as the clown. Restraint is important. From the ingredients available, you should think about a specific flavor direction. Is it Mediterranean (olive oil, olives, garlic, lemons, tinned fish) or East Asian (ginger, garlic, green onion, soy sauce, mirin)? Is it Southeast Asian (ginger, lemongrass, coconut, sugar, chile), Middle Eastern (olive oil, tahini, sumac, lemon), or Mexican (lime, cilantro, corn, dried chile).

Next, it's about picking a format. You can make a soup, a frittata, a pasta, fried rice, a stir-fry, a green salad, or a mayonnaise-based salad. Pick one and confidently move in that direction. If soup is on, make sure it's really on. If it's a noodle dish, stick to that program. For this kitchen-sink strategy to work, it's important to know how to make these basic recipes and to keep some staple items in your pantry and in the fridge. ●

DEB PERELMAN is behind the wildly successful Smitten Kitten website and cookbook series, and she lives by the motto of "fearless cooking from a tiny NYC kitchen."

How do you look at the clean-out-the-fridge, no-recipe meal?

First, I want to see what elements I have, and if I have onion, garlic, citrus, nuts, and cheese, I can make something great with any of the wilting vegetables or fruits. Those are my five key elements.

Can you give one example of an improvisational, jazzy meal?

I had a really old bag of carrots, and I soaked them in ice-cold salt water and cut them into really thin coins. I also had a handful of pistachios left, and I toasted them, dressing the carrots with lemon, sumac, olive oil, and chile flakes. I do a lot of these two- or three-ingredient salads, and it works out really well.

What about cooking with leftovers?

I'm not a fan of that. It feels like the dish starts two days behind, which feels old. It's like a ticking time bomb.

CHICKEN, CHEDDAR, AND TOMATO SOUP WITH MUSTARDY POTATO BUN CROUTONS

Every day for nearly a year, Daniel babysat his young niece and nephew and cooked them lunch using the kitchen-sink approach. They're part of a big family, so there was always a hodgepodge of ingredients in the fridge. Many memorable meals were born of his babysitting tenure, but one enduring recipe was this tomato, chicken, and Cheddar soup. Grilled cheese and tomato soup is a classic combo and a kid-friendly favorite, so this mash-up will be a welcome addition to your weekly roster.

Serves 6

2 tablespoons unsalted butter

1 yellow onion, minced

4 thyme sprigs

2 cloves garlic, smashed

Kosher salt

2 tablespoons all-purpose flour

1 (28-ounce) can crushed tomatoes

2¾ cups chicken stock (or substitute bouillon)

⅓ cup heavy cream

10 ounces Cheddar cheese, grated

Freshly ground black pepper

1 poached chicken breast, shredded

2 cups Mustardy Potato Bun Croutons (recipe follows)

1. Melt the butter in a large, heavy-bottomed pot over medium-high heat. Add the onion, thyme, garlic, and 2 teaspoons salt and cook, stirring frequently, until soft and translucent, about 10 minutes. Stir in the flour, mixing until completely incorporated.

2. Add the crushed tomatoes, stock, and cream, stir well, and bring to a boil. Lower the heat to a simmer and cook for 20 minutes to blend the flavors.

3. Turn off the heat and remove and discard the thyme stems. Add the cheese a handful at a time, whisking in each addition until melted and fully dissolved before adding the next.

4. Season to taste with salt and pepper. Ladle into bowls and top each serving with the chicken and croutons.

Mustardy Potato Bun Croutons

Makes about 6 cups

3 tablespoons butter, melted

1 clove garlic, minced

3 tablespoons Dijon mustard

1 tablespoon fresh tarragon or flat-leaf parsley leaves, chopped

1 teaspoon kosher salt

4 potato buns, torn into bite-size pieces

1. Preheat the oven to 375°F. Line a sheet pan with aluminum foil.

2. In a bowl, whisk together the melted butter, garlic, mustard, tarragon, and salt, then add the bun pieces and thoroughly toss to coat evenly.

3. Spread the bun pieces in a single layer on the prepared pan. Bake, stirring every 5 minutes, until just crisped and browned, about 30 minutes.

What is the best way to wash greens and dry lettuce?

→ **LEARNING TO WASH GREENS** properly may seem insignificant—or at least too trivial to find the task competing with one hundred pressing cooking and food culture questions—but improperly washing greens is one of the most common mistakes Daniel sees home cooks making. And anyone who has ever bitten down on a sandy piece of braised kale or a forkful of gritty arugula knows that any trace of dirt means it's curtains, lights out, game over for that course—or even the entire meal. This is not to say you can't wing a quick fix in the middle of a gritty produce emergency by adding fried bread crumbs or crispy capers and calling the dish "crunchy braised kale" and then praying no one notices. Daniel, dinner party for twelve, true story. But ideally, you're saving your relationship with God for a higher purpose than hoodwinking your dinner guests because of a produce-washing faux pas.

The good news is that washing vegetables isn't rocket science; there's a simple technique that works perfectly for every green, with a few common mistakes to avoid. The method involves submerging your leafy greens in a large bowl with enough cold water so there's plenty of room to agitate the floating foliage, allowing heavier particles (like sand) to sink to the bottom. Tightly packing your chard in a small bowl—or worse, rinsing romaine only one time through in a strainer—won't do the trick.

Once washed, it's *imperative* that you lift the vegetables out of their bath rather than dumping them—water and all—into a strainer (which only serves to reincorporate the grit back onto the vegetable). Do this three times and taste as you go. You shouldn't be reluctant to rinse and repeat. It's not uncommon to need multiple washes to persuade the more obstinate of sediment to depart its home.

To dry greens, there's no denying the power of the salad spinner. No better way exists, and it's worth the fifteen-dollar investment. Drying greens without a spinner is like measuring out a quart of milk using a tablespoon—you can do it, but it takes forever, and it isn't particularly pleasurable. Just make sure not to overcrowd the basket, which can impede the process and bruise the tender greens. How dry should the greens be? Completely dry. A good test is to place the greens against your shirt or a paper towel. If the greens leave any trace of moisture, they are not dried. Any extra water on salad greens will dilute the dressing and accelerate the wilting process.

And if you end up with some grit in your greens, even after washing and spinning and spinning some more, don't be afraid to wash them again. Or as the old adage goes, which Daniel and Matt stress throughout the book: when in doubt, throw it out. It's okay to make mistakes—it's not okay to serve your mistakes. ●

LET'S TALK ABOUT THE BLACK STUFF ON THOSE MUSHROOMS.

You've probably noticed that when you buy button or cremini mushrooms, there's often black "dirt" stuck to the caps and stems that is extra stubborn and resists cleaning. That isn't dirt but a heat-treated compost material that is actually completely edible. The bottom line with cleaning mushrooms is that it's okay to cook them without removing all of the black stuff. You can wipe your mushrooms down with a moist towel or give them a quick rinse, but don't obsess over the dirt. On the other hand, mushrooms gathered in the wild are often sandy or come clad with pine needles, insects, and other foreign interlopers. Wild mushrooms should be washed in a water-filled sink, using warm water to expedite the process. Also, wash them right before you are ready to cook with them. Otherwise they will get soggy—or, worse yet, moldy. All mushrooms absorb a ton of water and tend to get waterlogged, so it's best to keep them dry until you're ready to cook.

LEEKS GRIBICHE

Kosher salt

6 medium leeks

1 tablespoon Dijon mustard

1 teaspoon whole-grain mustard

1 tablespoon white wine vinegar

1 hard-boiled egg, peeled and minced

3 tablespoons extra-virgin olive oil

1 tablespoon capers, rinsed and chopped

3 cornichons, finely chopped

1 tablespoon chopped fresh tarragon leaves

1 tablespoon sliced fresh chives

1 tablespoon chopped fresh flat-leaf parsley

1 tablespoon chopped fresh chervil

Freshly cracked black pepper

This is a hearty variation on the French classic, leeks vinaigrette. Sauce gribiche, traditionally served with cold fish, is a simple vinaigrette with the addition of hard-boiled eggs, chopped cornichons, capers, and fines herbes (a French blend of tender green herbs: parsley, tarragon, chervil, and chives). It makes an excellent accompaniment for boiled vegetables, such as leeks, asparagus, potatoes, or green beans. Mincing eggs with a knife can be a tedious task. A good shortcut is to use a tablespoon to smash them through a strainer.

1. Bring a large pot of heavily salted water (⅓ cup salt per 4 quarts water) to a boil over high heat.

2. Trim off the root and the dark green tops of each leek, leaving the white and pale green parts. Then cut the leek partially in half lengthwise to expose its layers for washing. Don't cut all the way through to the base or the leek will fall apart. The dirt is concentrated in the upper portion of the stalk, so carefully wash the leeks, submerging them in warm water and fanning the layers to ensure all the sand is removed.

3. Add the leeks to the boiling water and cook until tender to the center when pierced with a knife, about 12 minutes. Drain, then immediately shock them in cool water until just warm. Finish cutting each leek in half lengthwise and set the halves on paper towels to drain.

4. Meanwhile, make the gribiche. In a small bowl, whisk together the Dijon and whole-grain mustards, the vinegar, egg, and 2 teaspoons salt. Slowly whisk in the oil to emulsify, then fold in the capers, cornichons, tarragon, chives, parsley, and chervil (feel free to leave one or two herbs out if you are unable to find them). Adjust the seasoning with salt and pepper.

5. Arrange the warm leeks on a platter or individual plates and spoon the sauce over them. Serve immediately.

My roasted vegetables never get properly crispy. How do I make that happen?

→ **THIS QUESTION DESERVES A** shout-out to the longtime Holzman collaborator and super-talented chef Daniel Sharp (aka the other Daniel). Chef Sharp was the one who course-corrected Daniel on his vegetable-roasting technique, and he's here to share it. Daniel Holzman's assumption was that, for definitively crispy cauliflower, broccoli, Brussels sprouts, carrots, and all the other vegetable sides universally loved at New American bistros, cooks needed to cut bigger pieces (he was thinking of whole-roasted cauliflower—the bigger the better) and give their vegetables plenty of time to brown and crisp before becoming overcooked. This is totally wrong.

You want *smaller* pieces so they can be properly dried out before they burn. The second piece of the puzzle is that you need more (sometimes much more) oil than you think. For a whole head of broccoli, this is several *glug glug glugs* (¼ cup, minimum). The third puzzle piece is spacing. You absolutely cannot crowd the pieces on the sheet pan, let alone stack the vegetables on top of one another. The vegetables cannot touch, period. This means that for a larger dinner crew for which you are roasting several heads of this or that, you need two and possibly three pans. Drop them into the oven at around 375°F. If your oven has a convection setting, use it! The goal is drying out before burning, and convection is your friend.

THE QUEST FOR THE CRISPY CHICKPEA

In recent years, the holy grail of fried vegetables hasn't been a vegetable at all but a popular legume: the chickpea. (Legumes are technically a class of vegetable, but you get the point.) When Daniel and Matt started writing this book, they polled friends for their top five cooking questions, and the question of how to get incredibly crispy chickpeas like the restaurants do came up several times. The short answer is that crispy chickpeas need to be deep-fried in a lot of oil—about a cup of olive oil per can of chickpeas—to achieve that incredible texture you've likely tasted at a restaurant and then attempted to replicate at home to big-bummer results. Frying in a cast-iron pan or a deep Dutch oven will do the trick. Dust with kosher salt, black pepper, and some lime zest, smoked paprika, or ras el hanout, and there is nothing that tops it. Roasting chickpeas with a few glugs of oil is perfectly fine, but ultimately, those will be harder and less crunchy than the fried version.

The last trick is knowing that certain vegetables will be okay a little more charred than others. Broccoli and cauliflower are excellent when roasted slightly beyond recognition—verging on a shade of black (note that the word *burnt* is not being used here). For sweeter vegetables like carrots and onions, you need to be more careful. When sugar caramelizes too much, it can turn very bitter. ●

REAL-DEAL CRISPY ROASTED BRUSSELS SPROUTS

2 jars

1 pound Brussels sprouts, trimmed and halved lengthwise

¼ cup extra virgin olive oil

Kosher salt

Juice of 1 lemon

Ever since David Chang started fervidly deep-frying Brussels sprouts at Momofuku Noodle Bar in the mid-2000s, the world has gone crazy for the crispy little cabbages. Chang served them extra well-done, with a sweet fish sauce dressing and crunchy puffed rice, and they were (and still are) one of the best things ever to come from the legendary East Village restaurant that closed in 2020. Brussels sprouts can stand up to high heat, so don't be afraid to cook them until they're on the verge of burnt–that's when they're at their very best. This is the base recipe technique, and it works perfectly as is, but feel free to build on it, adding toasted nuts, dried fruit, spices, fresh herbs, or Chang's fish sauce to best complement the meal you're serving.

1. Preheat the oven to 500°F, with the fan on. (If you don't have a fan, the recipe will still work, but the Brussels sprouts may take a few more minutes to cook.) Line a large sheet pan with parchment paper.

2. In a large bowl, combine the Brussels sprouts, oil, and 1 teaspoon salt and toss well, making sure all of the sprouts are evenly coated.

3. Spread the Brussels sprouts on the prepared pan. They should be neither touching nor crowded (use an extra pan if necessary). Roast the sprouts, stirring them every 10 minutes, until they are deeply browned, with crispy outer leaves and soft centers, about 40 minutes.

4. Season with the lemon juice and extra salt as needed just before serving.

What's the best way to stay organized in the kitchen and run recipe air traffic control?

→ **A VERSION OF THE** same question drops into Daniel's world on a weekly, and sometimes daily, basis, especially during the buildup to great cooking holidays like Thanksgiving and the Fourth of July: "How do I cook better?" It's not a simple answer, and this book you are holding is a testament to the complexities and nuance of trying to actually cook "better"—or at least more efficiently, happier, healthier, and without burning down the house in the process (though still possibly setting off the most annoying sound known to humankind, the smoke alarm).

All of that being said, there is a little bit of strategy that you can follow to get a head start on your journey to "cooking better," and it is being dropped right here. Cooking better means staying organized throughout the entire process. When the pressure is on, which—let's be honest—is the case during the bulk of the thirty minutes to three hours of your cooking journey, these four tips will help you stay calm, cool (except, of course, when the broiler is cranking), and cooking at a controlled speed. The mantra is simple: slow is smooth, and smooth is fast.

1. Your bowls are not big enough. Cooking is all about combining from small to larger, and you need the proper space to stir, mix, mingle, blend, and toss with abandon. Everyone has tried, and failed, to dress greens in a bowl that's just big enough to fit the lettuce. The inevitable outcome is a grim excuse for salad—a bruised mess with pools of dressing and pockets of dry leaves throughout. Daniel has twelve large bowls and very few small bowls in his kitchen, and he mostly cooks for himself. Bowls stack, and they're relatively inexpensive, so there's no excuse not to have an adequate supply of them. Daniel and Matt use bowls every time they cook, whether they're grating cheese for quesadillas, seasoning broccoli florets with chile and garlic, or whisking egg whites for baked Alaska. Large bowls are an essential tool that should never be treated as an afterthought.

2. You have too much clutter on your counters. Home cooks need counter space to cook, and lots of it. A cleared countertop is prime real estate, and it should be treated that way. It should be preserved and protected. The basic rule of thumb is that if you aren't using something on a daily (or weekly, at max) basis, there is no reason it should be out on your counter. A jar crammed with thirteen different specialty OXO utensils doesn't look good, and it's actually doing you a massive disservice. Here's what happens: You're almost finished cooking your pesto, and at the flicker of a burner, the sauce starts to stick. All of a sudden, you need a rubber spatula to stir it. But because the spatula is crammed in that jar with a bunch of useless equipment, you can't get to it in time. If you are a utensil hoarder—and let's be clear, everybody is a utensil hoarder in some way—keep your stuff stored away.

The countertop is sacred. Here is what's on Daniel's counter when he is cooking: the one or two utensils specifically necessary for the dish he's cooking, usually a wooden spatula or tongs; a knife and cutting board; and spoons for tasting along the way. The rest can be put away. Now, there's a big exception here. We all love our beautiful cooking objects: the Ankarsrum Original stand mixer, or the La Spaziale S1 Mini Vivaldi II espresso machine. Daniel has his fire-engine-red KitchenAid stand mixer, Baratza Encore coffee grinder, and Legend 300 prosciutto slicer proudly on display. He just keeps them tucked in a corner and out of action's way.

3. Clean as you go. This one is related to number two, because if you don't clear your cutting boards and (large) bowls as you are cooking, you will not be rewarded with counter space. When you're done cooking, you shouldn't have to wash more than the last few items you used. The rest should be cleaned, dried (don't skip this step!), and put away. The drying rack should hold only one layer—not piled sky-high—and the sink should be empty. This is so important that we're hitting . . .

3A. The sink is one of the most important tools of all. The sink is where you wash produce, drain, strain, dump off oil, and even toss the occasional oversize salad. Your sink is an available open surface (with the added benefit of possessing a drain and a water source). But a sink full of dishes cannot be utilized. The trick to staying ahead of the dishes is never to get behind, so take a few minutes between recipe steps to keep your cooking space clean and organized.

4. Read the recipe all the way through before starting to cook. This may sound obvious, but people often find themselves missing an ingredient or tool halfway through cooking a recipe—and that's how disasters happen. Take the time to read through the instructions and gather all of the necessary ingredients and tools you'll need before you embark on cooking. In a professional kitchen, this is called "mise en place." This is short for (if you ask Matt, at least), "I'm a show-off and going to say this French word meaning 'everything in its place' out loud when cooking dinner for friends." Even worse, you might shorten it to "mise" when a friend asks you why you have all these tiny bowls filled with ingredients splayed out on the counter.

The overuse of the term is a bit of a bee in Matt's bonnet. But mise en place is a critical part of cooking, and it's proof that a little forethought can save a whole lot of drama down the line. You don't want to go rummaging through the fridge for cream in the middle of making a caramel sauce, or you're likely to end up with burnt pudding. The fun part of cooking is the cooking. The work part of cooking is setting yourself up for success, but it really is the key to executing that next meal flawlessly. ●

CHEF HAND, KNIFE HAND

During our discussions about organization, Daniel's framing of the "chef hand" really resonated with Matt. The idea is simple: when a guest walks into the kitchen, she should always be able to shake the chef's hand. What this means is that you keep your dominant hand clean. You don't touch any food with it; you don't get it greasy or caked with raw chicken juice. Daniel often observes home cooks using both hands to a toss salad or salt a steak, then transferring that schmutz to the handle of a knife, the pepper grinder, and the clean plates being set out on the table.

The trick is to make your dominant hand your knife hand and the other hand your chef hand—the one you use to cook. That way, anytime you need to run to the refrigerator or grab a spice from the drawer, you are doing so with a clean hand. Does it take a little practice? Sure. But you will adapt much quicker than you think. Your knife hand is also a good Instagram hand for when you're popping off stories in the middle of your cooking.

FRIED RICE TO CLEAN OUT YOUR FRIDGE

Serves 4

3 tablespoons
vegetable oil

1 small yellow onion,
cut into ¼-inch dice

1 carrot, peeled and
cut into ¼-inch dice

1 cup fresh or
frozen peas

1 red bell pepper,
stemmed, seeded,
and diced

Kosher salt

2 eggs, lightly beaten

1 tablespoon minced
garlic

1 tablespoon peeled
and minced fresh
ginger

3 green onions, white
and green parts
thinly sliced and kept
separate

4 cups cold cooked
white rice (preferably
1 day old)

3 tablespoons
soy sauce

2 tablespoons
Shaoxing rice wine

1 tablespoon toasted
sesame oil

1 tablespoon sesame
seeds

Making fried rice will push your time-management skills to the limits. Most recipes try to simplify the process with a dump-and-stir approach, but to prepare the dish correctly, you need to cook the ingredients separately, then fold them together. Wok frying is fast and furious, so it's essential to have your tools and ingredients at the ready. You don't want to be digging around in your pantry for soy sauce or searching for a spatula while your eggs are overcooking. Fried rice is the perfect vehicle to clean out your fridge, so feel free to add, swap, or omit ingredients to utilize whatever you have on hand.

1. Heat 1 tablespoon of the vegetable oil in a wok or large sauté pan over high heat until smoking. Add the yellow onion, carrots, fresh peas (if using frozen peas, mix them in after the other vegetables are cooked), pepper, and 1 teaspoon salt and cook, stirring frequently, until just beginning to soften, about 4 minutes. Transfer the vegetables to a waiting bowl and wipe out the wok with a paper towel.

2. Return the wok to high heat, add 1 tablespoon of the remaining vegetable oil, and heat until smoking. Add the eggs and cook, mixing so they break up and scramble, until just set, about 1 minute, then transfer to another waiting bowl.

3. With the wok still over high heat, add the remaining 1 tablespoon vegetable oil and heat until smoking. Add the garlic, ginger, and white parts of the green onions and cook until they release their fragrance and just begin to brown, about 1 minute. Add the rice and fry, mixing to breaking up any clumps. When the rice is toasted and warm, after about 5 minutes, add the cooked vegetables, soy sauce, wine, and sesame oil and mix to incorporate. Turn off the heat, then fold in the cooked eggs and season to taste with salt.

4. Transfer to a serving dish, garnish with the green onion tops and sesame seeds, and serve.

When buying meat, how do I get the most bang for my buck?

→ **YOU CAN CATEGORIZE BUYING** meat, whether at the butcher shop or the grocery store, into one of two columns: buying a cut for a specific purpose or recipe, such as a veal breast for blanquette de veau or a lamb shoulder for Mike Solomonov's pomegranate-braised masterpiece, and buying meat spontaneously, which is often dictated by price—the organic London broil or bone-in chicken thighs that are on special. For most of us, cheaper (though still high quality) is better. This question addresses how to embrace the latter through smarter shopping and cooking techniques.

The pricing of meat in the United States—home to some of the world's best beef, pork, and poultry—is pretty straightforward. Commodity markets dictate the price, and the most prized cuts—usually the most tender and the easiest to cook, like tenderloins and rib chops—are more expensive than the less popular (and tougher) cuts, like brisket, sirloin, flank, and shank.

This is actually great news for price-conscious home cooks because, in general, these less expensive cuts are actually relatively higher in quality than the pricier ones. That's because they hold some of the best flavor, even though they are not as easy to cook. The meats we eat are mostly muscles, and the more a muscle is worked, the leaner and tougher—but also the more flavorful—it will become. The lesser-used muscles, like the tenderloin, are more tender ("cuts like butter" is the phrase that's often thrown around) but bland by comparison. You can put a tenderloin or New York strip steak in the pan, fry it up, and boom-bam, you're done. That's not the case for osso buco, the literal calf of a cow, or brisket. Think of how tough the calf meat of a thousand-pound animal would be,

but also think about all that flavor. When cooked correctly, these cuts pay off in extraordinary ways.

So how do you cook them? Low and slow with lots of moisture is the best first option—think braises, pot roasts, and stews. A low temperature and moist cooking break down the tough meat, which is inherently flavorful, to a tenderness that exceeds expectations. Braising is the reason the once lowly short rib—previously less desired and cheaper—became a restaurant staple in the early 2000s and is now quite a bit more expensive at the butcher counter. Pork and lamb shoulders are way less expensive than their high-on-the-hog counterparts (the loin, for example), and when they're cooked with care in a braise of anchovies and olives or sweet ginger and soy they end up being so much more.

And when it comes to poultry, chicken specifically, there is no more under-utilized (and cheaper) cut than the bone-in chicken thigh. Over the years, Americans have become obsessed with the boneless chicken breast. This is due to a number of factors, from health claims to ease of preparation to the promise of a "pure" chicken flavor. But in reality, there is no more delicious and versatile cut than the bone-in, skin-on thigh. Higher in fat (and rich with flavor), the bone-in thigh can be braised or pan roasted with great flexibility. It's much more difficult to overcook (read: dry out) a cut like the thigh, and many wise home cooks have been choosing thighs exclusively for years.

Salting and seasoning your meat in advance is especially important when braising these less expensive cuts, because it helps the meat retain its moisture and gives the salt time to permeate the larger pieces, seasoning the inside as well. Patience is key: The biggest mistake people make is trying to speed up the process. Cooking tougher cuts of meat is a marathon, not a sprint. •

CARA NICOLETTI is a butcher, sausage maker, and founder of Seemore Meats & Veggies based in New York City.

What makes a particular steak good?

People make a big deal out of tenderness, but I want a steak to feel like a steak, like I'm chewing on meat. Flavor comes from blood flow, and blood flow happens with work; the more a muscle is worked, the more flavor it will have. Marbling can also be overrated. The best steak I ever had came from a ten-year-old cow with butter-yellow fat. For the lean cuts, you need to serve them seared rare. Anything more than that and the muscles tense.

What's the deal with grass-fed beef?

The first time I ate grass fed I thought it was fishy and disgusting. The grass-fed movement is young in the US, and there are a lot of farmers who don't know what they're doing. It wasn't until I moved to England and spent a year butchering over there that I realized what grass-fed beef raised the right way tastes like, and now I crave it. Grain-fed beef tastes like butter to me now. It's delicious, but it doesn't satisfy what I want in a steak.

How can you tell if a butcher shop is good?

It sounds kinda snobby, but the easiest way is to ask the butcher where the meat is coming from. Do they have a relationship with the farmer? If they have no idea where the meat is from, then they have no idea how it was raised or how good it is.

As a proud butcher, why did you choose to start a sausage company that's part plant based?

Good meat is extremely expensive, and I was tired of working with products that only rich people can afford. I believe in the magic of regenerative farming, but it's not realistic for the mainstream unless you first reduce dependency. You need to go mass-market to turn the dial—we need to democratize the humane meat movement.

BRAISED CHICKEN THIGHS WITH APRICOTS, GARLIC, OLIVES, AND FRESH THYME

Serves 3 or 4

---

6 bone-in, skin-on chicken thighs

Kosher salt

2 tablespoons extra-virgin olive oil

2 heads garlic, cloves separated and peeled, then smashed

12 dried apricots, chopped

8 large green olives, pitted

6 thyme sprigs

½ cup dry white wine

1 tablespoon honey

1½ cups chicken stock (or substitute bouillon)

1 tablespoon soy sauce

Steamed basmati rice for serving

Braising chicken with apricots and olives is a classic French preparation appropriated from North African tagine cooking (see page 64) during the French colonization of Morocco. Stewing chicken in the sweet and salty combination seasons the meat, while the garlic and the apricots melt down to thicken the broth, glazing the skin a beautiful amber golden brown. Once you've mastered the technique, try swapping in other braising meats, like lamb shoulder or duck legs, and substitute other dried fruits, like figs, raisins, or prunes.

1. Season each chicken thigh with ½ teaspoon salt (for the best results, season them at least 2 hours before cooking and ideally the night before).

2. Heat the oil in a large Dutch oven or other heavy pot over medium-high heat. Sear the chicken thighs, skin side down, until they're a deep golden brown. Resist the urge to move them until the skin lifts naturally from the pan, after about 7 minutes, then flip and gently sear until the underside is brown, about 3 minutes. Transfer the chicken to a plate.

3. Lower the heat to medium, add the garlic, and cook, stirring frequently, until soft and lightly browned, about 4 minutes. Add the apricots, olives, and thyme and then deglaze the pan with the wine, scraping up any bits of caramelized chicken (fond) that have stuck to the bottom and cooking until the wine has reduced by half, about 5 minutes.

4. Add the honey, stock, and soy sauce, stir well, and bring to a boil. Lower the heat to medium-low and nuzzle the chicken thighs, skin side up, into the liquid. Cover and cook until the chicken is fork-tender, about 40 minutes.

5. Adjust the seasoning with salt before serving, then serve with the rice.

How do I know when meat is done without using a meat thermometer?

→ **DIGITAL MEAT THERMOMETERS ARE** an unfortunate crutch that can lead you into some pretty embarrassing territory. They're not necessarily a bad thing to own, but buyer beware: have a backup plan for when the batteries inevitably give out at the worst possible moment. And, most important, make sure you know when the meat is done without a gadget or tool. Because if you do miss the mark with the temperature, there's only so much you can do to sell your dinner-party guests on the idea that the roast is "purposely rare." And sure, black and blue steak, sometimes called "Pittsburgh style," may be fixable, but if you overcook your meat, there's no going back.

There are some dishes for which a meat thermometer comes in handy. There's no better way to tell the internal temperature of a large roast, such as a standing rib roast or a turkey breast. But with smaller cuts, it becomes much trickier. Meat thermometers read the temperature directly from their tip, and it's difficult to get that tip into the depths of a thin steak or chicken thigh without under- or overshooting the center and getting a higher temperature reading than is accurate. In general, the smaller the cut of meat, the more difficult it will be to get an accurate reading from a thermometer.

Daniel isn't saying that you should throw your meat thermometer out. Instead, he is offering a tip on how to double-check the accuracy. Take the sharp tip of the thermometer (a cake tester or a thin skewer will also work) and insert it straight through the thickest part of the steak until it reaches the bottom of the pan, then leave it in for ten seconds. Pull it out and press where it made contact with the center of the meat against your sensitive lower lip. If the metal is ice-cold, the meat is still raw; slightly cold is rare. If it's tepid, it's medium-rare, warm is medium, and if it burns your lip, well—shame on you and your burnt lip (for overcooking the meat). Peek into a busy restaurant kitchen and you may notice a cook constantly, and with lightning speed, poking a row of steaks cooking on the grill. Poke, test, wipe, repeat. It's a beautiful thing to observe.

The other method, which is more abstract and takes more practice, is the pressure test. Once mastered, this technique is fast and accurate, and it's how trained chefs in most restaurant kitchens tell the temperature of a steak. Press on a raw steak, and the texture has no memory; it doesn't bounce back, and your finger just sinks in. As the meat cooks, the outside starts to tighten, and you begin to feel some hardness just beneath the exterior when pressing. But your finger continues to sink in beyond that. The longer you cook the meat, the more hardness you will feel developing in the interior. That's why, when you watch a chef cook meat, she is pressing against it constantly. The first time you try this, of course, you aren't going to know exactly when the meat is cooked to temperature, so you'll need to use your meat thermometer. But over time, you will be able to feel for doneness using the rule of the palm: feel the meaty part of your palm and how the texture changes (the muscle flexes) as you gently connect your thumb to the tip of your index finger (medium-rare), middle finger (medium), ring finger (medium-well), and pinky finger (well-done). A helping hand, indeed. ●

THERE IS NO UNIFORM MEAT TEMPERATURE!

There's not much debate around here about when certain cuts of meat are done and when they are overcooked. There's a right way, and there's your eighty-six-year-old grandma's way that takes well-done to creative heights. That said, personal preference should always be taken into account when cooking for friends and family. We are not here to judge, but to advise. Here is a handy guide for cooking different cuts of meat.

Chicken: medium-well to well (140°F), or rare in some cases (mostly in Japan). **Beef**: rare to medium-rare (125°F). **Lamb**: medium (130°F). **Pork**: medium to medium-well (135°F). **Squab, pheasant, and other game birds**: medium-rare (125°F). **Hamburgers**: medium-rare (125°F) (though Matt approves the medium Shake Shack burger, and Daniel the well-done Double-Double from In-N-Out).

BIG-ASS BONE-IN RIB EYE WITH FRIED SHALLOTS

Serves 2

---

1 (24-ounce) bone-in rib eye

Kosher salt

3 tablespoons extra-virgin olive oil

4 thyme sprigs

2 cloves garlic, smashed

2 tablespoons unsalted butter

3 cups Fried Crispy Shallots (recipe follows)

2 teaspoons flaky finishing salt (such as Maldon or fleur de sel)

MSG for finishing (optional)

Cooking a great steak–in this case, a bone-in rib eye–is just about the easiest thing you can do in the kitchen, as long as you have the confidence to cook it really hot and pull it out when your gut tells you it's done. The key is to remember that you can always cook it longer (there is no embarrassment there), so if you're gonna err, err on the side of undercooked. Once you take the steak out of the pan, make sure to let it rest for at least five minutes before slicing, otherwise the juices will run out. These crispy shallots are my favorite accompaniment for a thick, juicy steak. They're also a great topping for fish, chicken, or vegetables, and they add a nice, salty crunch to salads.

1. Season the steak heavily on both sides with kosher salt (aim for 1.5 percent by weight, or about 2 teaspoons) and refrigerate for at least 2 hours and preferably the night.

2. Remove the steak from the refrigerator 1 hour before cooking. A room-temperature steak will cook more evenly, which is especially critical for a thick cut. Thinner-cut steaks are best cooked directly from the cold fridge to help prevent the center from overcooking.

3. Heat a cast-iron or heavy-bottomed pan over high heat until smoking hot, about 4 minutes. Add the oil and then carefully lower the steak into the pan, dropping it away from you so as not to splash any hot oil toward you. Cook the steak until deeply golden brown on the first side, about 4 minutes, then flip and continue cooking until you've reached your preferred temperature, about 5 more minutes for 125°F or medium-rare. Test the temperature using the cake-tester method mentioned above or an instant-read thermometer.

4. Two minutes before the steak is finished, add the thyme, garlic, and butter to the pan and baste the steak repeatedly with a spoon, ladling the hot butter over the meat to season and crisp the top.

5. Let the meat rest in a warm place for at least 8 minutes before slicing to serve. Top with the fried shallots, a sprinkle of flaky salt, and a light dusting of MSG, if using.

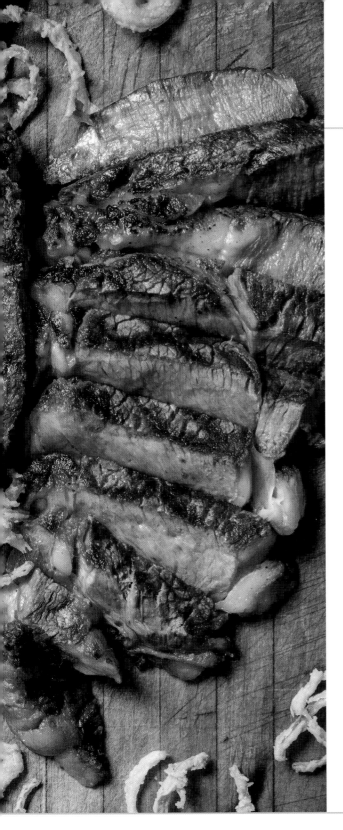

Crispy Fried Shallots

Makes about 6 cups

4 large shallots, thinly sliced crosswise into rings on a mandoline or with a sharp knife

2 cups buttermilk

4 cups vegetable oil

3 cups all-purpose flour

Kosher salt, finely ground in a mortar and pestle

½ teaspoon MSG

1. In a bowl, mix together the shallots and buttermilk. Let sit at room temperature for 1 hour.

2. In a large, heavy pot, heat the oil over medium-high heat to 375°F. A test shallot will bubble vigorously and float but not brown immediately. (Oil triples in volume when deep-frying, so be sure to use a large pot to keep it from boiling over.) Line a plate with paper towels and set it near the stove.

3. Put the flour in a bowl. Working in small batches, drain the shallots (discard the buttermilk) and toss them in the flour, breaking up the rings and making sure they are completely coated. Shake off any excess flour, then add the shallots to the hot oil and fry until just golden brown, about 2 minutes.

4. Using a fine-mesh strainer, transfer the shallots to the towel-lined plate. Season them immediately with a healthy pinch of kosher salt mixed with 10 percent MSG by weight (see page 32). Repeat with the remaining shallots. The shallots will remain crispy in an airtight container at room temperature for up to 2 days.

How do I know if meat has gone bad? And when is bad actually okay?

→ **DANIEL LIKES TO BRING** up the oyster example often—and for a pretty animated dude, the anecdote is more animated than his usual animated self. It's impassioned. It might be written on his headstone. Dear reader, did you know that if you were to eat a dozen oysters every single day for the rest of your life—and lucky you, Mrs. Hypothetical Bivalve Fan— you would get sick from those oysters exactly once every seven thousand *years*? Only one time. Once. Let that sink in.

The point of this is to illustrate that the chances of you getting sick from a "bad oyster" is literally a million to one. To put it in perspective, you are about three thousand times more likely to get struck by lightning. But even more important, it taps into Daniel and Matt's belief that many eaters—even the most ambitious and well seasoned (see what happened there?)—are missing out on some of the most delicious foods simply because they got some bad press in the past. Here are a few examples: Roast chicken is way better when it's served pink in the middle, and sometimes chicken should be served rare or even raw. (And it is absolutely unnecessary to cook pork all the way through. Pork chops are at their best when cooked to medium at most.) There is no difference, from a health safety perspective, between a rare burger (tough for some eaters) and steak tartare or Korean yukhoe (extremely tough for some eaters).

There's an unfortunate paradox here. A great many people are fearful of foodborne illness—which is, in general, something that they don't completely understand—while also being ambivalent toward other, more imminent dangers. Take meat, for

example. When meat has become bacterially spoiled, it smells really, really bad. It smells like, well, rotting meat, and it's certainly not something you would mistakenly eat. And if you did manage to ignore the warning shot to your olfactory system, it tastes even worse. So when somebody eats a cut of meat that maybe tasted a little funny or off, it hasn't gone "bad" exactly, or at least not in a way that would harbor dangerous foodborne illness.

There's no accidentally eating bad meat. There are flavorless and odorless pathogens that can get you sick, but those aren't the types of sick that people complain about, laying the blame on last night's steamed mussels. It's the type of sickness that lands you in the hospital and triggers a CDC investigation, complete with stool sample analysis and possibly a mention on the five o'clock news. Oysters are the same. Anyone who has opened a rotten oyster will tell you it's potent enough to make your entire house smell foul.

The other thing to keep in mind is that when food goes bad, it goes bad from the outside in. You'll have some chicken in the fridge for a day or two too long, and the liquid on the outside of it will start to have some bacterial growth and smell a little funky. Rinse it off and smell it again? Chances are, it's going to smell fine. That funkiness is the warning shot, but it's definitely okay with a quick rinse in the sink. There is no reason to throw out that slightly funky chicken. The only time it's gone truly bad—the kind of bad that causes bad things—is if the sourness has gone deep into the meat. This is the reason why ground meat can be so dangerous and is often the source of massive recalls. Grinding the bacteria-rich exterior and mixing it in with the clean center is not good. In fact, it can be deadly. Yet many unsuspecting home cooks trust the pound of chopped chuck over the slightly funky rib eye sitting in their fridge since last week. (See page 119 for some thoughts on dry-aged beef.)

But, of course, food poisoning does exist. Those who have been unfortunate enough to have it know the feeling of inescapable GI trauma that rips through your body, sucking your soul of life and likely causing you to wince at the sight of that Italian trattoria down the block that may have caused a special kind of poo de grâce. What's likely to blame is not meat but raw foods such as salads or green juices. Why? Because cooking kills most of the bacteria that cause foodborne illness. Raw vegetables are a main source of many of the nasty things, like E. coli, salmonella, and listeria, you hear about on the news. A poorly washed tomato can give you a case of shigellosis. Cooked meat is less likely to be the culprit, and oysters are definitely not to blame either. And remember, those two bottles of cheap cava you drank with those dozen bivalves might have something to do with your morning heaving. They call that the wine flu. ●

REFRIGERATOR CHICKEN RICE BOWL

Serves 2

1 cup leftover roast chicken meat, shredded (or substitute poached chicken, page 197)

½ cup Nước Chấm (recipe follows)

1 English cucumber, thinly sliced (about 1 cup)

¼ white onion, thinly sliced

Juice of 1 lime

Pinch of kosher salt

2 cups warm cooked jasmine rice (or substitute cooked rice noodles)

2 cups shredded lettuce greens

1 large carrot, peeled and shredded

1 cup mung bean sprouts

¼ bunch cilantro,

¼ bunch basil, tough stems discarded

¼ bunch mint, tough stems discarded

¼ cup salt-roasted peanuts, chopped

Nobody advocates serving old chicken that tastes like the refrigerator, but let's face it, we've all kept cooked chicken for a few too many days and then vacillated on whether to throw it out or prepare it in a way that freshens it up. Enter nước chấm, the glorious Vietnamese sweet-and-sour dipping sauce and dressing that is insanely delicious and is Daniel's go-to sauce for cold noodle bowls, rice bowls, fresh spring rolls, and, yes, refrigerator chicken. Nước chấm is a blend of fish sauce, sugar, and freshly squeezed lime juice, and it will transform all but the most questionable meat into something you really want to eat.

1. In a small bowl, toss the chicken in the nước chấm and let marinate while building the bowl.

2. In a bowl, combine the cucumber, onion, lime juice, and a pinch of salt, toss to mix, and let marinate. Scoop 1 cup of the warm rice into each bowl (90 seconds in the microwave in a bowl covered with plastic wrap warms rice perfectly), then arrange the lettuce, carrot, sprouts, basil, mint, and mixed onion and cucumber around the edge, nestling them in to create a beautiful nest-like arrangement.

3. Spoon the chicken and nước chấm over the top of the rice. Garnish with the peanuts and cilantro and serve.

Nước Chấm

Makes about ¾ cup

½ cup water

2 tablespoons sugar

2 tablespoons fresh lime juice

2 tablespoons fish sauce

1 small clove garlic, minced

1 fresh bird's eye chile, thinly sliced (if you like it spicy)

1. In a small saucepan, combine the water and sugar over low heat and stir to dissolve the sugar. Let cool thoroughly, then transfer to a small bowl.

2. Add the lime juice, fish sauce, garlic, and chile, if using, and stir to mix. Any leftover sauce will keep in an airtight container in the refrigerator for up to 1 week.

CALLING A LITTLE BULLSHIT ON THE DRY-AGING OBSESSION

Daniel doesn't love dry-aged meat that much, and Matt thinks there's an easy punch line for the people who covet the forty-five-day dry-aged rib eye—and for the restaurants that make a killing selling these cuts. Aging steaks is important, no doubt, and a week to ten days of bacterial growth time can add more complex flavors and help tenderize a well-marbled New York strip.

There are animals that benefit greatly from a longer aging process: game birds like pheasant, pigeon, and quail. Some hunters swear that hanging a pheasant in a barn for any less than a month is a travesty. Dry aging beef for forty-five days is an expensive price to pay, however, and Matt and Daniel argue that it's a gimmick that doesn't taste *that* great. Matt hypothesizes that there's a connection between Scotch whisky drinkers and dry-aged beef fans: a fetishizing of age that ultimately doesn't add up to much. And adding dry-aged beef to a boutique hamburger blend is akin to grating a thirty-six-month aged Parmigiano Reggiano over a bowl of spaghetti and meatballs (see page 31). For burgers, by the way, freshly ground 80 percent lean ground chuck is all you need to get the job done right.

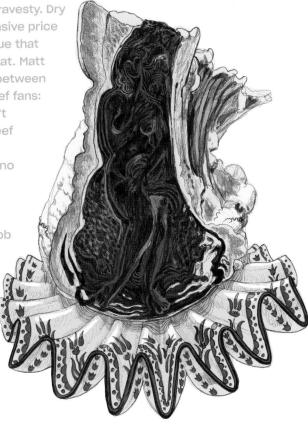

What is deglazing?

→ **MATT WAS A LITTLE** iffy on including this question among the one hundred. Deglazing felt dated and a little too cheffy—about the same level of excitement as a visit to the eighteenth-century French furniture case at the Met. But Matt *is* a fan of cooking spatchcocked chickens and double-cut heritage pork chops in a cast-iron pan. He also loves a good, restaurant-quality sauce on his meats, but he could never really execute one at home. It turns out he was overlooking an important step called, you guessed it, deglazing—the step that fully utilizes the incredible flavor so often left behind in the pan.

Next time you sear a piece of meat and set it aside to rest, take a look in the pan. You'll notice a deeply browned crust of crispy, caramelized goodness stuck to the bottom. Most red-blooded humans who love the flavors of salt and fat will be salivating at the sight. It's like the muffin top of meat cooking. This stuff is called "fond" (French for "base"), and it's these leftover bits that flavor a pan sauce or gravy. The key is getting all of this fond off the pan and onto your plate before it burns. Enter deglazing.

While the pan is still hot and your meat is resting, drain off any excess fat and oil, then add whatever sauce ingredients will match up with your meat— peppercorns and shallots for a quick steak au poivre, a handful of capers for a perfect chicken piccata, a few cloves of garlic and a sprig of rosemary to flavor your lamb chops. Next, shower the freshly caramelized fond with a healthy splash of white wine (start with ¼ cup) and cook, scraping all the bits and pieces off the bottom over medium-high heat.

Depending on your sauce of choice, you can play with different liquids. Add sherry for its sharp, dry bite, Marsala for its subtle sweetness, or apple cider vinegar for a hit of bright acid. Once the initial splash of liquid has reduced, you can add some stock or cream or both, a couple of knobs of butter, and swirl it all together as you boil the sauce down to the perfect nappe consistency (coats the back of a spoon). That's all it takes to make an incredible sauce that will elevate your next pork chop or New York strip.

Deglazing isn't a technique reserved only for stove-top meat cooking. You can employ it at all different stages of the cooking process, depending on the dish you're preparing. After searing meat for a stew in a Dutch oven, you deglaze with wine to capture all the meaty flavor before adding the stock. When your turkey comes out of the oven on Thanksgiving, you deglaze the pan (Daniel's dad used ginger ale—think about that!) for the perfect gravy. Even with a simple process like caramelizing onions, you can deglaze with a few drops of water to help scrape up the sweet sugars that are sticking to the pan, reincorporating their flavor. Deglazing is a crucial technique that Matt regrets thinking was too fancy. Deglazing is essential. ●

PAN-ROASTED AIRLINE CHICKEN BREAST

An airline chicken breast is a beautiful thing: a skin-on chicken breast with the bones removed save the first joint of the wing bone, or drumette. Wing = airline . . . get it? This is one of the very first recipes a young cook learns in culinary school: it teaches the fundamentals of properly pan roasting a chicken breast and serving it with pan gravy. It's quintessential wedding food, but when perfectly executed, it's delicious. The trick is, wait for it, deglazing the fond so the sauce picks up the roast chicken flavor. All in all a good pan sauce shouldn't take more than three to four minutes to cook, about the time you'll want to rest your breast anyway. Once you get the hang of it, for additional twists and turns, try adding herbs like tarragon, parsley, or a dollop of grainy mustard.

Serves 2

- 2 (5-ounce) airline chicken breasts
- Kosher salt
- 2 tablespoons extra-virgin olive oil
- 2 thyme sprigs
- ¼ cup dry white wine
- ½ cup chicken stock (or substitute bouillon)
- 3 tablespoons butter
- Freshly ground black pepper

1. Season the chicken breasts heavily on both sides with salt (aim for 1.5 percent by weight, or about 1 teaspoon each) at least 2 hours before cooking and preferably the night before and refrigerate until ready to cook.

2. Set a wire rack on a sheet pan or tray and place near the stove. Heat the oil in a large sauté pan over medium-high heat until it just begins to smoke. Pat the chicken breasts dry with a paper towel and then gently lower them, skin side down, into the pan, dropping them away from you so as not to splash any hot oil toward you. Cook the chicken breasts until the skin is deeply golden brown, about 5 minutes, then flip them and add the thyme to the pan. (If the skin sticks, the chicken isn't ready to flip; give it another minute or two and it will loosen on its own.) Continue cooking until the breasts are firm and just pink in the center, about 4 minutes, or until an instant-read thermometer inserted into the center registers 140°F. Transfer the breasts to the waiting rack and let rest in a warm place while making the sauce.

3. Deglaze with the wine, scraping up any fond that has stuck to the pan with a wooden spoon. Raise the heat to high and boil the wine until almost completely evaporated, about 2 minutes. Add the stock and boil until reduced by half, about 3 minutes, then whisk in the butter. The sauce is ready when it has thickened to nappe consistency (coats the back of a spoon, and when you trace a trail with your fingertip across the back, the trail holds its shape without dripping).

4. Slice each chicken breast on the diagonal, then transfer to individual plates and fan the slices. Spoon the sauce over the top.

Crispy skin is the holy grail of fish cooking. How do I do it?

→ **THERE ARE MANY GREAT** ways to cook a fish. You can poach halibut in butter, court bouillon (deeply flavorful broth), or olive oil; steam whole snapper with ginger and green onions; or grill swordfish steaks over gas or charcoal. But cooking fish in a pan, and crisping the skin to shattering perfection, is the climbing K2 of fish cookery. High-heat cooking without burning the skin or overcooking the fish is an exercise in humility. Flip the fish a moment too early, and the skin sticks to the pan, ruining Christmas Eve. A minute too late, and it's a charcoal-black, burnt, bitter nightmare—again, no presents for anyone. This is to say that the technique can be tricky, and many home cooks balk at attempting it.

Crisping fish is difficult because the skin is high in moisture and rich in collagen. Heat plus moisture melts the sticky collagen, gluing the fish to virtually any surface, and fish skin is quite delicate. This dynamic presents a challenge for even the most seasoned restaurant chefs, and it's a real pitfall for less experienced home cooks. Cooking the skin properly comes down to patience and timing. Home cooks tend to panic halfway through cooking the fish and, afraid the fish is burning, prematurely try to flip it. Wrong decision. Confronted with the skin's obstinate determination not to budge, they pry harder, ultimately separating the flesh from the skin or tearing it apart, and all involved are sad.

What many don't realize is that this skin will eventually release its grip, offering itself up to be flipped easily when it's ready. The trick is to manage the heat and simply wait for the moment to arrive—and avoid the temptation to help the process along with any prodding or prying. But how will you know when it's ready? Channel your inner Yoda, use all of your powers of observation, and the moment will reveal itself—that and a little shake of the pan from time to time to look for evidence of loosening.

Yes, successfully cooking a fish also hinges on proper preparation, and to do this, you start not in the pan but several minutes (or even hours for larger fish) earlier. Make sure to salt the skin at least twenty minutes in advance of cooking, which both seasons it and draws out some of the moisture. Moisture is the enemy of crispy fish, so dry the fish thoroughly with a paper towel just before cooking it. Next, heat your oil in a carbon-steel or cast-iron pan until it's smoking hot. Grapeseed or vegetable oil is ideal, as they have a higher smoke point than olive oil. Place the fish skin side down, pressing it with a spatula to ensure even contact with the pan (fresh fish will often tense and curl when first encountering heat and can take up to a minute to relax). Once flattened, lower the heat to medium and continue cooking for several minutes, gently shaking the pan and checking the edges of the fish to see if it's ready to flip. You are going to cook the fish 95 percent of the way through on the skin side and then merely kiss the flesh side to finish before plating it. Ready your accompaniments beforehand—crispy skin is a fleeting promise and best served immediately. •

CRISPY SALMON WITH LEMON, PINE NUTS, AND WILTED BUTTER LETTUCE

Serves 2

---

2 (5-ounce) skin-on salmon fillets

Kosher salt

1 cup torn bread, soaked in water to cover

½ cup pine nuts

¾ cup extra-virgin olive oil

Grated zest and juice of 1 lemon

1 clove garlic

1 head butter lettuce, cored and cut into 1-inch-wide strips

1 cup fresh or frozen peas

Daniel developed this dish for the winter menu at the Inn of the Seventh Ray, a creek-side fine-dining restaurant in Los Angeles. This recipe employs two lesser-utilized techniques: cooking lettuce and blending bread. Gently sautéing lettuce brings out the sweetness in the leafy vegetable and offers a refreshing crunch, which pairs beautifully with the earthy and acidic pine nut sauce. And blending bread soaked in water works to emulsify the sauce, giving it a rich and creamy texture akin to a Caesar dressing. The technique works as a thickener for soups as well and is a great use for stale bread.

1. Season each salmon fillet on both sides with ½ teaspoon salt.

2. To make the sauce, drain the bread and add to a blender along with ¼ cup of the pine nuts, ½ cup of the oil, the lemon juice, garlic, and 1½ teaspoons salt. Blend until smooth, adding a few tablespoons water if necessary to achieve a thick, pourable consistency. Set aside.

3. Heat 1 tablespoon of the remaining oil in a large sauté pan over medium-high heat until it just begins to smoke. Pat the salmon fillets dry with a paper towel and then gently lower them, skin side down, into the pan, dropping them away from you so as not to splash any hot oil toward you. Lower the heat to medium and cook until the skin is crispy, about 4 minutes. Flip the fillets and continue cooking until just cooked through, about 2 minutes, depending on thickness.

4. Meanwhile, in a small bowl, mix together the remaining ¼ cup pine nuts, the remaining 3 tablespoons oil, the lemon zest, and a pinch of salt and reserve.

5. Transfer the salmon to a plate. Add the lettuce, peas, and a pinch of salt to the pan and cook over medium heat, stirring constantly, until just warmed and wilted.

6. Divide the wilted lettuce mixture between individual plates. Place the fish on the lettuce, then spoon the pine nut sauce over the top. Garnish with the lemony pine nuts and oil.

What is baker's math, and why is it the secret to perfect pastry?

→ **BAKER'S MATH, SOMETIMES CALLED** the baker's ratio, is an idea that was foreign to Matt at the start of working on this book. He's more of an arts and letters kind of guy, and for anybody who used their TI-83 more for tic-tac-toe than for computing logarithms, you know how math can be . . . challenging. But math came up nonetheless after Daniel credited "the ratio" for a recent at-home sourdough success. It turns out it's a topic that requires some deeper discussion, and it starts by going back to the idea of cooking by weight instead of volume (see page 56), which is the way professional kitchens are widely run—and generally a much easier way to bake.

The baker's ratio is based around the weight of flour as the constant in relative proportion to other ingredients, including water, salt, and yeast. For a simple white bread, the ratio is typically 100 percent flour, 66 percent water (often referred to as "hydration"), 2 percent salt, and 1.2 percent yeast. The key is that these ratios can be scaled up and down to fit your exact needs—from 500 grams flour for a small loaf to 22 kilograms for an industrial bake. Hydration is the key to switching between different doughs. Lower hydration rates (52 to 58 percent) are used for stiffer doughs (bagels and pretzels), and medium hydration levels (59 to 65 percent) are typical for most common breads and rolls. Higher hydration creates larger holes, as is common in artisanal loaves, baguettes, and ciabatta. Baker's math can be used for all types of baking, and we've compiled a chart on page 126 for some of our favorite recipes. •

SHERRY YARD is a renowned pastry chef, restaurateur, author of several seminal cookbooks on the art and craft of baking, television personality, and all-around amazing human being. Sherry exudes hospitality from the depths of her soul, sharing her immense knowledge with the world. She also bakes extremely delicious cookies.

How can I become more creative with my baking?

First off, you need to understand the basic format and principles, ingredients, and what role they play in your recipe. What is butter and is it a liquid or a solid? What is the butterfat percentage? Each ingredient is a tool. Once you have your foundation set up, you will understand how any change will affect the end product.

When developing a new recipe, what does your creative process look like?

When I'm working on a new recipe, a brownie for instance, I try to find every brownie recipe I possibly can. I convert all of the recipes to percentages (percent of butter for brownies, percent of flour for breads), then write them next to one another on a graph. From there I can see what the basic range is for each ingredient, I can tell the evolution of the recipes—who's copying whom—and then land on a recipe.

How do you judge a new bakery?

I always try a croissant, then something chocolate to see if they are using cocoa powder. But most of all I'm looking for color. Does the pie have great color? Because color equals flavor. I like to say the only blond thing in my bakery is me.

A PERCENTAGE TABLE FOR EIGHT CLASSIC YEAST BREADS

Take a look at the following table presenting baker's percentages for a few of the more popular styles of yeasted breads. While the recipe variation among breads is subtle, a small percentage change in hydration or fat makes a big difference in the final product, so it's easy to see why precision matters (and cooking with a digital scale—see page 56—gives you the most precise results). Familiarizing yourself with the general ratios will help you analyze a bread recipe quickly and get an idea of what the outcome will be.

	FLOUR	HYDRATION	YEAST
challah	100 g	45% water	0.9%
brioche	100 g	25% milk	1.5%
sandwich bread	100 g	58% water	3%
French bread	100 g	65% water	0.55%
focaccia	100 g	78% water	0.8%
pizza	100 g	62% water	0.5%
bagel	100 g	53% water	0.3%
pretzel	100 g	56% water	1.25%

FAT	EGGS	SWEETENER	SALT
5% vegetable oil	25%	5.5% sugar	1.5%
50+% butter	45%	7% sugar	2%
8% shortening	4%	7% sugar	2%
			1.9%
			2.2%
2% olive oil			2.25%
		2% malt	2%
5% butter		2% malt	1.8%

Grill, steam, or fry: what's the best way to cook a whole fish?

→ **THERE'S SO MUCH TO** love about cooking a whole fish, whether it's grilled slowly in the backyard or carved tableside at a restaurant minutes after an innocuous gesture toward a tank sent the flipping fish on its journey to gustatory glory. Chefs love the drama of a whole fish, too. Matt's *Koreatown* coauthor, Deuki Hong, goes nuts for it, and he ordered it every chance he got, introducing Matt to a sea of whole fishes during their book tour around the country. Daniel is no different, and he has trouble picking a favorite. Covered in salted seaweed, then steamed slowly in clay that is cracked tableside with a hammer in Italy. Skewered and deep-fried in the shape of a swimming *S* in Singapore. The whole poached Dover sole at La Grenouille in New York City. And perhaps the most memorable of all: grilled turbot at Elkano in northern Spain. Those grill baskets are really great, and you should invest in a couple of them.

But if Daniel had to choose one way to cook a whole fish at home, the answer would be steaming. Steaming highlights the flavor of the fish rather than overpowering the subtle nuance of the flesh and the skin. You can steam a whole fish with very little equipment in any oven in the world. All you need is a piece of paper (well, a very large piece of parchment paper). Cooking en papillote (in paper) is a great technique with a wonderful sense of theater: you seal the fish, along with vegetables, seasonings, and a little stock, inside a folded piece of parchment paper and bake it. The paper locks in the steam, puffing up and browning beautifully, and then exhales a powerful statement when cut open, ideally in view (and olfactory range) of the diners: "It's time to eat fish." The technique is especially convenient for larger cuts that would otherwise be challenging to steam for lack of properly sized cookware. Enter the whole fish.

It's hard to argue against steaming a whole fish, or even just a nice piece of fish, for that matter. (Shout-out to your Jewish grandparents, Team Nice Piece of Fish.) It's a quick preparation, and it consistently nails the landing with very little cleanup required. When buying a whole fish, freshness is obviously the key, so look at the eyes to make sure they are clear. The flesh should be perky, shiny, and bright. Give the fish a poke and a sniff. You should be looking for the flesh to bounce back and for a fresh odor akin to a day at the beach (and not Jones Beach). You can cook all sorts of fish whole, but Daniel prefers flaky white fish like branzino, striped bass, dorade, and the whole-fish daddy of them all, the snapper.

When buying a fish for a group dinner, you can estimate weight at a pound per person—factoring in about a 40 percent yield after carving. And about those bones: they're a pain in the ass! The key to deboning is patience. If the fish is undercooked, it's an uphill battle. But provided you cooked the fish through, you can gently trace the bones with a butter knife or the back of a flat spoon, and the flesh should lift away in whole fillets. If you're uncomfortable with the idea, do your research. There are plenty of tutorials online that will walk you through the process. ●

friend of FOOD IQ

ERIC RIPERT is a legend in food popular culture, a longtime Bourdain friend and television sidekick, and a master of cooking fish. His New York City restaurant Le Bernardin has won every major award several times over, and it is where Daniel got his start working on a professional kitchen line at the age of fourteen. This interview was conducted by Matt.

Why do chefs love the whole fish so much?

The whole fish has more flavor because it's cooked on the bone. So first of all, the bones are very gelatinous. Gelatin is basically a magnet for flavor. Also, the flesh doesn't shrink, or doesn't change its structure. It stays the way it's supposed to be, and you keep a lot of the juice of the fish, a lot of flavors, and the texture is better. If you cook the whole fish, very often you have the skin that protects the flesh from the heat as well.

Do you prefer grilled, steamed, or fried?

Depending on the size of the fish, I mostly bake it at very high temperatures. Let's take a snapper, for instance—a five- or six-pound snapper. Inside, in the belly, I put some butter and citrus, like limes and lemons and oranges, and herbs like rosemary and thyme and so on, and then I season the fish on the outside with olive oil and put it into the oven. The skin becomes kind of crispy if it's cooked at a very hot temperature. And then the flesh is very moist.

What's the temperature? North of 450°F?

I go to 500°F because my oven is always super clean and there's no smoke in the house [laughing].

What's a whole fish to cook that is maybe less known?

Well, if you catch a bluefish and it's out of the water for just a few hours before you [cook] it, it's one of the most amazing fish that you can eat. It's very rich, it's very fatty, and it's very flavorful.

What do you remember of Daniel in the kitchen of Le Bernardin at age fourteen?

I remember how young he was, and I remember how surprised I was at how interested he was to come to our kitchen. He was not hired in the beginning; he was coming to observe and learn and so on, and we treated him like a normal cook. He didn't have special treatment. And I thought he was doing really well. He was hardworking, very quick with his mind, and he came for many, many years like that. And then at one point he became an employee of Le Bernardin as well.

Well, thank you for that memory. He thinks the world of you and of his experience in the kitchen.

Oh, I think the world of him, too, but I never see him. He's too busy!

WHOLE FISH STEAMED IN PAPER

Serves 2

---

1 (2¼-pound) whole snapper, cleaned and scaled

Kosher salt

6 thyme sprigs

1 lemon, thinly sliced

2 tablespoons extra-virgin olive oil

2 tablespoons unsalted butter, cut into three or four pats

¼ cup dry white wine

Steaming en papillote (cooking in a folded parchment-paper envelope) never ceases to enchant Daniel and Matt. The technique works well for almost any type of fish or for quick-cooking vegetables like asparagus, broccoli, or green beans. You can experiment with different vegetables and flavor profiles using different sauces, such as sake, butter, and soy sauce for a Japanese direction or chipotle, tomatillo, and lime for a Mexican inspiration. Just be sure that if you're cooking more than one item (like halibut and asparagus) in the same envelope, everything cooks in roughly the same amount of time. Cutting vegetables into smaller pieces can speed up their cooking. But if you're trying to cook salmon and butternut squash in the same package, you'll be hard-pressed not to overcook the salmon by the time the squash is soft enough to serve, so pay attention when matchmaking.

1. Preheat the oven to 425°F.

2. With a sharp knife, score the fish skin on the diagonal three or four times on each side. Season both sides of the fish and inside the cavity with 1½ teaspoons salt. Stuff the cavity with the thyme and lemon slices.

3. Place the fish on a large piece of parchment paper, then drizzle with the oil and arrange the butter pats evenly spaced on top. Add the wine, fold the long sides of the paper up to meet in the middle above the fish, and then roll the edges over to seal. Roll in the edges on the sides to seal and then fold the sides under the fish. Place the whole package on a sheet pan.

4. Bake until the parchment inflates and begins to brown, about 25 minutes.

5. Slice the package open tableside for maximum effect.

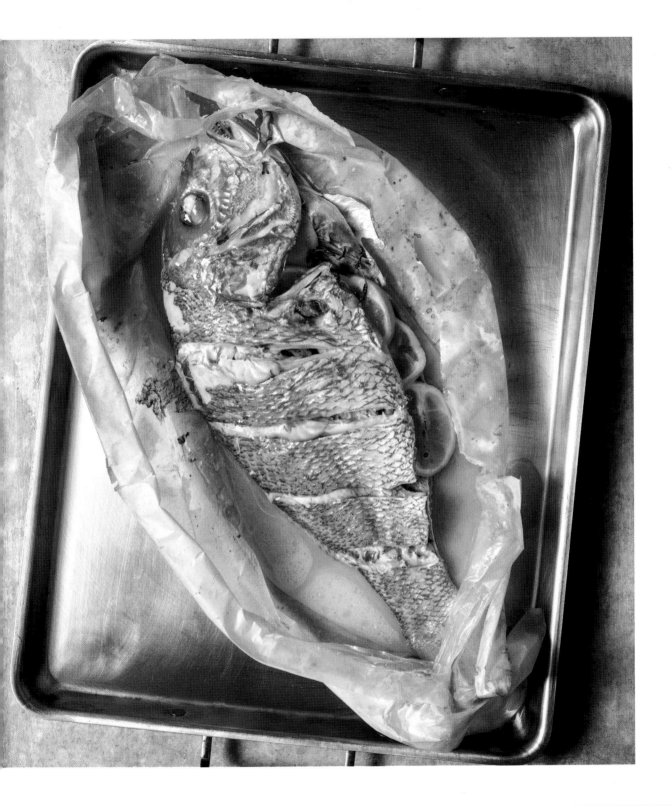

How do I make fluffy gnocchi like my favorite Italian trattoria?

→ **WHEN DANIEL AND MATT** started writing *Food IQ*, they sent out a survey to a couple of dozen friends and family asking for their burning food questions, and the request for an "easy way to make really good potato gnocchi at home" came up more than any other. So here it is. Daniel has been making this foundational northern Italian dish for almost twenty-five years, and he believes firmly that the key to a good gnocchi game is all about timing—and burnt fingertips.

Potato gnocchi are a gift from the culinary gods—the transformation from simple spud to something fluffy, ethereal, and soaked in brown butter. But that truth is lived only when the gnocchi are made fresh. Store-bought gnocchi (and we've all gone in this direction; there's no shame in it) fall into a different category—gummy, chewy, and definitely not what you order at your favorite neighborhood trattoria. This is because shelf-stable gnocchi have way more flour in them (flour = gluten = toothsome), and they're extruded under pressure and dried so they won't lose their shape. Pillowy Platonic-ideal gnocchi are made mostly of potatoes, with just enough flour and egg to bind them together. It's executing this balance that will win the day.

The key is to use starchy potatoes (see page 38) and to remove as much moisture as possible. Baking the spuds works well, but the microwave is the fastest dry-heat method to cook them through. You can also boil the potatoes in their skin, but make sure to drain them thoroughly before peeling. This all leads to the critical ricing step. Ricing the potatoes while they're still hot (using a kitchen tool called a ricer, akin to a garlic press) allows the steam to escape, drying the potatoes further. Yes, your fingertips may suffer a little. And yes, your gnocchi will be the best possible gnocchi.

The real challenge with gnocchi is judging how much flour to add. Add too little and your gnocchi will fall apart; add too much and your fluffy pillows will more closely resemble dense bricks. No recipe can account for the exact moisture content of the potatoes or the yield once the potatoes are riced, so it's up to the home cook to pick the proper amount of flour and adjust as necessary. The challenge is compounded by the tendency for potatoes to become gummy when worked, so the more you mix, the worse your gnocchi become.

Ideally, you'd add the perfect amount of flour at the beginning, give the dough a quick mix, and knead. But unless your name is Nadia Santini, you'll likely have to add a few extra scoops to get the consistency right. You'll know it when you nail it because your pile of mashed potatoes will magically transform into a soft and malleable dough just barely tacky to the touch but not sticky enough to adhere to the table or your fingers. Once you have your dough done, you can chill out a little bit, maybe cool your scorched fingertips in an ice bath, and roll the pile of potatoes into long, fragile logs, then cut and shape your gnocchi.

Cooking these clouds is a cinch. Gently drop them into boiling salty water and wait for them to float, which shouldn't take more than a minute or two. Scoop them out and they're done. Once you're comfortable with the process, try taking the next step and frying the gnocchi in butter and oil to brown them on all sides. This takes some forethought and timing—you'll have to get your butter hot and ready at the same moment your gnocchi come out of the water. Otherwise, they will lose their composure in the pan. Given all of the opportunities for disaster along the way, it's pretty remarkable to think about that plate of pillowy perfection landing in front of you in a restaurant.

Once you've got the technique down pat, you can try your hand at some of the more uncommon cousins and distant relatives of gnocchi. The technique works with other starchy vegetables like pumpkin or sweet potato, though their additional moisture adds an extra level of difficulty. **Ricotta gnocchi** call for fresh cheese instead of potato. The curds are drained overnight and then mixed with flour and egg before shaping. **Gnudi** are made by burying dollops of ricotta in semolina flour and waiting for them to dry. The semolina absorbs the moisture from the cheese, hardening after a few days into a crusty dough around each orb. The end result is a soft ball of delicious cheese held together by an impossibly thin layer of seamless dough that bursts open when bitten. ●

FLUFFY POTATO GNOCCHI WITH PISTACHIO PESTO

Serves 4

---

3 large russet
potatoes (about
1½ pounds total)

Kosher salt

1 egg, lightly beaten

1½ cups all-purpose
flour, plus more for
dusting

1 cup Pistachio Pesto
(recipe follows)

Potato gnocchi are an easy entry point into the world of fresh-pasta cookery. The biggest issue is drying out the potatoes so the gnocchi require only a minimal amount of flour to bind them. The more flour you use, the stiffer and gummier the texture becomes. A microwave cooks the potatoes quickly and without any extra moisture. You'll need a potato ricer to make the recipe, but it's a worthy investment. You can also use a food mill, which is a little more expensive but more versatile as well. Rice the potatoes while they're still steaming hot so as much moisture evaporates as possible.

1. Stab each potato with a fork about ten times, piercing the skin in different places. Cook the potatoes in an uncovered microwave-safe dish in the microwave on high power, flipping them twice at 5-minute intervals, until cooked through, about 15 minutes.

2. Bring a large pot of heavily salted water (⅓ cup salt per 4 quarts water) to a boil over high heat.

3. Peel the potatoes while still piping hot (rubber gloves will help combat the heat), then rice them onto a lightly floured work surface.

4. Make a well in the middle of the still-warm potatoes, add the egg, 1½ teaspoons salt, and 1 cup of the flour. Using a metal spatula or bench scraper, fold the ingredients together, forming a loose, sticky dough and adding more flour as necessary, a tablespoon at a time, to help the dough come together. Knead just until smooth and incorporated, about 1 minute. Overmixing will stiffen the gnocchi.

5. Working in small batches, roll the mixture with your hands into penny-thick logs. Use a butter knife to cut the logs into 1-inch pieces. (You can dimple each gnocco with a fork or gnocchi board if you choose.)

6. In portion-size batches, add the gnocchi to the boiling water and boil until they float, about 2 minutes. Using a slotted spoon, scoop them out, sauce with the pesto, and serve immediately.

Note: Any extra gnocchi can be dusted with flour, transferred to an airtight container, frozen for up to 1 month, and then cooked directly from the freezer.

Pistachio Pesto

Makes 1½ cups

1 cup unsalted shelled roasted pistachios

1 small clove garlic

¼ cup fresh mint leaves

¼ cup freshly grated pecorino romano cheese

¼ cup extra-virgin olive oil

Kosher salt and freshly cracked black pepper

1. In a food processor or with a mortar and pestle, pulse or grind together the pistachios, garlic, mint, and cheese until just chopped but still chunky. Drizzle in the oil while pulsing the processor or pounding the pestle to incorporate. Be careful not to over-puree the sauce, as you want to retain the texture from small pieces of nuts and cheese. Alternatively, mince the pistachios, garlic, mint, and cheese together with a knife, transfer to a bowl, and slowly drizzle in the oil while stirring constantly.

2. Season to taste with salt and pepper. Leftover pesto will keep in an airtight container in the refrigerator for up to 3 weeks.

Why doesn't my homemade guacamole taste as good as the one at my favorite Mexican restaurant?

→ **SALT AND ACID—OR, MORE** specifically, a lack thereof—is the sticking point for most grand guacamole plans (failed plans). It's a sad fact when things go badly because there is really no better example of perfection in food's great taxonomy of dips than a super-salty tortilla chip loaded with a mound of exquisitely balanced guac. Be it freshly pounded at your favorite Mexican restaurant or served at a Super Bowl house party, guacamole never makes anybody sad. The ripe, fatty tree fruit, in its trademark verdant green, is scooped into a bowl and showered with salt, lime juice, cilantro, and other components that we may or may not suggest. For the record, tomatoes and hot sauce are not the way for these authors. But all guacamole does need *something* to take it over the top, to make it the star of the backyard barbecue. And Daniel says that something might just be mayonnaise.

First, the recipe. What's challenging about guacamole is that it doesn't really have a recipe. It's more of a concept or a feeling. To get guacamole right requires tasting it along the way. Home cooks are a little scared of adding the right amount of salt (you need a lot of it), leaving many guacamoles flabby and flavorless. Mayonnaise can solve a lot of your problems, though Daniel wants to be clear that it's never required. But when you add a couple of tablespoons of Hellmann's or Best Foods mayo, you're adding a perfectly seasoned dollop of salty, acidic richness that contributes to the flavor while adding an inexplicably silky texture.

Let's talk about buying avocados for a moment. When presented with a bin containing hundreds of choices, you need to be judicious. First, feel the leathery outer skin for a hint of the inner texture. Chances are, you know the difference between a hard avocado and a ripe one, but to refresh your memory, the right texture is soft but not mushy. Next, pull the nub off the top of the avocado, revealing the color of the flesh inside. That should be bright green, with no hint of brown. When avocados are overripe, the flesh under the little nub turns brown, just like a cut avocado does after it has been exposed to the air for a period of time. Like bananas, they are still okay to use when they're slightly brown, but you should avoid any black or gray spots, and taste the flesh to make sure it doesn't have a rotten flavor. Finally, guacamole is meant to be served à la minute. With too much exposure to air, the lime juice turns bitter and the color transforms from green to brown. This is why pricey tableside guacamole service is hardly a gimmick. It's truly the best possible way to eat it. •

QUICK AND CREAMY GUACAMOLE

Serves 2

¼ cup minced white onion

Juice of 1 lime

2 large, ripe avocados, halved, pitted, peeled, and diced

1 tablespoon mayonnaise

2 teaspoons kosher salt

¼ cup chopped fresh cilantro

Tortilla chips for serving

The trick to extra-creamy guacamole is adding a dollop of mayonnaise. People tend to overthink guacamole, but the truth is that less is more, so resist the temptation to add too many ingredients. Balancing the salt and acid is the hard part, and no recipe will get you there, so taste as you go. Your guacamole should be a little too salty and a little too acidic when you first mix it. With time, the avocado will absorb the seasoning, so a little extra is the right amount. Pro tip: Pickling the onion in the lime juice for a few minutes before mixing them with the rest of the ingredients helps mellow the raw onion flavor and keep your guacamole fresher for longer. This recipe serves two, but it is easy to scale up for a crowd.

1. In a large bowl, mix together the onion and lime juice and let sit for 5 minutes.

2. Add the avocado, mayonnaise, salt, and cilantro and mix gently to incorporate. Serve immediately with tortilla chips.

Busting Some Myths

Food facts and food fiction—there's a lot of subjectivity and fanaticism swirling around people's tastes and diet. And with the internet accelerating trends and coining buzzwords faster than ever, it can be hard to know who and what to trust. In this chapter, Daniel and Matt answer several questions based on myths, conjecture, and general confusion.

Is canola oil inferior, and why shouldn't I always use olive oil?

→ **IT COMES DOWN TO** PR. Good PR and bad PR. Olive oil, the golden child of cooking oils, popularized by TV chefs (Rachael Ray) and Mediterranean-diet acolytes, has not just good PR, but exceptional PR. Most of you have cooked with a bottle of EVOO (that's extra-virgin olive oil thanks to RR) as of late, and you regularly reach for the bottle for a number of reasons: flavor, health benefits, and primarily habit (turn to page 6 for a thorough breakdown of EVOO). Rapeseed oil, on the other hand, did not have great PR. Beyond the fact that the name shares its first four letters with a heinous act, the oil itself was plagued with a sketchy past tied to an association with high levels of erucic acid, which can be toxic to humans in large amounts. The toxicity was later proven erroneous, and with modern oil production, there is no risk of harm at all. But as with so much of our inaccurate institutional knowledge, the reeducation process is slow and unreliable. So, in stepped the Canadians. With a lock on the rapeseed market, which is cultivated in Western Canada, a sharp marketer came up with the rebrand "canola"—an acronym for "Canadian oil, low acid"—and canola oil was born.

Daniel is a fan of cooking with canola oil, and he uses it interchangeably with other neutrally flavored oils, such as vegetable, corn, and sunflower. Too often, home cooks reach for olive oil by default, even if it means injecting the clashing flavor of olives into a dish. Lime and olive oil, for instance, don't generally pair particularly well. Sautéing ginger and garlic in a wok for Chinese long beans with XO sauce? Olive oil doesn't match. Daniel's general thinking is that if you wouldn't eat something with an olive, then don't use olive oil. It's really that simple. Would you eat a piece of warm focaccia with olives? For sure. Would you eat a ten-ingredient fried rice that contains sambal, bok choy, and cumin ground pork with olives? Hopefully not. On the baking side, would you eat chocolate brownies with olives? No. Would you eat a warm semolina–olive oil cake with olives? Probably! Now, of course, food is like fashion, where the rules are meant to be broken, but just because you make an exception doesn't make it the rule. It's surely a sign of culinary genius to take seemingly incompatible ingredients and work them into something truly remarkable, and there are plenty of examples of just that. But the goal of *Food IQ* is to lay down the basics and explain the rules of engagement.

This is all to say that having a really good neutral oil around is important, and canola is one of the best. And the benefit is not only about flavor. Sometimes you need to cook with an oil at a hotter temperature. Each oil has a smoke point (the temperature at which the oil starts smoking, rapidly breaking down and approaching the temperature of spontaneous combustion), and olive oil has one of the lower ones (325° to 350°F). In contrast, the smoke point of canola oil is 450°F. Burning oil, and its acrid results, means starting over, so working with canola oil offers greater flexibility for high-temperature sautéing and frying.

Finally, here's a word about oils and expiration dates: they have one! Store your oil in a cool, dark place (that is, not next to the stove or above the oven) and be aware of the date on the label. Bad oil smells like crayons or a dusty attic. Throw that stuff away. ●

GREEN CHILE ENCHILADAS

Enchiladas made from (relative) scratch are one of Daniel and Matt's all-time favorite dishes, and they're worth the extra time this slightly more involved recipe requires. Braising the pork takes time, so make a double or triple batch. The stew is fantastic served over rice as a stand-alone main course if you don't have the time to roll and bake the enchiladas.

_____

1 pound boneless
pork butt, cut into
½-inch cubes

Kosher salt

½ teaspoon MSG

4 ounces Anaheim
chiles

4 tablespoons
vegetable oil

½ medium white
onion, minced

4 cloves garlic,
smashed

2½ cups chicken
stock (or substitute
bouillon)

8 ounces tomatillos,
husks removed and
chopped

¼ bunch cilantro,
stems and leaves
separated and
chopped

Juice of 1 lime

12 (6-inch) corn
tortillas

1 cup crumbled
queso fresco

1. Preheat the oven to 325°F.

2. Season the pork with 1 tablespoon salt and the MSG and set aside.

3. To fire-roast the chiles on a gas stove top, turn on a burner to high. Then, one at a time, place the chiles directly on the metal grate of the burner and roast, rotating with tongs as needed, until completely blackened and blistered, about 6 minutes. As the chiles are ready, transfer them to a bowl, cover the bowl with plastic wrap, and allow the chiles to steam and cool for about 10 minutes. If you don't have a gas stove top, preheat the broiler. Position an oven rack about 8 inches from the heat source and broil the chiles on an oven-safe tray, turning them as necessary to char them completely on all sides, then place them in the covered bowl. Once the chiles have steamed and cooled, cut them open, remove the stems and seeds, and scrape and wipe away the charred skin. It's okay if a few burnt bits remain. Cut the flesh into 1-inch dice and reserve.

4. While the chiles cool, heat 2 tablespoons of the oil in a Dutch oven over high heat until smoking. Add the pork and cook, turning as needed, until browned on all sides, about 10 minutes. Add the onion and garlic and continue cooking, stirring frequently, until soft and translucent, about 6 minutes. Add the stock, tomatillos, cilantro stems, and fire-roasted chiles and bring to a boil, scraping up any stuck food.

5. Transfer the pot to the oven and cook uncovered, stirring every 15 minutes, until the pork is fork-tender, about 1 hour.

6. Remove from the oven and season the stew with the lime juice and with salt to taste, then let cool for 15 minutes. Drain the stew into a fine-mesh strainer set over a bowl. Skim off and discard the fat from the surface of the braising liquid. Reserve the drained stew and the liquid. Increase the oven temperature to 400°F.

7. Heat the remaining 2 tablespoons oil in a large sauté pan over medium heat. One at a time, fry the tortillas for 20 seconds on each side. As the tortillas are ready, set them aside on a plate.

8. To assemble the enchiladas, spoon ⅔ cup of the pork braising liquid into the bottom of a 9-by-13-inch baking pan. Spoon 2 to 3 tablespoons of the pork in a line along the center of each tortilla, roll the tortilla around the filling, and then place seam side down in the pan, fitting the enchiladas snugly alongside one another to ensure they don't unravel. Ladle the remaining cooking liquid over the top and sprinkle with the cheese.

9. Bake until bubbling and browned, about 15 minutes. Garnish with the reserved cilantro leaves before serving.

When making pasta sauce, must I use those fancy canned San Marzano tomatoes?

→ **PLUM TOMATOES THAT ARE** grown in the volcanic soil near Italy's Mount Vesuvius are really quite spectacular. This prized Campania fruit is still cultivated in the area surrounding its namesake town, San Marzano sul Sarno, in ideal conditions (hot and sunny days develop sugars, while cool nights promote a prized concentration of acidity) for growing perfectly balanced sauce tomatoes. Regulated by the Italian government, tomatoes stamped with the dignified and official DOP name "San Marzano" have been cherished around the world for decades for their thick, sweet flesh and their minimal number of pesky seeds. That translates to higher prices and prime placement in recipes and restaurant menus, most commonly in Neapolitan-style pizzerias, which often exclusively use San Marzanos for their pies' delicate sauce.

But two things have changed in the last decade that should influence the way home cooks think about canned tomatoes. First, the canned tomatoes in California have gotten way, way better. Second, there has been a growing swell of shady import practices surrounding tomatoes arriving from Italy. In 2011, Edoardo Ruggiero, the president of the organization tasked with preserving the sanctity of the San Marzano DOP, said that only 5 percent of tomatoes sold in the United States as San Marzanos are legitimate. That's not a typo: from the tomato police chief himself, 95 percent of the so-called San Marzanos in the United States are fraudulent. This is coupled with the fact that the name "San Marzano" can appear on virtually any can of tomatoes—the naming is unregulated. That popular brand called San Marzano, with the white label and striking tomato watercolor, is actually a product of California (and sells a very good product, despite the misleading advertising).

Which takes us back to the Golden State. The canned tomatoes from California are pretty extraordinary, and Daniel prefers them, using the Stanislaus Foods brand out of Modesto (sold under brand names Alta Cucina or Valoroso) and the smaller Bianco DiNapoli brand, founded by famed American pizzaiolo Chris Bianco (these are hands down the best tomatoes available, and Daniel has tasted dozens). Both brands utilize state-of-the-art packing equipment, ensuring their tomatoes are picked, sorted, washed, canned, and sealed within hours of harvesting—locking in every drop of sweetness the California sun doles out.

Does any of this make a difference for your Sunday sauce or pizza? There are many brands of high-quality tomatoes on the market, and any will do the trick. Muir Glen (California), Cento (Italy), and Redpack (Indiana) are all good labels, and if you've got one you prefer, stick with it. But if you're asking a chef for advice, then the goal is to use the best possible product available, and most chefs these days have switched over to domestic tomatoes—and not just for the diminished carbon footprint, another added plus. ●

FORTY-MINUTE RED SAUCE THAT WORKS WITH EVERYTHING

Makes about 5 cups

---

1 head garlic, cloves separated and peeled, then smashed

⅓ cup extra-virgin olive oil

Pinch of red chile flakes

2 (28-ounce) cans good-quality whole peeled tomatoes with their juice

Kosher salt

6 fresh basil leaves

Here's the thing about red sauce. If you start with high-quality tomatoes, it's extremely easy to make a delicious utility sauce with only five ingredients plus salt. Whether you're making pizza, dipping calamari, building a lasagna, or topping chicken parmesan, this sauce will be the answer. Save this recipe and share it with friends (you can take a photo of this page and text it on—we are very okay with that). The trick is to slowly confit the garlic in the oil before adding the tomatoes. That step will add a few extra minutes, but the sauce will always be scented with raw garlic otherwise.

1. In a large Dutch oven or heavy-bottomed pot, slowly heat the garlic and oil over medium-low heat. Cook slowly, being very careful not to brown the garlic, until the smashed cloves are soft and pungent, about 8 minutes. You should watch the garlic for the entire duration, as it can burn quickly. Toss in the chile flakes at the very end.

2. Add the tomatoes and 2 teaspoons salt, raise the heat to medium-high, and bring to a boil, stirring frequently. Lower the heat to a simmer and cook, stirring frequently and mashing the tomatoes to break them up as they cook, until one-fourth of the liquid has evaporated and the sauce begins to thicken, the color darkens, and the oil begins to float and separate, about 30 minutes.

3. Stir in the basil and adjust the seasoning with salt as needed. Use immediately or let cool and then store until needed. The sauce will keep in an airtight container in the refrigerator for up to 2 weeks or in the freezer for up to 2 months.

When is it okay to cook with frozen vegetables?

→ **THERE'S A LONG ANSWER** and a short answer when addressing the question of cooking with frozen vegetables. The latter is simply that it's best to use frozen vegetables when the fresh ones aren't available or in season. As for the longer answer, some vegetables freeze better than others. Depending on how you plan to use the vegetables (snap peas served raw in a salad, spinach braised in a stew, cut potatoes deep-fried in oil), the choice of fresh or frozen will influence the final dish in a number of ways. The overall benefit of cooking with frozen vegetables is that it saves time and (usually) money, and that leaning into the freezer is a good way to pull together quick meals when you are in a pinch: a yakisoba stir-fry with green beans or lentils with braised spinach over rice comes to mind.

The biggest issue with freezing vegetables is changing or eroding texture, not flavor. As the water inside the cells of a vegetable freezes, it forms sharp, crystalline structures that expand, slicing trillions of microscopic cuts and rendering the thawed vegetables relatively mushy or mealy. They are fine in soups, not so fine in salade niçoise.

Therefore, the desired texture and moisture level are key to determining if a previously frozen vegetable will pass muster. Drier vegetables, such as carrots, tend to retain most of their texture when thawed, whereas wetter vegetables, like onions, tend to lose their snap, which is fine for a caramelized burger topping but less so for a crunchy addition to salad. But the most important factor in determining whether to go fresh or frozen is your dinner guests' expectations.

Substituting legumes that are soft and inherently mushy, like English peas, with their frozen counterpart will most likely go unnoticed, whereas crisp snow or snap peas will lose their pleasing crunch when thawed. So which frozen vegetables are best? Luckily, there are plenty to choose from, so you don't need to be a scientist or be familiar with crystalline structures to decide what to make for dinner. Carrots, corn, cauliflower, Brussels sprouts, broccoli, butternut squash, and spinach all work great. Start there. French fries are perhaps the best example of when it's okay to reach for a freezer bag. Indeed, every chef knows that fresh fries are a fallacy, and it's an industry secret that the frozen variety is always a better option.

When Daniel was still living in Williamsburg, Brooklyn, he and Matt once found themselves hungry and in Daniel's local Key Food supermarket. They'd been talking about frozen vegetables that day and hesitantly decided to test their luck in the freezer section with a vegetable-centric recipe they were developing for a column: spring vegetable risotto. The recipe relies on both the fresh flavor and the varied texture of the vegetables to cut through the rich and creamy rice, which is cooked slowly with chicken stock and finished with a fistful of grana padano cheese (page 28) for maximum umami.

Daniel and Matt grabbed a trio of frozen vegetables (Birds Eye brand asparagus, petite peas, and spinach) and were shocked with the quality of the resulting dish. The asparagus stalks, in particular, were impossibly crunchy and a really inviting shade of green. Even better, there was no need to blanch the vegetables, as the freezing process softened them to perfection, simplifying the recipe and cutting down on prep time.

As a jaded chef whose restaurants work with primarily local and seasonal vegetables, and a food writer who is constantly reading and writing about the virtues of quality ingredients, Daniel and Matt wholeheartedly expected to be underwhelmed by the outcome of using frozen vegetables. On the contrary, however, the risotto was really great: flavorful and embodying a texture that rivaled the farm-stand vegetable cooking you last saw hyped in Ruth Reichl's hyperlocal, seasonal, picked-that-afternoon Twitter stream. For the record (this book is bound for the Library of Congress), Ruth is and always will be a national treasure. ●

FOOD IQ

FROZEN SPRING VEGETABLE RISOTTO

Serves 4 as a main course or 6 as a side dish

4½ cups chicken stock (or substitute bouillon)

2 tablespoons olive oil

½ yellow onion, finely chopped

Kosher salt

2 cups Arborio rice

½ cup dry white wine

1 cup frozen snap peas, cut into ½-inch pieces

1 cup frozen English peas

1 cup roughly chopped frozen spinach

1 cup cut-up frozen asparagus, in 1-inch pieces

2 tablespoons unsalted butter

¼ cup chopped fresh flat-leaf parsley

2 tablespoons chopped fresh mint leaves

2½ cups freshly grated pecorino romano cheese

Freshly ground black pepper

This simple and seriously flavorful recipe was born as an experiment to put frozen vegetables to the test, and they passed with flying colors. Because the freezing and thawing process breaks down the cell structure of the vegetables, softening them in the process, there's no need to precook the ingredients (as would be the traditional method) before adding them to the rice. If you haven't cooked with frozen vegetables before, you'll be shocked by their quality. Even the asparagus (which is notoriously easy to overcook) maintains its vibrant green color and snappy texture.

1. In a saucepan, bring the stock to a simmer over medium heat, then adjust the heat to keep the stock at a bare simmer.

2. Heat the oil in a large, heavy-bottomed pot over medium heat. Add the onion and 2 teaspoons salt and cook, stirring frequently, until soft and translucent, about 4 minutes.

3. Add the rice and cook, stirring constantly, until coated with oil and lightly toasted, about 4 minutes. Pour in the wine and stir vigorously until the liquid is completely evaporated, about 3 minutes.

4. Add 1 cup of the simmering stock to the rice and continue to cook, stirring vigorously, until the stock is almost completely absorbed, about 4 minutes. Add another cup of stock and continue to cook, stirring gently, until it is almost completely absorbed. Add the snap peas, English peas, spinach, asparagus, and the remaining 2½ cups stock and cook, stirring gently, until the stock is absorbed and the rice is fully cooked but still al dente, about 15 minutes.

5. Remove from the heat and gently stir in the butter, parsley, mint, and 2 cups of the cheese. Transfer to a serving platter and garnish with pepper and the remaining ½ cup cheese.

Why is the farmers' market so damn expensive?

→ **THE STICKER SHOCK AT** your local farmers' market can be, well, shocking. A pint of locally grown Boyne raspberries is twelve dollars. "Heritage-breed" eggs are going for a dollar apiece. A massive Brandywine tomato can cost you the price of lunch. To help put this question into perspective, Daniel and Matt must first try to answer another question completely: Why is the food in the supermarket so cheap? The answer to that question is not straightforward. It involves decades of political lobbying influencing government sanctions and subsidies, the consolidation of thousands of small family farms across the country into multinational conglomerates, and many billions in advertising dollars training generations of Americans to believe that cheap is a good thing. This means that smaller farms—the ones setting up each weekend morning at your farmers' market—must operate without checks from Washington, let alone the efficiencies realized from modern robotic technologies and a genetically modified, ultrahigh-yield seed crop (see page 188).

Second, when shoppers buy apples or baby carrots or celery (or chickens or eggs or pork chops) in the grocery store, they are very likely coming from a massive factory farm. These farms, whether they're located in California (fruits and vegetables), Iowa (hogs), Nebraska (beef), or Mississippi (chickens), operate like literally any factory, realizing massive economies of scale, with each part of the process carefully designed to minimize inefficiency and maximize profit. And if you want a thoughtfully grown heirloom carrot, you'd be hard-pressed to find one growing in a factory field.

In viewing farming by size, scale, and government subsidies, that three-acre farm in Chester, New York, doesn't have a chance of competing with the big boys from Modesto. To survive, they must charge more—double or triple the commodity price—just to keep the tractors running. On a small farm, the harvest is often managed by hand, which costs more than machines, but that's the cost of growing vegetables that haven't been bred to work within the factory system. The farmer at your farmers' market has a name, not a serial number.

And there's something else to keep in mind. The farmer who shows up at your farmers' market—often having risen at one or two in the morning to load the truck and drive four hours to arrive at the stretch of pavement or empty parking lot that you ritualistically show up to each week—simply cares more about the food they are selling than the robots do. She cares more about the quality of the baby sweet corn placed on the folding table, and the well-being of the cows whose milk made that block of tomme-style cheese possible. It's this dedication to showing up each morning and choosing to do the right thing ethically (and putting up with snarky, sticker-shocked customers) that should be supported with your pocketbook. Small farmers play an important role in the world's food security. The fewer varieties of vegetables being grown, the more susceptible the remaining crops become to widespread blight and disease. Small farmers support biodiversity, which is at the very core of our food-safety system. So after knowing all of this about the farmers, how much should you pay? Daniel and Matt will say it together: More! Much more. ●

SEASONAL FRUIT GALETTE WITH YOGURT ALMOND CRUST

**Makes 2 galettes;
each serves 4 to 6**

**For the Yogurt
Almond Dough**

Makes two 10-inch
piecrusts

1 cup / 130 grams
whole raw almonds

1¾ cups / 220 grams
all-purpose flour

Pinch of kosher salt

10 tablespoons / 140
grams cold butter, cut
into small pieces

1 teaspoon pure
vanilla extract

½ cup / 100 grams
white sugar

1 egg

¼ cup whole-milk
plain yogurt (or
substitute sour
cream)

Having a go-to piecrust recipe and universal fruit filling technique
is an absolute necessity for all home cooks. This crust works in a
traditional pie pan, but Daniel and Matt love the rustic beauty of a
free-form galette, and knowing how to make one will come in handy
if you don't have a pie pan at your disposal (hello, impromptu Airbnb
baking). Grinding your own almond flour adds not only a distinctly
nutty flavor but also a great crunchy texture from the roughly ground
bits. Adding an egg and yogurt makes this piecrust bomb-proof.
The recipe works with all kinds of seasonal fruit, including cherry,
strawberry, peach, quince, apple, apricot, and pear.

1. In a food processor, pulse the almonds until finely chopped but not
completely pulverized. Add the flour and salt and pulse to incorporate.
Transfer the almond flour to a bowl and reserve.

2. Add the butter, vanilla, and white sugar to the food processor
and pulse until just mixed and incorporated. Add the almond
flour, egg, and yogurt and pulse just until the mixture comes
together to form a crumbly dough.

3. Lightly dust a work surface with flour and turn the
dough out onto it. Knead the dough just long enough
to bring it together into a ball. Wrap in plastic
wrap and refrigerate for 30 minutes. The
dough will keep in the refrigerator for up
to 3 days or in the freezer for up to 1
month. If refrigerated for longer than
30 minutes, let the dough sit at room
temperature for a few minutes before
rolling it out, and if frozen, thaw
overnight in the refrigerator
before using.

For the Fruit Filling

Makes 4 cups; enough for two 10-inch galettes

5 pounds fruit of choice

⅔ cup white sugar

2 tablespoons cornstarch

4 tablespoons butter, melted

2 tablespoons fresh lemon juice

Pinch of kosher salt

1. Preheat the oven to 375°F. Line two sheet pans with parchment paper.

2. Trim and pit or core the fruit as needed, then cut stone fruits and pome fruits into thick wedges. Cut smaller fruit such as strawberries and cherries in half. Transfer to a large bowl, add the white sugar, cornstarch, butter, lemon juice, and salt, and toss to coat evenly.

3. Spread the seasoned fruit in a single layer on the prepared pans. Bake until soft and beginning to brown, about 30 minutes. Let cool to room temperature before building a galette.

To Make a Galette

All-purpose flour for dusting

½ recipe Yogurt Almond Dough (recipe above)

2 cups Fruit Filling (recipe above)

1 egg white, lightly beaten

4 teaspoons turbinado sugar (for crunch and flavor)

1. Preheat the oven to 350°F.

2. Lay a sheet of parchment paper on a work surface and dust the parchment with flour. Top the parchment with the dough, then roll out into a round 12 inches in diameter and ⅛ inch thick. Transfer the dough round on the parchment to a sheet pan.

3. Starting in the center of the dough round, arrange the fruit in an even layer and stopping when a 2-inch lip of dough remains uncovered. Working your way around the edge of the dough round, fold the uncovered dough up and over the filling, pleating as needed as you go, to create an envelope at the edge of the entire galette. Pour any liquid remaining in the bowl into the center of the galette.

4. Brush the egg white around the upturned crust and sprinkle with the turbinado sugar.

5. Bake the galette until the crust is golden brown and crisp, about 35 minutes. Let cool to room temperature before slicing to serve.

Is it okay to use bouillon cubes?

→ **BEFORE HE AND DANIEL** talked this question through, Matt observed that there is a general assumption—one shared by many of his peers in food media—that the aseptic boxes of chicken and vegetable stock sold in the grocery store are basically useless. No better than water. (Some food writers even live in the fantasy world where making homemade stock is a regular weekend activity, like laundry and Sunday HBO. Matt knows no such world.) The other assumption was that bouillon cubes are to be avoided—a misguided shortcut for adding possibly detrimental flavor to soups and stocks.

Daniel was aghast at these snobbish suggestions. He first ordered Matt to read the book *Factfulness: Ten Reasons We're Wrong About the World—and Why Things Are Better Than You Think*, a critical 2018 work by Hans Rosling that, when boiled down, draws the conclusion that people need to stop assuming that what they learned as kids in school is still true and realize that the world is changing fast, in critically important ways. And, in fact, bouillon cubes have been changing along with us—for the better.

So, yes, if you time machined back to 1957, the bouillon cubes you bought likely weren't that great. The flavor from these tiny cubes was unnatural and chemical. Today, though, there are some pretty great products out there, including from some of the bigger brands like Knorr, which makes an excellent all-natural chicken bouillon. Better than Bouillon is a concentrated paste that offers a similar flavor. These products are so good that Daniel has used them in more than one restaurant that he has worked at or consulted for. He won't name names, but he says it would shock you to know how many high-quality restaurants lean into these products. This all goes without saying that, for years, Daniel turned his nose up at them, too. But as Rosling wrote in his book, don't assume that popular knowledge is correct or current. Always question the fore-drawn conclusions and draw your own based on the evidence you collect.

So, why make stock? To Matt, it seems impractical to dump a bunch of bones and vegetable trimmings in a pot and simmer them for hours with water—eventually to use it for what exactly? He needed a reminder from Daniel why this practice is such a foundational element in cooking. Daniel often roasts chickens, and when he spatchcocks them, he pulls out the backbones, tosses them in a pot with water, and makes a collagen-rich stock. It's really that simple. Okay, but why make stock in the first place? Well, that depends on how you're planning to use it. If the recipe will highlight the stock itself, as in a soup, risotto, or brothy sauce, go for it. But when the stock is more of a building block for flavor, as in a braise or stew, then bouillon is more than fine. Daniel says using the canned or boxed stuff is fine, too, but it's important to choose a low-sodium option. Otherwise, the recipe can turn out oversalted when you reduce the stock. ●

ARROZ CON POLLO
CHICKEN AND RICE

Serves 6

1½ pounds chicken drumsticks and thighs

Kosher salt

1 tablespoon apple cider vinegar

2 cups basmati rice

1 green cubanelle or green bell pepper, stemmed and seeded

2 cloves garlic

1 large yellow onion, peeled and finely diced

½ bunch cilantro

1 tablespoon vegetable oil

1 red bell pepper, stemmed, seeded, and finely diced

2 (5-gram) packets Goya brand sazón con culantro y achiote

1 teaspoon garlic powder

½ teaspoon sweet paprika

½ teaspoon dried oregano

1 teaspoon ground turmeric

2 bay leaves

1 (6-ounce) can tomato paste

3 bouillon cubes

dissolved in 3 cups water

1 (15-ounce) can pigeon peas, drained

¼ cup drained capers

2 cups fresh or frozen corn kernels

½ cup Spanish green olives, pitted and chopped

You'll find an example of arroz con pollo in nearly every Hispanic country around the globe, and each has its nuanced individuality. The Puerto Rican version is the one Daniel grew up eating in New York City. While there are as many versions of the dish as there are Puerto Rican households, the common thread is recaíto (or sofrito), a blend of peppers, onions, and herbs that the dish is built upon. This recipe calls for chicken bouillon as well as an achiote and culantro seasoning paste that both colors the rice and flavors the dish.

1. In a large bowl, toss the chicken with 1 tablespoon salt and the vinegar. Let marinate at room temperature while you prepare the sofrito.

2. In a second large bowl, combine the rice, a pinch of salt, and water to cover generously and let soak until needed.

3. To make the sofrito, in a food processor, combine the cubanelle pepper, garlic, half of the onion, and all but a few cilantro leaves (reserve the leaves for garnish) and process until smooth. Reserve until needed.

4. Heat the oil in a large Dutch oven over medium-high heat. Add the chicken and cook, turning as needed, until browned on all sides, about 8 minutes. Transfer the chicken to a plate.

5. Add the remaining onion and the red pepper to the pot and cook over medium-high heat, stirring frequently, until soft and translucent, about 8 minutes. Add the sazón, 2 teaspoons salt, the garlic powder, paprika, oregano, turmeric, bay leaves, tomato paste, and sofrito and continue cooking, stirring constantly, for 5 minutes.

6. Drain the rice and add it to the pot. Then add the reconstituted bouillon, pigeon peas, capers, corn, and olives and bring to a boil. Drop in the chicken, lower the heat to a simmer, and cook, stirring once or twice, for 12 minutes. Then cover the pot, turn down the heat to the lowest setting, and continue cooking until the rice is cooked through and the chicken is tender and beginning to fall from the bone, about 40 minutes.

7. Garnish with the reserved cilantro leaves just before serving.

Should I feel guilty for loving fat so much?

→ **DANIEL AND MATT GREW** up in the 1980s and early 1990s, and they were hammered with a "fat is evil" public information campaign that promoted a sugary "low-fat" diet (remember SnackWell's?), which accelerated a historic downturn in overall health that culminated in the first declining life expectancy recorded in modern history. Yet to this day, a general belief remains that if you cut fat out of your diet, you won't get fat.

Thankfully, this mentality is fading, and the world is getting out from under the anti-fat blanket. People—smart food people like yourself—are learning that there are different kinds of fat, some good and some bad (although they are mostly all delicious): saturated and unsaturated fats. The basic modern-day thinking is that if the fat is hard at room temperature, it tends to be worse for your health. So that means more olive oil and less bacon, Crisco, and lard.

Setting aside the impact on our health for a moment, we need fat in our cooking. It's a fundamental element to building a balanced and delicious recipe. Daniel recalls a cauliflower soup he made while working at Le Bernardin from onions, cauliflower, and chicken stock (or so he thought). It was a puree for the amuse-bouche course, and when the three ingredients were blended together, he just couldn't taste the cauliflower—it was nonexistent, even after adding more of the vegetable to the mix. He asked his boss, Chris Mueller, for help. After a quick taste, Chris dumped a quart of whipping cream into the puree, and viola, it immediately tasted like the cruciferous vegetable.

The same principle held true for Daniel years later when he was adapting a tomato sauce recipe at the Meatball Shop and couldn't figure out why it tasted so flat. It turned out that the kitchen hadn't properly scaled up the amount of olive oil used to sweat the onion. No fat, no flavor. Nobody should feel guilty for wanting their dishes to bubble and braise with excitement. It's just important to be aware of what you are eating.

While writing this book, Daniel was maintaining an 1,800-calorie diet, and he bragged to Matt over Zoom—many times—that he was eating extraordinarily well. Was he buttering bread? No, there wasn't much bread to speak of. Was he cooking a rich duck confit for dinner? Yes! Daniel was just staying aware of what was going into his body and saving up for those moments when he wanted to go big.

Matt pressed Daniel to pick his favorite fat, and it wasn't that tough of a call. He uses olive oil as his go-to fat all day, every day. Yes, olive oil tastes like olives, and it clashes with many ingredients that are native to lands without olive cultivation. "If it grows together, it goes together" is the line Daniel uses often. Lime juice and olive oil? Not so great. How many olive trees grow in Mexico? Not many (though they do pop up on the Baja Peninsula). When asked for a memory of fat that sticks with him, Daniel heads to Italy and its lardo di Colonnata—fatback that is salt cured in large marble tubs and served as a salumi with grilled bread or over grilled vegetables like asparagus. When you taste it, and the months of work that go into producing it are translated onto your tongue, you learn the true meaning of the chef's favorite phrase: "Fat equals flavor." ●

CHILE FLAKES, WATER, AND OIL

Here's a little experiment to illustrate how fat delivers flavor. You'll need two pinches of red chile flakes. Drop the first pinch into a small saucepan with ¼ cup water and bring the water to a boil. While the water heats, in a separate small saucepan, combine ¼ cup olive oil with the second pinch of chile flakes and heat gently until the oil is simmering hot. Let both mixtures cool down and then taste them. Capsaicin (the chemical compound that causes the piquant element of spice) is fat soluble. You'll notice right away that the chile oil is much "spicier" than the chile water. That's because the spice has dissolved into the fat, which allows it to disperse onto your tongue. There are many, many other fat-soluble compounds like capsaicin that carry a variety of flavors in our food, but in the absence of fat, those flavors are lost to our sense of taste.

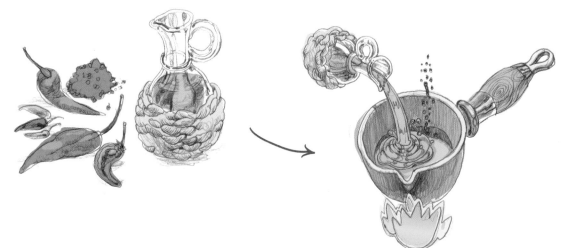

THE BEST EGG SALAD SANDWICH

Makes 2 sandwiches

---

4 farm-fresh eggs

4 tablespoons good-quality mayonnaise (such as Best Foods, Hellmann's, or Kewpie)

1 tablespoon thinly sliced fresh chives or green onion

Juice of ½ lemon

½ teaspoon kosher salt

¼ teaspoon freshly ground black pepper

4 slices soft white bread

Ten minutes and four dollars worth of ingredients will bring you one of the world's greatest sandwiches: egg salad. Originally popularized in Britain in the early 1800s, egg salad has been a diner and Jewish deli fixture in the United States for more than a hundred years, though it had recently fallen out of fashion. Thankfully, Japan (specifically Japanese convenience stories, or konbini, like Lawson and FamilyMart) have resurrected the decadent antiquity, mixing perfectly boiled eggs with MSG-rich Kewpie mayonnaise and serving the salad between slices of ethereal, untoasted milk bread. Daniel prefers toasting his bread to add texture, but only if the sandwich will be eaten right away. Success depends on the quality of the eggs you use, so spring for the expensive farmers' market kind.

1. Place your eggs in a small pot and add water to cover by at least 1 inch. Bring the water to a boil over medium-high heat, remove from the heat, cover, and let rest for 10 minutes. (Once cooled, the eggs will keep in their shell in the refrigerator for up to 2 weeks.)

2. Peel the eggs, then chop into ¼-inch pieces. Transfer to a bowl, add the mayonnaise, chives, lemon juice, salt, and pepper, and mix thoroughly.

3. Toast the bread, then divide the egg mixture evenly between two toasted slices and close the sandwiches with the remaining two slices. Cut in half and enjoy.

Should I feel embarrassed to cook with canned beans?

→ **THIS QUESTION WAS NOT** from a friend, a reader of a *TASTE* or *Saveur* column, a random person on the street, or Twitter (but shout-out to all those folks, who legitimately helped shape this book). No, this question came directly from Matt—though not really as a question. It was more of a reflexive defense mechanism after Daniel saw him cooking with canned chickpeas one night on Instagram and lit up his DMs like the eighth night of Hanukkah. Daniel could not fathom a reality in which Matt, a Food Writer® with some years of experience and skill, and a few cookbooks under his belt, was accompanying his roasted za'atar chicken with two fistfuls of aluminum-encased chickpeas. Things got a little ugly. But then, after a bit of a cooling down period for Daniel, and some heartfelt and slightly earnest legume logic from Matt, the answer to this question became a little more interesting.

Beans have been trendy for the past couple of years, with dried bean buyers' clubs—essentially monthly drops of pounds of heirloom ayocote, flageolet, and cranberry beans landing on doorsteps—becoming really popular. Steve Sando, the outspoken founder of specialty food distributor Rancho Gordo, is certainly to thank for prophesying the pinto, that underappreciated—perhaps due to a touch of xenophobia toward our fine neighbors to the south?—though extremely creamy and versatile bean. More and more home cooks have gravitated toward cooking beans for their value proposition, health properties, and deliciousness. Soaking and cooking beans can be a weekend project (see the final chapter for more of those) or even a form of self-care.

There are some culinary benefits to choosing dried beans over their precooked, canned counterparts.

First, there's variety. Farmers' markets, specialty food stores, and the Internet are overflowing with an abundance of specialty options that you can't find in tinned form. Just like tomatoes, beans have a season, and dried beans taste best the same year they were grown. Second is cost. On average, dried beans are a quarter to half the cost of canned ones. A one-pound bag of dried beans (priced between one dollar for the cheapest and five dollars for those at the highest end) yields the equivalent of four fifteen-ounce cans. And last—and most important—there's flavor, texture, and mouthfeel. Ever wonder why beans served at restaurants just taste "better" than what you make at home? This comes down to the simple fact that how you cook your beans, and what you cook them in, matters. With canned beans, you can't choose the cooking liquid, the spices, or how much salt to use— all of those choices have been made for you.

But, of course, canned beans are still what many of us cook with (Matt—and, admittedly, sometimes Daniel—included) because there are great canned beans on the market, and it's just way more convenient. Many of us don't have the time, or weren't blessed with the planning gene, that allows for the low-and-slow method. Daniel argues that the process is unfairly pegged as complicated. The soaking step is as simple as covering the beans with water overnight. And for cooking, he says just to stick them on the stove and simmer them for forty-five minutes, and they'll be pretty much perfect. But he's a chef, and to him, nothing is complicated to cook. Matt pushed back a bit on this notion—the ease of the planning and the cooking. But he agrees with Daniel that the whole process can be enjoyable and meditative.

In the end, Daniel came to terms with the reality of it all. "You shouldn't be embarrassed, but you certainly shouldn't advocate it," he instructed, while Matt looked at the cubby filled with emergency cans sitting next to his desk. (All New Yorkers have some level of prepper in them.) Matt did end up making this recipe, which was truly incredible, and he did share it—without embarrassment. ●

BRAISED AND FRIED WHITE BEANS WITH GARLIC AND OREGANO

Serves 4 to 6

2 cups dried cannellini, Great Northern, or other medium-size white beans

3 quarts water

1 head garlic, top cut off to expose the cloves

1 bay leaf

1 small carrot

½ yellow onion

Kosher salt

½ cup extra-virgin olive oil

1 tablespoon fresh oregano leaves, or 1 teaspoon dried oregano

Pinch of red chile flakes

Beans are often sidelined as a filler ingredient, but quality beans can be so much more. Daniel first encountered this extraordinary recipe for slowly poached white beans with aromatic vegetables while traveling on a restaurant research trip in southern Italy. The tender poached beans were then gently refried in olive oil with marjoram and topped with bread crumbs. Over the years, he's made many versions—one of his favorites includes braising the beans with whole heads of garlic, then frying them with the tender cloves to give the dish an extra-rich and creamy texture.

1. In a large bowl or other large container, combine the beans and water, cover, and let soak for at least 4 hours or ideally overnight.

2. Transfer the beans to a pot along with enough of the soaking water to cover by 4 inches. Add the garlic, bay leaf, carrot, and onion and bring to a boil over medium-high heat. Turn down the heat to low and simmer uncovered, skimming any foam from the surface from time to time, until the beans are soft and tender, about 40 minutes.

3. When the beans are cooked, add 2 tablespoons salt, remove from the heat, and let cool. The beans can be stored in their liquid in an airtight container in the refrigerator for up to 1 week.

4. To serve, drain the beans, discarding the onion, bay leaf, and carrot. Using your hand, squeeze the soft, paste-like garlic cloves from their skins and reserve, being careful to discard all of the skins.

5. Heat the oil in a medium pot over medium-high heat with the oregano and chile flakes. When the oregano starts to sizzle, add the beans and garlic and cook, stirring gently, for 10 minutes. Remove from the heat and season to taste with salt before serving.

Does it really take an hour to caramelize onions?

→ **THE TERM** *CARAMELIZED ONIONS* is a little misleading, as the process of slowly cooking raw onions until they reach a browned state of nectary ambrosia has little to do with the scientifically defined technique called "caramelization." The confusion comes down to the fact that cooking onions on low heat until they are soft and browned relies not on the caramelization of sugars but instead on the Maillard reaction (the browning of proteins and sugars, with heat, over time). Sautéing onions, on the other hand, uses high heat in a dry pan, quickly browning them while retaining some of their snappy, raw texture. Sautéing is actually an act of true caramelization (requiring a temperature in excess of 320°F for most sugars), but that's not the focus in these pages.

So why the mistaken nomenclature? The term *caramelized onions* was coined well before Dr. Maillard discovered his eponymous reaction more than a hundred years ago. Calling them Maillard onions just didn't have the same ring to it, so the name "caramelized" stuck (in all fairness, they do taste sweet like caramel). The bottom line is that these onions are hardly recognizable from the sharp, spicy, sulfuric state of their raw form (see page 2). They are sweet and sticky, with a deep, nutty complexity and balanced acidity. And, like caramel, they take time to cook down—with patience and attention required. Caramelized onions are both the foundation and the garnish of some of the culinary world's greatest dishes, from French onion soup to Arabic mujaddara to the animal-style Double Double at In-N-Out Burger.

The reason caramelizing onions takes so long comes down to water. Onions consist of a lot of it—close to 90 percent—and as they are cooked, the water boils and evaporates, in turn cooling them and slowing down the process. The trick is maintaining the right temperature: too hot and the sugars will burn; too low and the magical Maillard reaction will never take place. At the right speed, the alchemy occurs, and the onions are transformed into the jammy and golden alliums we love. How long it takes depends on how dark you want the onions to be.

"Soft, dark brown onions in five minutes. That is a lie," writes Tom Scocca in one of the cooking Internet's greatest polemics, a 2012 *Slate* article debunking the widely misstated cooking time. Indeed, five minutes for true caramelization is impossible. Thirty minutes is more like it. Can you go for a full sixty minutes? Sure! But it's probably not required. Daniel is sometimes asked if there is an ideal onion for caramelization: Spanish yellow onion is the most common, but all onions will caramelize equally given enough time. ●

SOUR CREAM AND ONION DIP

Makes 2 cups

---

1 cup vegetable oil

2 large Spanish yellow onions, finely diced

1 teaspoon sugar

Kosher salt

1 head garlic, cloves separated, peeled, and thinly sliced

1 (16-ounce) tub high-quality sour cream

1 teaspoon garlic powder

1 teaspoon onion powder

½ teaspoon MSG

It's no joke: sour cream and onion dip is Daniel's favorite thing to take to a potluck. When a professional chef rolls into a party, people sometimes expect a lot, so he's found that it's wise to arrive with something that starts the event on a strong note, though in a simple and unpretentious way. A really righteous onion dip has been the answer, time after time. The big secret here is—you guessed it—taking your time to caramelize the onions. By the end, they should be deeply golden brown and beginning to crisp. A few burnt pieces will look beautiful mixed with the pure white sour cream, and the crunchy bits will give the dish some texture, so take your time and don't be afraid to cook the onions down thoroughly. And, of course, serve this with your favorite chips. In Daniel's case, classic Ruffles are a no-brainer.

1. Heat the oil in a heavy-bottomed frying pan over medium heat. Add the onions, sugar, and 2 teaspoons salt and cook, stirring frequently, until the onions are soft and beginning to brown, about 30 minutes.

2. Add the sliced garlic and continue cooking until the garlic begins to brown, about 10 minutes. Meanwhile, set a fine-mesh strainer over a heatproof bowl. When the onions and garlic are ready, drain them into the strainer, then transfer them to a bowl and let cool in the fridge. Let the onion- and garlic-flavored oil cool, then store in an airtight container and reserve for another use.

3. In a large bowl, mix together the caramelized onions and garlic, sour cream, garlic powder, onion powder, and MSG. Season to taste with salt. The mixture should be just a little too salty, as the apparent saltiness will subside as it rests—just in time for you to roll into the party with a bag of your favorite potato chips.

Preparing raw fish and beef at home? Me? Is it really safe?

→ **DANIEL LOVES THIS QUESTION,** because most American home cooks have had the fear of god (and the ICU) placed into them that consuming even the smallest amount of raw chicken, beef, lamb, or fish will cause a sudden and cartoonishly graphic death. All this while dishes like steak tartare, beef carpaccio, and scallop ceviche remain extremely popular in restaurants. So what's up with this disconnect? Are restaurants really that much safer than a kitchen run by a diligent home cook? Certainly not, as you will find out shortly. Serving a plate of raw oysters or fluke crudo as a dinner-party first course is a really nice way to kick off a festive meal. Raw fish is light, healthy, and shows your guests that they are in for something really special. And a rib-sticking steak tartare course, followed by some vegetables and cake, can be the perfect spring three-course meal to make your collected guests think, who is *this*? When handling these raw ingredients, there are just a few things you should keep in mind to ensure everyone's safety—or at least plausible deniability.

A good fish counter—from the local shop you visit weekly to Whole Foods or even grocery chains like Kroger and Safeway—will respond to your probing questions. Ask them for a selection of fish that they consider "sushi grade" (a universal code if you are thinking about serving something raw). Tell them you want to make a ceviche or crudo with a firm white fish like fluke, and ask if they have anything that will work for this. If the person behind the counter's voice pitches to Larry David levels ("yeahhhhh, it's pretty, pretty, pretty fresh"), you know you should think twice. Japanese and Korean grocery stores often have an entire section of fish that is cut specifically to eat raw—another reason to visit your local H Mart often.

For meat, the butcher is the same. Ask if there's a lean and tender cut like tenderloin that would work well (and is safe) for a carpaccio. Many home cooks forget that you can order meat in advance. Give your butcher a call and say that you need something for tartare next Thursday. It's ideal if they are able to cut it fresh for you. But if not, remember, meat spoils from the outside in (see page 116), so in a pinch, trimming the outside layer of a precut packaged filet will work.

When serving raw beef, it's important to keep in mind that the leaner, more tender cuts are best, and cutting across the grain into thin slices or small pieces will yield more tender results. An eye of round is better than a rib eye, which has a lot of fat and sinew. For steak tartare, it's really easy to chop up a cut and fold in a raw egg, shallots, capers, mustard, and cornichons. For beef carpaccio, you're quickly rolling the well-seasoned meat into a screaming-hot pan to sear it—about ten seconds all around—then placing it in the freezer for ten to fifteen minutes to firm up, and finally slicing it superthin with a very sharp knife. Serve with shavings of well-aged Parmigiano Reggiano, a tangle of baby arugula, a healthy dose of finishing olive oil, a splash of fresh lemon juice, and a sprinkle of crunchy salt like Maldon and freshly ground black pepper. ●

WHAT'S THE DIFFERENCE BETWEEN CRUDO AND CEVICHE?

Crudo means "raw" in both Italian and Spanish, and a dish called a crudo (be it fish or meat) is served simply dressed with olive oil or with a dressing like a vinaigrette. New York City chef David Pasternack is credited with coining the term and launching a crudo boom in the early 2000s at his restaurant, Esca. Ceviche is fish "cooked" in acid, and it has a long history tracing back to Spanish influence in colonial Peru. Cooking something without heat may seem strange, but acid coagulates proteins, which is effectively the same thing heat does (albeit way slower), so when raw seafood is marinated in large amounts of fresh citrus juice (lemon, lime, orange), the acid in the juice effectively cooks the fish. This is not always a quick cure, and ceviches can take time—from an hour to overnight, depending on the size of the cut, the density of the protein, and the concentration of acid—to work their magic.

THREE CRUDOS FOR THREE MOODS

Serving raw fish is something of a balancing act. You need a sauce that is flavorful enough to be discernible and interesting, yet subtle enough to allow the delicate flavor of the fish to remain at center stage. Sticking to three or four ingredients is generally advised, so as not to overcomplicate and overpower. All three of the following recipes utilize a balance of salt and acid, with a spicy or earthy component delivering the flavor. Each recipe yields enough sauce for about 1 pound fish, or 1 teaspoon room-temperature sauce for each ounce of fish. Serve the fish cold from the fridge and dress it with the sauce at the last minute. Otherwise, the acid will cook the fish, discoloring it.

Smoky, Spicy Southern Italian Crudo

3 tablespoons extra-virgin olive oil

1 tablespoon crushed Calabrian chiles in oil (preferably Tutto Calabria brand)

Juice of 1 lemon

Pinch of smoked Maldon salt

1. In a small sauté pan, combine the oil and crushed chiles and heat over medium-low heat, stirring constantly, until the chiles turn a deep brick-brown color and cease to spatter, about 5 minutes. Let cool to room temperature.

2. Transfer the chile mixture to a small bowl and stir in the lemon juice.

3. Spoon over the sliced fish and top with the salt.

Japanese Yuzu Ponzu Crudo

¼ cup light soy sauce

¼ cup fresh lime juice

1 tablespoon salted yuzu juice (available at Asian markets)

1 (8-gram) packet instant dashi (available at Asian markets)

1 green onion, white and green parts, thinly sliced

1. In a small bowl, stir together the soy sauce, lime juice, and yuzu juice. Drop in the dashi packet and let steep at room temperature for at least 1 hour or ideally overnight.

2. Discard the dashi packet. Spoon the sauce over the sliced fish and garnish with the green onion. This robust sauce will keep in an airtight container in the refrigerator for up to 1 month and also works as a sauce for cooked fish, chicken, vegetables, or rice.

Mexican Chipotle Lime and Sesame Crudo

2 tablespoons toasted sesame seeds

4 teaspoons fresh lime juice

1 teaspoon kosher salt

½ teaspoon adobo sauce from canned chipotle chiles in adobo sauce

1. In a small bowl, stir together all of the ingredients.

2. Spoon over the sliced fish.

Why do some people love chicken breasts so much?

→ **IF YOU ARE A** chef, you very likely have a chip on your shoulder about chicken breasts—specifically the boneless, skinless kind—and toward the many people who prize (prize!) what is obviously an inferior cut on the bird. A true technical foul with the fowl. The chicken drumstick and thigh, on the other hand, have more flavor and more fat, retain their moisture, stand up to long cooking techniques like braises and stews, are more versatile, and are, simply put, more interesting to cook with. Think of chicken thighs marinated in miso and soy sauce or soaked in buttermilk overnight and shallow fried. Tagine, Basquaise, lacquered with gochujang—the list goes on and on. No matter what direction you choose, a properly cooked chicken thigh (or even one that has been overcooked by several minutes) is tender, lip-smacking, finger-licking unctuousness. (Matt allotted the criminally overused food-writerly word *unctuousness* exactly one use in this book, and here we are. Chicken thighs are the definition of unctuous meat.)

With all that said, there's a faction of (possibly, slightly) older folks who love themselves a juicy breast. Some people equate white meat with quality, and in general, the breast is more expensive because breasts are more sought after, with around 60 percent of chicken sales falling into the white-meat category. That allegiance has been shifting, however, and thigh sales have been quickly catching up in recent years. To be fair to our venerable wiser generations, some people simply enjoy a leaner cut of meat—meat that has no sinew, gristle, or fat (ask any bodybuilder or NBA power forward, and they'll tell you what it's all about). The breast is just a big, juicy cut of meat, and there is a certain appeal there.

The real issue with chicken breasts is this: they are often overcooked, which dries them out. Breasts, particularly skinless ones, are very low in fat, and fat is the texture the human palate equates with moisture (see page 154). That means chicken breasts, with very little intramuscular fat (called marbling), have an extremely narrow margin of error, drying out the moment they overcook. And don't get Daniel started about cooking chicken to 165°F (the temperature suggested by the US Food and Drug Administration as safe). That figure is garbage, in his opinion—hammered, as they say in the industry. Think more like 135° to 140°F max for a barely opaque, and truly delicious, juicy breast.

So now that you've been convinced to relinquish your preference for the paler meat in favor of the darker variety, whatever should you do with all those breasts? Japanese cooks have a very interesting suggestion: meatballs (tsukune). In the West, the breast is the most expensive cut, and with its lean and dry texture, it makes a poor candidate for a meatball. But in Japan, chicken breasts are less popular and therefore less expensive. Making up for the breasts' lack of fat and flavor, tsukune are made by chopping the lean meat and mixing it with aromatic vegetables, chicken skin, and cartilage for flavor, moisture, and texture, then forming the blend into football-shaped meatballs that are skewered and grilled over charcoal and served with a sweet and salty dipping sauce and raw egg yolk. ●

BREEDING FLAVOR OUT OF FOOD, AND THE PROBLEM WITH "THE OTHER WHITE MEAT"

Thinking about industrialized agriculture in the United States is a big bummer, and chicken, in particular, is one of its greatest monstrosities. For decades, the chickens you find in your grocery store and those served at many inexpensive restaurants have been bred not only to produce oversize breasts to feed the above-mentioned demand but also to create both a uniform shape for ease of mechanical processing and a bland flavor to suit the typical American palate. Pork has gone through the same sad evolution. Do you remember that slogan "the other white meat" that brainwashed a generation of home cooks to view pork, like chicken breast, as a blank canvas? Erase that from your memory.

Pork has a huge personality, and if you've ever had a chop or a shoulder or charcuterie from a heritage breed like Berkshire (sometimes called Kurobuta), Duroc, Red Wattle, or Mangalitsa, you know how exciting pork can be. Each breed yields pigs with a distinctive flavor profile that has been developed over centuries by passionate farmers slowly selecting for the optimum flavor and fat content. Luckily, a network of these farms is working hard to maintain these special heritage breeds, and you can do your part to support the cause as well. All you have to do is eat more good-quality, heritage-bred, non-commodity meat. Call your local butcher and ask for the good stuff. It's certainly waiting there. And if they don't have it, ask them to carry it.

CLASSIC CHICKEN CUTLET

Makes 4 cutlets

---

2 (5-ounce) boneless, skinless chicken breasts

Kosher salt

½ cup all-purpose flour

2 eggs

1½ cups fine dried bread crumbs

4 tablespoons extra-virgin olive oil

Milanese, katsu, schnitzel, Popeyes—Daniel and Matt have always debated who makes the best chicken cutlet. But the truth is that virtually every culture has its own version, and they're all delicious. These classic Italian-style cutlets are one of their favorites. They're simple to prepare and freeze well for up to two months, making them an ideal candidate for meal prep. Serve them on their own with a slice of lemon and a simple arugula salad, slathered in tomato sauce and covered in melted mozzarella, or cold on a roll with provolone cheese and grilled rapini. It's worth learning to butterfly a chicken breast, but if you're not very comfortable with a knife, you can ask your butcher to prepare and pound them for you. The breading technique works equally well with pork, veal, lamb, and even flounder.

1. Butterfly each breast, slicing horizontally through the breast and stopping short to leave the opposite side intact. Open one breast up flat, place on a lightly oiled sheet of parchment paper, top with a second sheet of oiled parchment, oiled side down, and pound with the flat side of a meat mallet until uniformly thin. Repeat with the second breast. Cut each pounded breast into two evenly sized pieces (your cutlets) and season each cutlet with a pinch of salt.

2. Prepare a breading station. Set out three shallow bowls. Pour the flour into the first. Crack the eggs into the second, add a few tablespoons water, and give them a whisk. Spread the bread crumbs out in the third. Working in stages, and with one piece at a time, dip the chicken into the flour, then the egg, and finally the bread crumbs. Make sure to coat the breast completely at each stage, pressing down firmly, and shaking off the excess before moving onto the next coating. As the cutlets are coated, set them aside, not touching, on a large plate.

3. To cook the cutlets, heat 2 tablespoons of the oil in a large sauté pan over medium-high heat. When the oil is just beginning to smoke, gently lower two cutlets into the pan and cook until golden brown on the first side, about 3 minutes. Then flip the cutlets and continue cooking until crispy golden brown and cooked through, about 2 minutes. You can hold the cooked cutlets on a sheet pan lined with paper towels in a low oven. Repeat the process with the remaining cutlets and the remaining 2 tablespoons oil.

Cooking with livers and hearts . . . isn't that gross?

→ **IN ANCIENT ROME, BUTCHER** apprentices were paid in offal. Tongue, tail, innards, and other extremities—known as the quinto quarto, or the "fifth quarter"—were what was left over after the four quarters of the cow were broken down and separated. Today, being paid in these lowly bits may not be as prized as a paid vacation or a flexible spending account, but these young Roman meatcutters made the most of their "wages," and years of developing and perfecting recipes made the Italian capital's cuisine famous for its delicious utilization of lesser-regarded cuts.

Coda alla vaccinara (oxtail cooked in tomato), trippa alla romana (tripe with tomato, mint, and pecorino), pajata (milk-filled intestines of an unweaned calf), sweetbreads, hearts, lungs, brains, and liver all have their place in the noble cuisine of Rome. And most of the world shares Rome's romantic view: that an animal is a sacred being, and to kill one without using it in its entirety is a cruel and unusual punishment—and a wasteful one at that.

Regretfully, not all Americans share this view. Innards rarely make it to the local supermarket, and when they do, they are relegated to a back corner of the case, rather than highlighted for their unique qualities and complex deliciousness. And let's face it, cooking a steak is a whole lot easier than cooking an oxtail, especially if you've never learned how. Not to mention that, with a lack of firsthand experience, the imagination is left to run wild, and brains sound a lot scarier than they taste in real life.

If you are looking to delve into fifth-quarter cuisine, look beyond your traditional Western supermarket or butcher shop. Daniel lives in Los Angeles, home to one of the world's most diverse and vibrant food cultures west of Queens, New York, and he often shops at Mexican, Thai, Korean, Japanese, and Chinese markets where offal proliferates. He brings home beef tongues, duck hearts, and lamb kidneys. A grilled beef heart has a texture like nothing else in the world. Daniel was lucky to work under people—like the great Marlboro Red chain-smoking chef Jean-Louis Palladin, for example—who were willing to serve these underappreciated delicacies to New York society despite their reputation. There are limits for Daniel, however, and pork liver is among the offal that gives him pause. "It can be quite . . . pronounced," he muses diplomatically. But the offal world is vast—and often inexpensive—and they think there are a lot of opportunities for home cooks to expand their culinary worldview right in their local markets.

You may be wondering, where do Matt and Daniel come down on foie gras, the world's most polarizing offal? Daniel believes that the only reason foie gras has gotten such a bad rap (foie gras has been banned in restaurants and its production was once outlawed in California) is that it's a crime of convenience. As Daniel says, "If you think those ducks or geese are being treated any differently than the chickens you buy in the grocery store, you are out of your mind—they're treated a good deal better, in fact." Yet most of the critics have never had foie gras, may never encounter foie gras, and can protest against its existence because there are few proponents of it to argue against. Blue Hill Farm chef-owner Dan Barber gave a popular TED Talk in 2008, and the general takeaway was that the controversial "force-feeding" of the ducks, called gavage, is not really needed, nor is it actually forced (the ducks come of their own accord to be fed). Barber introduced the audience to a farmer in Spain, Eduardo Sousa, who had recently won France's highest award for culinary products, the Coup de Coeur. Sousa won with a foie gras that doesn't rely on gavage. Instead, Sousa's ducks and geese graze naturally on local flora and fauna during the cool autumn months. Barber confirms that it's the most delicious foie gras he's ever had, and you can buy it to this day at eduardosousafarm.com.

Foie gras is an important part of Europe's culinary heritage, and it supports farmers whose livelihood depends on its continued production. To eat meat is to take the life of an animal. Who are we to argue that a duck's life is more sacred than a chicken's, a goat's, or a cow's? Animals should be raised and slaughtered humanely, whether it's for the production of a McDonald's Quarter Pounder or a pâté de foie at The French Laundry. And neither should be singled out simply because there are fewer people to protest on their behalf. ●

FOOD IQ

BEER-BRAISED BEEF TONGUE

Makes 12 slices; serves 4

---

1 (2½-pound) whole beef tongue

1 teaspoon freshly ground black pepper

Kosher salt

3 tablespoons vegetable oil

2 large white onions, peeled and thinly sliced into rings

4 cloves garlic, thinly sliced

1 (12-ounce) can light Mexican lager (such as Tecate or Modelo)

1 oregano sprig

2 bay leaves

In spring 2020, near the start of the COVID-19 crisis, Daniel's dear friend, Meatball Shop chef, and longtime culinary co-conspirator, Daniel Sharp (Sharp from here on out, to avoid confusion), visited Daniel in Los Angeles, planning to stay for a few days. The pandemic struck, and Sharp ended up stuck and living with Daniel for months. There were many good times, a few too many bourbon drinks, and a few pounds gained in the process. This recipe was one of Sharp's early creations, inspired by his recent trip to Mexico, and his more recent visit to Northgate Market near MacArthur Park in Los Angeles. Slowly braising the tongue with onions renders out the fat, self-basting the meat as it cooks, and breaks down the sinew, coaxing out the offal's uniquely tender texture.

1. Season the beef tongue at least 12 hours (or up to 48 hours) ahead of time with the pepper and generously with salt (aim for 1.5 percent by weight, or about 1 tablespoon) and refrigerate in a covered container.

2. Preheat the oven to 300°F.

3. In a Dutch oven, heat 1 tablespoon of the oil over medium heat. Add the onions and garlic and cook, stirring frequently, until just soft, about 5 minutes. Add the tongue, beer, oregano, and bay leaves and bring to a simmer.

4. Cover, transfer to the oven, and braise, flipping once halfway through, for 4 hours. The tongue will shrink to half of its original size and be tender, offering little or no resistance when pierced with the tip of a knife.

5. Let the tongue cool in the liquid in the pot until tepid, then transfer to the refrigerator and let cool completely. Remove the cooled tongue from the pot. To peel the tongue, make a shallow lengthwise cut along the center of the tongue and then, using your hands, peel off the skin. Reserve the cooking liquid and onions.

6. To reheat and serve, cut the tongue crosswise into 10 to 12 thick slices. Heat the remaining 2 tablespoons oil in a large sauté pan over medium-high heat. Working in batches if needed, add the tongue slices and sear, turning once, until piping hot and crispy deep golden brown, about 3 minutes on each side. Reheat the braised onions and their liquid and spoon them over the hot slices.

Is the broiler good for anything other than melting cheese?

→ **DANIEL HAS HAD A** two-decade love affair with his many broilers, which includes not only the ultrahot section of the floor of his rental-apartment gas oven in Brooklyn and the more updated gas "with electric assist" located at the top of his KitchenAid oven in Venice but also all those he has used throughout his professional cooking career. Daniel thinks about a broiler differently than many home cooks do. First, he sees it as a big, upside-down grill with a roaring fire on the top that can reach upward of 1,000°F. He thinks of the steaks at Peter Luger in New York being slid under that inferno that grills and sears and roasts and bakes simultaneously. This is not to be confused with the commercial kitchen's salamander, which is used more for finishing, toasting, and melting cheese, and which operates with a lower intensity. Matt always confused the two.

The home kitchen broiler may not be as powerful as the professional-grade ones found in restaurants, but it can be used in the same way—expanding beyond crisping a frozen pizza. The broiler should be thought of as a real tool, and Daniel uses it often to cook meat, fish, and vegetables (as well as toasting and melting cheese, naturally). He'll broil a whole side of salmon slathered in porchetta seasoning (see page 59), or he'll slide a frozen New York strip steak (hard as a rock, though well seasoned) in there. Broil for under six minutes until crackling hot and deeply browned, then flip and repeat for four minutes, and you have a perfect medium-rare steak. This, of course, isn't the perfect way to cook a steak (look to the cast-iron pan for that), but if you come home famished after a Peloton or jujitsu session, it's hard to argue against fourteen minutes from frozen with zero cleanup. The broiler works so successfully because of the combination of a superhot oven to roast the meat along with direct radiant heat from the fire to sear the outside.

The broiler cooks full meals as well as it works to brown, crisp, toast, and finish. Try crisping the skin of a roast chicken after resting, or finishing a frittata, browning the top. There's no other way to get the signature melted Gruyère that crowns a bowl of French onion soup. For those without a grill, a thick cast-iron grill pan and a broiler can serve as a worthy substitute. You can grill raw vegetables, char peppers, and fire-roast eggplant. Daniel uses the broiler to toast slices of sourdough bread and melt cheese on a tuna melt. Many people don't have the counter space for a toaster oven, Matt included, so the broiler is their go-to option. What an underrated kitchen tool. •

FIFTEEN-MINUTE FROZEN BROILER STEAK

Serves 1

1 (10-ounce) frozen New York strip steak, about 1 inch thick

1 teaspoon kosher salt

1 tablespoon extra-virgin olive oil

½ lemon

Pinch of flaky finishing salt (such as Maldon or fleur de sel)

Freshly ground black pepper

Daniel almost always has steaks sitting in the freezer, but he rarely has the forethought to plan on cooking one (and setting it out to defrost) the night before. One evening, after a particularly vigorous jujitsu match (he wrestles competitively), he was famished and had a strong hankering for a steak. Without the time or patience to defrost one, he tossed the seasoned, though still frozen, block of icy beef under the broiler for ten minutes. To his surprise, the steak cooked beautifully this way, with rendered, crispy, golden fat and a deeply browned crust. As with all meat cookery, resting the steak for a few minutes when it comes off the flame is key to redistributing the juices and getting an even medium-rare cook temperature from edge to edge.

1. Preheat the broiler. Position an oven rack about 8 inches from the heat source.

2. Place the steak on an ovenproof tray. Season the top with ½ teaspoon of the kosher salt (the salt won't stick to the frozen meat, so only season the top side until ready to flip).

3. Broil the steak until sizzling golden brown on top, about 6 minutes. Flip the steak, season with the remaining ½ teaspoon kosher salt, and broil until medium-rare, about 4 minutes more.

4. Remove from the broiler and let the steak rest for 5 minutes before cutting. Drizzle with the oil, squeeze the lemon half over the top, and season with the flaky salt and pepper.

What's the difference between dried and fresh pasta? And can I make my own pasta without a pasta machine?

→ **THE SHORT ANSWER TO** the pasta machine question is yes, you can make fresh pasta with your bare, flour-dusted hands. Machines just make things a lot easier. Either way, you will be rewarded with a lifelong skill: fresh pasta whenever and wherever you want it. This question also gives Daniel an opportunity to dive into one of his favorite things not just to make at home, but to do at home—fare le spaghetti, fare le tortellini!

There are two different types of pasta machine: an extruder (squeezing the flour and water through pasta-shaped dies) and a laminator (squeezing the flour and water between rollers into a flat sheet that is then cut into shapes). Most dried pastas, including spaghetti, rigatoni, rotini, and linguine, are extruded. Their dough is made from golden semolina flour, milled from hard, high-protein durum winter wheat. Your stand mixer likely has an attachment that claims to extrude pasta, but the results won't be like what you buy in the grocery store. These pastas require an immense amount of pressure to force the dough through pasta-shaped dies, so without industrial equipment, you won't be able to rival the quality of store-bought products. A small professional machine would take up most of the free counter space in a home kitchen and cost a year's grocery budget, plus an additional few hundred bucks for each brass die, as a different one is needed for every shape you want to make.

Fresh pastas use a laminator (sometimes called a sheeter), which rolls the dough through ever-tightening pins until the desired thickness is achieved. This is the hand-crank model you more than likely associate with pasta making. Alternately, instead of a laminator, you can buy a mattarello—a long, thin rolling pin made famous on Aziz Ansari's Netflix show *Master of None*, and slightly less famous by a bearded dude in Venice, California. This is how you make pasta like they did during the time of Da Vinci. Rolling pasta with a mattarello takes a lot of practice, and even more elbow grease. If you're intent on making pasta without any specialty equipment at all, there are a number of shapes found in Italy's south, like cavatelli, orecchiette, and lorighittas, that traditionally use an eggless water-and-semolina dough and are formed completely by hand.

The first time Daniel made pasta was with his mom at age six. The family didn't have a pasta maker, so they rolled them out by hand and cooked them, and they turned into incredibly thick and chewy worms. No grazie. What he now knows is that a traditional fresh pasta dough that can fit through one of those hand-crank rollers has a much lower hydration, and the less water in a dough, the more toothsome it becomes. If you don't have the tools to roll it, the dough will be way too tough to eat, so you're better off working with a softer dough if you are going to do things by hand.

Some might ask, why even make fresh pasta when there are so many high-quality dried (and frozen fresh) pastas available at the grocery store? Why spend all that time with the bag of flour and the eggs and messing up your clean kitchen when you can reach for a box of De Cecco or Ronzoni? It's sort of an extrapolation of the question, why don't I just drink Soylent for every meal instead of spending the time chewing? You make fresh pasta because it's special. It has a unique flavor and texture. It's a labor of love and a communication of passion in the kitchen. And, as with oral history, tribal dance, and visual art, with every batch of strozzapreti rolled or cappelletti filled, a little piece of history and tradition is kept alive and passed on to the next generation.

The bottom line is that you don't know how easy it is to make fresh pasta until you make fresh pasta. Daniel first made cavatelli while working at the San Francisco Campanian restaurant A16. It takes a little practice to get the hang of it, but once you learn how to do it right, it requires less than an hour, start to finish, for a bowl of perfect—and Daniel promises that you'll have more friends and get invited over for dinner more often if you do. ●

FRESH HANDMADE ORECCHIETTE

Makes 2 pounds

---

2 cups all-purpose flour

2 cups semolina flour, plus more for dusting

1¼ cups lukewarm water

This recipe is designed to prove to you how fun and easy it is to make pasta at home with little or no equipment. Daniel and Matt hope you will make orecchiette (little ears) at least once, because there is nothing like the flavor and texture of freshly made pasta. Italy's south has historically been a poorer region of the country, so the pastas tend to be made without eggs, relying on semolina flour from protein-rich durum wheat to give the pasta its toothsome bite. This eggless dough will work for nearly any hand-shaped southern pasta, such as cavatelli or lorighittas. Orecchiette is a versatile shape, and Daniel and Matt prefer a meat ragu, but feel free to serve it with your favorite sauce.

1. In a large bowl, mix together the two flours. Add the water and stir until the mixture gets pebbly and begins to come together as a dough.

2. Lightly flour a work surface and turn the dough out onto it. Knead the dough until it becomes silky smooth and elastic, about 7 minutes of continual, vigorous kneading (this is no joke).

3. Wrap the dough in plastic wrap and let rest in the refrigerator for at least 20 minutes. The dough will keep in the refrigerator for up to 48 hours or in the freezer for up to 2 months.

4. To shape the pasta, dust one or more sheet pans with semolina flour. Transfer the dough to a clean work surface. Work in small batches, keeping the remaining dough covered so it doesn't dry out. Cut a small piece (1 to 2 ounces) of dough and, using your palms, roll it into a rope ¼ inch in diameter (if the dough slips, sprinkle a few drops of water onto the work surface). Cut the rope crosswise into ¼-inch pieces. One by one, flatten and stretch each piece with a butter knife into a penny-sized disk, then invert the disk, stretching it over your thumb to make it concave, giving it its namesake ear-like shape. As the orecchiette are formed, transfer them to the prepared pan in a single layer. Repeat until all of the dough is shaped.

5. Let the pasta dry uncovered at room temperature. If you cook the pasta right away, they will be done in 2 to 3 minutes, but the longer they dry, the longer they will take to cook. If you dry the orecchiette fully (which will take 48 hours), they will last for months in an airtight container in the pantry and will take 8 to 10 minutes to cook.

Is shrimp overrated?

→ **SHRIMP ISN'T OVERRATED. IT'S** overcooked and poorly sourced. But this doesn't have to be the case. Like any other food product, there's amazing shrimp, decent shrimp, and shrimp that should always be left behind on that giant platter at the grocery store. Yet all shrimp, when improperly cooked, is no good. You can think of the target cooking time as really fast or really slow, and it's the middle preparations where you can end up chewy, rubbery, and just wrong. Shrimp needs to be either poached for only a couple of minutes and served, or it must be braised for an extended time, which slowly breaks down the tough proteins in the crustacean—think of that seriously tender shrimp that has been long cooked in a gumbo.

Why do we love shrimp so much? Well, first, because they are delicious and easy to eat. They are on the pleasant side of innocuous—the opposite of fishy or gamy. And their texture is unanimously adored. Shrimp is versatile and works as an amazing vehicle for sauces: Butter, garlic, and white wine in a scampi, fish sauce and sugar in a Vietnamese-style braise, fried giant Gulf shrimp, or baby shrimp Louie. Everybody has a favorite. Shrimp cocktail (poached shrimp served chilled with a piquant ketchup-and-horseradish sauce) has come in and out of style several times over since its popularization in the 1950s, when modern freezing technologies first allowed the shrimp to travel farther from the sea, and crimson cocktail sauce made the jump from its long-standing relationship with oysters to crowning the little-legged crustacean king of cocktail. As for shrimp cocktail's parturition, there are a lot of claims but little evidence as to whether it originated in Mexico and traveled northward, or was invented elsewhere in the Americas and found its way south. The bottom line is that for a tref animal that looks an awful lot like a baby cockroach (sorry, it's true), shrimp is impressively popular. Matt's close family friends in Kalamazoo, Michigan, the Maiorano-Stivers, have been bringing platters of jumbo shrimp and cocktail sauce to Thanksgiving for years. It's perfect.

When sold in bulk, shrimp are assigned a unit number per pound to account for variation in size. For example, U/32 means thirty-two pieces per pound, so the smaller the number, the bigger the shrimp. Cocktail shrimp or fried jumbo shrimp are typically larger, in the eighteen to twenty-four pieces per pound range. There are thousands of species of shrimp in the world, but the ones found in supermarkets are primarily farm raised and frozen, and many are very good. When buying shrimp, take note of whether they are whole or have been previously peeled and deveined. Should you care about where your shrimp come from? Absolutely, but that information can be tough to suss out. Wild-caught shrimp are typically of higher quality than farm raised, but they can carry a hefty price tag.

If you can find fresh shrimp or spot prawns, which are absolutely delicious, make sure they're still alive or freshly killed, as they spoil quickly. Whether you prefer to peel your own or enjoy the convenience of a composed bite, shrimp served head-on are always the way to go when available. The head keeps the juices in (like the lid of a pot), and when fried, the head (and the squishy flavor bomb that may or may not include shrimp blood, guts, brains, and exoskeleton) is by far the most delicious bite of the entire crustacean. ●

LET'S UPDATE THAT SCENE FROM *FORREST GUMP*

Daniel and Matt agree with Benjamin Buford "Bubba" Blue: shrimp is the fruit of the sea, and it's pretty great barbecued. But the film is now nearly thirty years old, and we figure that it might need an update. With shrimp, you can (1) braise them in fennel, tomato, and saffron; (2) scampi them with butter and white wine; (3) pile them on toast; (4) shrimp Louie them; (5) Thai salad them; (6) smother grits with them; (7) poach them with Old Bay; (8) teppan them; (9) tempura them; (10) ajillo them.

POACHED SHRIMP LOUIE SALAD

Serves 2

Salad

Kosher salt

6 asparagus spears, tough ends trimmed

10 large shrimp (18/24), peeled and deveined

2 eggs

½ head iceberg lettuce, quartered

1 large ripe tomato, cored and cut into bite-size wedges

Freshly ground black pepper

Dressing

½ cup mayonnaise

2 tablespoons ketchup

1 tablespoon fresh lemon juice

2 dashes of Tabasco sauce

1 teaspoon Worcestershire sauce

2 teaspoons kosher salt

¼ teaspoon sweet paprika

1 small clove garlic, finely minced

2 green onions, white and green parts, minced

Shrimp Louie salad is a long-standing iteration of the California classic crab Louie salad, whose ambiguous origin is debatably San Francisco circa 1900. The composed salad of iceberg lettuce, asparagus, tomato, shrimp, and Russian dressing makes a deliciously satisfying lunch more than a hundred years later. Daniel's version is fairly austere (a good austere), sticking to the classic ingredients, but go ahead and add or substitute vegetables and seafood with whatever seasonal offerings you prefer.

1. To make the salad, bring a large pot of heavily salted water (⅓ cup salt per 4 quarts water) to a rolling boil over high heat. Add the asparagus and blanch until just cooked through, about 2 minutes. Using tongs, remove the asparagus and place under running cold water to stop the cooking. Add the shrimp to the boiling water and cook until just firm and cooked through, about 3 minutes. Using a slotted spoon or spider, transfer to a plate and let cool to room temperature. Gently add the eggs and boil for 8 minutes, then remove and place under running cold water to stop the cooking.

2. While the eggs are cooking, make the dressing. In a bowl, whisk together all of the dressing ingredients, mixing well.

3. Peel the eggs and carefully cut them lengthwise into quarters.

4. To assemble the salads, divide the lettuce wedges evenly between two individual plates and arrange the asparagus, tomato, shrimp, and eggs around the wedges. Season with a pinch of salt and a few grinds of pepper, then spoon the dressing over the top.

When is it okay to eat fruits and vegetables out of season?

→ **THERE'S A WIDESPREAD MISUNDERSTANDING** of seasonal fruits and vegetables, and it's time to clear some things up. Listen, Daniel and Matt consider themselves fairly intuitive seasonal eaters—and you likely are, too. That is, you probably seek out (and cook) produce with the best possible flavor based on the time of year. But this timing is more critical for certain fruits and vegetables than others. Asparagus is more widely available, and way better, in the spring. Sweet corn is absolutely a late-summer vegetable. Watermelon is best in the summer. Peaches are to be avoided until sometime in mid-July, and tomatoes are best from late summer through early fall, as are peppers, eggplants, and zucchini. Citrus like limes, lemons, tangerines, grapefruit, and blood oranges are all winter fruits. These are some pretty complicated rules to remember (unless you shop at the farmers' market, where Mother Nature regularly reminds you of what is available and when).

Then there are the more idiosyncratic items that you find only at certain times. You see quinces and pomegranates only in the fall; ramps, fiddlehead ferns, and cherries are in markets for just a few weeks in the spring; and most wild mushrooms have short, weather-dependent seasonal availability. But if you are reading this in August, you might be asking, didn't I just buy a perfectly good pear yesterday at Whole Foods? Yes, you probably did, but that pear sitting in your fruit bowl was picked *last* winter and was chilling in a massive nitrogen-cooled locker, its flavor and texture gradually degrading, until it was pulled out and sold to you. And those apples in your Fourth of July pie were likely picked the previous October and kept in a cold-storage facility. They may even still be crisp—the technology is that good now—but why would you serve an apple pie in the summer when there is so much great summer produce to celebrate?

The more you learn about seasonality, the more you realize how short each crop's season really is, with many fruits and vegetables available for only a few weeks when purchased locally. Luckily, modern storage and transportation systems extend humans' natural reach and allow people to vary their diets beyond what is available within a day's mule ride. The goal shouldn't be to limit your diet, but rather to understand the ingredients you are using and when they're at their best so you can make informed decisions. You can find greenhouse-grown tomatoes year-round, and they are usually good enough for a slice on a burger. But a tomato salad should be reserved for when tomatoes are at their best, in the late summer and early fall. For Daniel, this is a pretty hard-and-fast rule. Another advantage of eating seasonally available produce is that price is directly related to abundance—and fruits and vegetables are at their most abundant at the peak of their season. Translation: seasonal produce is both cheaper and better.

So which fruits and vegetables are okay to buy year-round without hesitation? Lemons and limes are typically winter produce, but they are certainly okay to use any time of year. They travel well. (Of course, if it's Meyer lemon or finger lime season, you'd be well served to feature those fruits.) There are also a number of fruits and vegetables for which we forget about seasons completely. When is romaine lettuce in season? It's technically late winter, but it doesn't really matter, as good romaine is always in stores. Broccoli, cauliflower, and green grapes all fall into this category as well. The first two have a season (fall and winter), but nobody really remembers it because the difference in quality at other times of the year is negligible.

In 2020 (pre-pandemic), the US Department of Agriculture projected that US fresh produce exports would reach $7.1 billion, while imports of fresh fruits and vegetables would total $23.4 billion. This is a huge difference, and it's growing as the country increases its demand for fresh produce despite seasonality challenges. ●

BRAISED BELGIAN ENDIVES

Serves 4

2 tablespoons
unsalted butter

6 Belgian endives,
halved lengthwise

2 thyme sprigs

1 cup chicken
stock (or substitute
bouillon)

1 teaspoon kosher
salt

Juice of ½ lemon

Belgian endives are a winter vegetable, but they're successfully grown year-round indoors in the dark. It's a fascinating process that yields an extremely versatile leafy chicory most often served raw in salads for its crunchy texture and mildly bitter flavor. Here, the endives are first seared in browned butter, then they are braised in chicken stock with thyme to coax out their nutty flavor and highlight their sweetness. Serve them warm as a side dish or vegetable accompaniment to fish or chicken.

1. Melt the butter in a large sauté pan over medium heat and heat, swirling from time to time, until bubbling and beginning to brown, 3 to 4 minutes. Add the endives, cut side down, and raise the heat to high. Cook until the endives begin to brown, about 4 minutes (resist the urge to flip them).

2. Add the thyme, stock, and salt, lower the heat to medium, and bring the stock to a simmer. Cook until all the liquid has evaporated, about 15 minutes.

3. Serve with the lemon juice sprinkled over the top.

Are organic fruits and vegetables worth the extra money?

→ **WHEN DANIEL AND MATT** started talking through this question over Zoom (there were hundreds of hours of Zoom involved in the writing of this book during the spring and summer of 2020), the chef's answer was quick, firm, and final: "No." Matt joked that they were done talking, and they could simply move on to the recipe. But joking aside, the answer is pretty much just that. The idea of organic fruits and vegetables (and we're talking strictly produce here, not meat and dairy) started in a very good place and has been eroded, twisted, and misused over time. But when it first gained steam, the concept of organic food was extremely important.

Starting in the 1960s, farmers, as well as environmentalists and the swelling counterculture movement in places like Berkeley, Ann Arbor, and the Hudson Valley, came together to argue passionately that the earth was not being treated well. The widespread use of pesticides, irradiation techniques, fertilizers, and generally reckless farming practices was harming both the planet and the health of society. By the 1970s, the organic food movement had grown to the point where the government needed to step in and set some standards (as governments sometimes do). Farms were calling themselves "organic" in a very haphazard way, without following any sort of protocol. Thus came the birth of organic certification, and with it, a number of problems began.

Today, achieving organic certification is a costly, labor-intensive process that requires farms to invest thousands of dollars each year to confirm practices that some would follow regardless of the government's oversight. At this same time of strict regulation, large food companies began to realize

that consumers were willing to pay much more for "organic" apples, carrots, broccoli, and lettuce. Loopholes in the system abound, and the use of "synthetic substances allowed for use in organic crop production" (read: organic pesticides per USDA guidelines) has become widespread. In fact, counter to the original hippie impulse to clean things up, farmers are today allowed to use organic pesticides with impunity, and many certified organic farms are spraying even more pesticides than the standard noncertified farms.

This is not to say that all organic produce is compromised. There are certified farmers out there who are growing fruits and vegetables that should absolutely cost more and be treasured. But in general, the best bet when choosing where to buy your produce is simply to know your farmer, or, at the very least, purchase your vegetables from a trusted source rather than relying strictly on a USDA sticker to guide your choices. If you go to a farmers' market week after week and you like what the farm is selling—as well as its sustainability and labor practices (that is, the workers are paid a fair wage)—you don't need to concern yourself with whether the produce is organic or not.

This translates to the grocery store as well, but in a different way. When Daniel goes to his local Ralphs to buy standard produce (yellow onions, Belgian endives, green onions, Savoy cabbage), he makes his decisions based on how the produce looks and tastes (please don't be shy with that tester taste!) as much as on the labeling. Buying organic can be better for the environment (*can be* is the key term here), but taste-wise, the difference is not consistent. Use your mouth and eyes. Talk to the farmer if you can, approach produce on a case-by-case basis, and don't judge the fruit by its label. ●

TALK TO YOUR BUTCHER

On the topic of buying meat, Daniel cares more about whether a side of beef or pork cutlet comes from an animal that is raised responsibly than any organic certification. The issue at hand is extremely complicated, and it's further obfuscated by the lack of traceability built into the US meat production system. The United States produces a lot of meat, and it's consistently available and affordably priced. In order to make that happen, animals are handled by multiple farms throughout their life, shuffled from region to region depending on seasonal rainfall, price, and availability of feed. Because there are so many touch points throughout the process, it's difficult to know how each animal was treated and what it was fed, which is why it's even more important with meat than with produce to get to know your local farmer, talk to your local butcher, and make sure you're asking the tough questions so you can find out, to the best of your ability, the source of your meat. If your butcher can't tell you the name of the farm where your meat was grown, consider looking for a butcher who can.

SLOW-ROASTED TOMATOES

Makes about 1 quart

---

8 medium-size vine-ripened tomatoes, cored and quartered lengthwise

4 teaspoons extra-virgin olive oil

Kosher salt

4 cloves garlic, smashed

6 thyme sprigs

Slow roasting tomatoes concentrates their sweetness and preserves their flavor, making a delicious, versatile ingredient that can be used in many dishes. Roasted tomatoes are equally good in a cold salad as they are served warm on their own or with green beans, asparagus, or other vegetables. They can also be blended with olive oil and a little vinegar to make an especially delicious sauce for fish or meat. This roasting technique works with any variety of tomato, from grocery store Romas to the heirlooms brought home from the farmers' market, and the result is well worth the investment of time. Plus, once roasted, they will keep in an airtight container in the refrigerator for up to three weeks, so feel free to make a big batch.

1. Preheat the oven to 300°F. Line a sheet pan with parchment paper.

2. Place the tomatoes, skin side up, on the prepared pan. Drizzle with the oil, sprinkle with salt, and scatter the garlic and thyme over the top.

3. Roast the tomatoes until they have shrunken and shriveled and are beginning to brown around the edges but are not completely dry, 1 to 1½ hours, depending on their size. Use warm, at room temperature, or cold.

Are all GMOs bad?

→ **ON THE SURFACE, THE** idea of GMO (short for "genetically modified organism") feels pretty icky when it's associated with our food supply. A dive into the nuts and bolts of the process will reveal terms like *genome editing* and *in vitro nucleic acid techniques*, fraught with images of labs, test tubes, and sinister food companies monkeying around with the natural order—all in the name of profits. Some of this is grounded in reality, but some of it is not.

Yes, it's true that there are many food companies that do not align with Daniel and Matt's values—and very possibly yours. Big Ag can be a pretty depressing industry to read about (see why farmers' markets are so expensive on page 148). But a closer look at GMOs, writ large, reveals a much more nuanced answer that may make you question your instinct to resist them, or your tendency to prefer products labeled "GMO-free" on the merits of that claim alone.

Generally speaking, GMOs exist in farming as a way to improve efficiency and yield. Many GMO crops grown in the United States are specifically cultivated for one reason: to resist a specific herbicide and pesticide called Roundup. You may have purchased Roundup yourself at the home and garden store. It's made by the mighty Monsanto, a multinational agro-chemical and biotechnology company that has grabbed headlines over the years. You may have strong thoughts about Roundup and Monsanto. GMO plants have been genetically modified to grow even when sprayed with glyphosate (Roundup's main active ingredient). Using the shorthand "Roundup Ready," these seeds for corn, soybeans, and canola (among many other crops) are resistant to the broad effects of glyphosate, which is not only great at killing weeds but also great at killing crops. The genetically modified seeds allow the glyphosate to work on the weeds but not on the crops, which allows for more targeted (read: less) use of the chemicals. Once grown, these crops are transformed into many of the foods we eat today, including milk, cereal,

tofu, carbonated soft drinks, meat, baby formula, and canned soups. Roundup Ready is not without controversy, and critics suggest that the wide use of the herbicide may be weakening Roundup's ability to control weeds in general. Critics also point to genetically modified, insect-protected corn (crops grown with built-in resistance to things like corn rootworm and the European corn borer) as also having lost its effectiveness.

But for the supporters, the GMO upside is both better yield and a positive environmental impact, with the ability to spray less than without genetic modification, and with using only glyphosate rather than more harmful products. This curbs toxic runoff that can contaminate underground water sources. The downside is twofold. First, is the reliance on Roundup's maker, Monsanto, a good thing? Should so much of the United States' food supply be controlled by a single massive corporate entity? It's debatable, of course, but overall, the farming industry is going to protect itself using whatever means possible. The second downside—and this one is more perceived—is the long-term effects of GMO crops on our health.

Today, there is zero proof that consuming genetically modified crops has an adverse effect on long-term health, with research dating back to GMO's introduction to the food supply in 1994. That said, research is still relatively slim, and the thirty-plus-year effects from the proliferation of GMOs are only now coming into focus.

So, are GMOs bad? For Daniel and Matt, evidence suggests that there is slightly more good than bad. And they fully recognize that the system can be improved, particularly in terms of ecological impact. Agriculture and food science, along with changing consumer tastes and habits, is swiftly shifting the way we think about how our food is grown and what labels mean (and don't mean). GMOs will likely remain amidst the controversy. The best bet is to stay informed about where your food is produced and how science is altering farming as a whole. ●

EDAMAME WITH HOMEMADE CHILE CRISP

Serves 4 to 6

Kosher salt

1 (10-ounce) bag frozen unshelled edamame (young green soybeans)

3 tablespoons Taberu Rayu (recipe follows)

1 tablespoon light soy sauce

Juice of ½ lime

Daniel and Matt have been obsessed with chile crisp since the early days of their friendship. Daniel once sent Matt a jar of the crunchy garlic condiment (a ramen bar staple) by mail as a surprise—a fine use of the USPS if there ever was one. The condiment, sold by brands like Lao Gan Ma (Chinese) and Momoya (Japanese), is a gently spicy mix (although you can make it extra spicy if you want) of crispy fried onions, garlic, sesame seeds, and chiles. While the stuff bought at the store is excellent, it's also great homemade. Daniel learned this recipe from his good friend Kyle Itani, a talented chef who owns and operates Japanese restaurants in Oakland, California. The process takes patience and time, but it will make your whole house smell divine, and the batch will keep for up to three months in the fridge. If you have the crisp on hand, putting together this dish takes only five minutes and makes a delicious snack or appetizer.

1. Bring a large pot of heavily salted water (⅓ cup salt per 4 quarts water) to a rolling boil over high heat.

2. Add the edamame (no need to thaw) and boil for 3 minutes, then drain well.

3. Transfer the edamame to a large bowl, add the taberu rayu, soy sauce, and lime juice, and toss to coat evenly. Season to taste with salt.

Taberu Rayu (Japanese Chile Crisp)

Makes 2 cups

1½ cups vegetable oil

1 yellow onion, thinly sliced

1 head garlic, cloves separated, peeled, and thinly sliced

¼ cup gochugaru (mild Korean chile flakes)

2 tablespoons sugar

2 teaspoons kosher salt

½ teaspoon MSG

2 tablespoons dried minced onion

1 tablespoon dried minced garlic

1 tablespoon sesame seeds

¼ cup toasted sesame oil

1. Preheat the oven to 300°F.

2. Mix together the vegetable oil, fresh onion and garlic, gochugaru, sugar, salt, and MSG in a 3-quart oven-safe saucepan. Bake uncovered for 2¾ hours. The onion and garlic should be soft and blackened but not bitter or burnt.

3. Let cool to room temperature. Add the dried onion and garlic, sesame seeds, and sesame oil and mix well. The condiment will keep in an airtight container in the refrigerator for up to 3 months.

Does sulfur give you a wine headache, and is natural wine the future?

→ **DANIEL AND MATT AGREE** on this: Drink the wine you like. Don't drink the wine that your friends, or some dude in a boxy suit, tell you to like. Of course, there is something to be said for taking advice from a seasoned wine professional who is helping you train your palate and teaching you to appreciate some aspect of wine that you may be unfamiliar with, whether that's the wine's origin, a grape variety or style, or the food that it best pairs with. This information can come to you from many sources— the pages of a magazine or website (shout-out to *PUNCH*, where Matt has pitched in as an editor), or through a sommelier at a restaurant. Daniel and Matt embrace beverage education and really respect those who thirst for information about natural Lambrusco from Emilia-Romagna or orange glou from the Czech Republic. But it's another story entirely to subscribe to the individual who says it's simply not cool to drink a white Zinfandel. Remember, you should drink what you like.

As for sulfur, wine people love to disagree about it. So here's a little information on the wine-making process and where sulfur fits into the equation to help you make a more informed decision about your own position on the matter. At its most basic level, wine is grape juice that has been fermented by yeasts, which eat sugars and turn them into alcohol (among other things). The fermented juice (wine) is aged in wooden barrels, steel tanks, or concrete tubs and then bottled, aged again (in a warehouse or in your closet), and finally opened and drunk.

At each stage of the process, the wine comes in contact with oxygen and bacteria; the oxygen oxidizes the wine, and the bacteria adds flavor. All wine is oxidized to some extent, and that process, along with bacteria, is responsible for many of the complex nutty, earthy, and grassy flavors that we love. But as the wine continues to oxidize, those vegetal flavors become more pronounced, replacing the fresh, vibrant, and fruity flavors of the grapes over time (wines are constantly changing, which is why they need to be drunk within a particular window of time, or they go bad—that is, become "oxidized"). The color also shifts from vibrant straw yellow or cherry red to a rusty orange or brick brown. To slow and control the oxidative process, sulfur is added, inhibiting bacterial growth and preventing the oxygen from reacting with the wine. Often, when you first pour a glass, there is an unpleasant (two clicks right of farty), though thankfully fleeting, scent of rotten egg that quickly dissipates. That is the sulfur evaporating, and scientifically speaking, it has no further effect on the flavor of the wine or on the drinker's health.

There is more sulfur in your diet than in the wines you drink, and the link between sulfur and hangovers has been debunked for years. Tannins are a different story, and some drinkers have an adverse reaction to more tannic red wines, like Nebbiolo, Cabernet, and Syrah. Consuming tannins has been linked to the brain's release of serotonin, which has, in turn, been linked to headaches. Some drinkers might not realize that wine is highly quaffable, and is also a boozy AF beverage, and when you've drained a few bottles over the course of an evening, that storm cloud might be arriving the next morning.

What about natural wines? People in the food media live and die by buzzwords, and for the past couple of years, the press has been captivated by the natural wine movement. In general, the term *natural wine* describes a wine that is produced without chemicals, pesticides, and other additives (sulfur included). There has been a debate about whether certain farming techniques disqualify a wine from being "natural," particularly the use of machines. But overall, natural wine has been broadly defined by an aesthetic—funky, fizzy, slightly pickled, perhaps a little rude to some palates—and a culture of small farms run by younger (though not always), broke winemakers who are making it work on a smaller budget. If the established houses of Burgundy were bumping Coldplay, the natural winemakers of the Loire Valley are certainly blasting Ty Segall.

There are many delicious natural wines on the market and many excellent winemakers producing a widely varied selection of styles under the natural wine banner. But more and more, the term has become associated with an abrasive, oxidative style that is often driven by a flawed wine-making process, rather than a purposefully oxidative technique, such as those used to make sherry and the vin jaune of the Jura. So, is this wine-making style (as many seem to believe) the future? As with all food trends, there are peaks and valleys. Right now, we are at one of the peaks for natural wines (or what some would argue is the nadir for wine overall). Sommeliers, who are as much in the storytelling business as they are in the business of giving guests great wine, will continue to pimp out bottles, and magazines will continue to write their stories. Taste evolves over time, both individually and as a community. Just because you can doesn't mean you should produce wine in that manner. This is Daniel's last word on natural wines. He has a few unprintable notions as well, which will remain just that. ●

HOW DO I ORDER A GREAT BOTTLE OF WINE AT A RESTAURANT?

A really good sommelier won't pressure you into making a decision, but will most certainly help steer you toward a wine that you will like. The advice here is to have some opinions about wine going in and not to be afraid of communicating them. Know the type of wine that you like—Daniel likes "leaner, old-world-style" wines. Matt's good friend Scott always asks for an "earthy red." And you should feel comfortable communicating how much you want to spend, taking into account tax and gratuity, which will make the $80 bottle cost more like $110 on your Amex. Being straightforward about your budget is the best strategy. "I'd like to spend between $50 and $60" is a perfectly polite thing to say. With this information, a good wine pro can help you make a selection, and will usually hit the price target, rarely offering bottles that are far from your price range.

As we learned above, wines are constantly changing, and a wine steward's job is to know the wine list and help guide you to the best bottle based on your tastes that is within your price range. So the more information you give, the better he or she will be able to help you—just as you wouldn't tell a waiter that you're hungry and simply expect that waiter to bring you something you're in the mood for. Remember that there are no hard-and-fast rules, only guidelines about what you like. Daniel often orders two or three bottles and has them arrive at the same time. It gives everyone at the table the fun of tasting different options with their food and talking through which ones they prefer and why. If you are dining out with a group, you're likely going to get a second bottle eventually, so why not strategize from the jump?

friend of
FOOD IQ

SKYE LATORRE has worked as a sommelier, wine buyer, and beverage director, designing programs for restaurants, bars, and wine shops from New York to San Francisco. She currently resides in New Orleans, Louisiana, where she owns and operates Pluck Wine, a bar and restaurant.

How do I know whether to trust the sommelier at a restaurant? Aren't they just trying to upsell me?

No! Wine professionals become wine professionals because they are passionate about wine, and they don't get paid extra for selling you an expensive bottle.

How do I know if the person helping me at the wine store knows what they're talking about?

First of all, if the person approaches you and asks if you need help, they probably know what they're talking about. The inexperienced salespeople usually hide, scared you'll ask a question they can't answer. When they approach you, ask what's drinking well in a certain price range. If they ask a follow-up question, that's a great sign. If they avoid the question, find someone else to help you. Also, rely heavily on the store's descriptor cards. They're great to give the wine context, like whether it's a "porch pounder" or "great with BBQ," but don't rely on the flavor descriptor. The wine doesn't actually taste like cherries.

What's the biggest misconception about wine?

Vintage matters way less than you think. A good winemaker will produce good wine despite the year's conditions. Unless you're celebrating an anniversary or a birthday and you need a specific vintage, or you're planning on becoming a collector, don't worry about the year the wine was produced. Wines do have a sweet spot, though—a time when they're drinking best—so ask about when the wine will be drinking best. For most inexpensive wines, the fresher the better. Age isn't always a good thing.

KIR ROYALE

Serves 1

---

5 ounces sparkling wine, chilled

½ ounce crème de cassis

1 lemon twist

A bottle of crème de cassis is a good thing to keep sitting around in one's liquor cabinet. The black currant liqueur comes in handy to brighten an underwhelming bottle of sparkling wine or revive a three-day-old bottle of Aligoté. Cassis is thick and sweet, with a deep, cherry-red color and a vibrant, ripe-currant flavor. It's strong enough to hold its own alongside gin and vermouth in an Arnaud martini, or to play center stage in a cassis spritz. The sweet liquor is useful behind the stove as well, making an excellent additive to fruit pie fillings, jams, and jellies. It even works well on the savory side, as a flavorful sweetener for braises and sauces.

Pour the sparkling wine into a Champagne glass, then slowly add the cassis. Garnish with the lemon twist. A simple Kir (not royale) can be made in the same way. Just substitute chilled still white wine for sparkling.

This Sounds Fancy. This Sounds Intimidating. What Is It?

What do these foods and cooking terms that you hear thrown around on food television competition shows and that you see written about in the pages of your favorite magazines actually mean? In this chapter, Daniel and Matt answer questions related to some of these favorite fancy-pants foods—many of which are not actually that fancy.

What is dashi?

→ **IF FRENCH CUISINE IS** built on the bones of chickens (simmered into stock, that is), then dashi, built from natural products from the sea to form an overarching flavor profile, is the Japanese equivalent. It is the central theme in countless iconic Japanese dishes, sauces, condiments, marinades, and dressings, including miso soup, ponzu, chawanmushi, tamago, and okonomiyaki, to name a few. While it does add a subtle wisp of seaside flavor, the stock's beauty lies in the healthy dose of umami it delivers with every ladleful, enhancing each ingredient's inherent flavor profile and making every bite crave-worthy.

Contrary to common assumptions, dashi is not made from a single static recipe. It is instead a family of stocks made with different ingredients depending on the intended use. Kombu (seaweed) is steeped in water to create the most basic dashi, with the frequent addition of katsuobushi (shavings from a dried and often fermented and smoked bonito or skipjack tuna), shiitake (mushrooms), and niboshi (dried sardines) to create increasingly complex and flavorful broths.

While making dashi by using the above-mentioned raw ingredients is easy, most home cooks (and many respectable restaurants) use premixed dashi packs (essentially tea bags) or instant dashi (Japanese bouillon). Both are available at most Asian markets, and they can be simply dropped into water to steep or dissolve. Hon Dashi, made by Japanese conglomerate Ajinomoto (of MSG fame), is the most popular form found in American kitchens. It can be used in traditional Japanese cooking, but it has been newly popularized as an ingredient added directly to scrambled eggs or sprinkled as seasoning over noodles. ●

OYAKODON
CHICKEN AND EGGS POACHED IN SWEET DASHI

Serves 2

2 chicken thighs, skinned, boned, and cut into bite-size pieces

½ yellow onion, sliced

½ cup Dashi (recipe follows)

2 tablespoons mirin

2 tablespoons sake

2 tablespoons light soy sauce

3 tablespoons sugar

2 large eggs, lightly beaten with a pinch of kosher salt

2 green onions, white and green parts, thinly sliced

2 cups warm cooked short-grain white rice

One of Daniel and Matt's favorite kinds of donburi (rice bowl) is also one of the simplest to prepare. Served over warm rice, oyakodon, which roughly translates to "parent and child," is a one-pot meal of chicken and eggs (get it? parent, chicken; eggs, child) gently simmered together in a sweet dashi broth until the eggs are just set. In Japan, a special pan is used for making the dish, but any small nonstick pan with a lid works perfectly well. The trick is cooking the eggs so they're just set but still runny.

1. Arrange the chicken and yellow onion in a 10-inch nonstick frying pan with a tight-fitting lid. Add the dashi, mirin, sake, soy sauce, and sugar and bring to a simmer over medium heat. Cook, stirring from time to time, until the chicken is just cooked through, about 4 minutes.

2. Mix the beaten eggs with the green onions, then drizzle into the pan, making sure to distribute them evenly. Cover and continue cooking until the eggs are just set, about 2 minutes.

3. While the eggs are cooking, divide the rice between two bowls. As soon as the eggs have set, scoop them, the onions, and the chicken over the rice. Serve immediately.

Dashi

Makes 4 cups

1 sheet kombu (about 4-by-5 inches square)

4 cups water

1 cup loosely packed dried bonito flakes

1. In a pot, combine the kombu and water over medium-low heat and slowly bring to a simmer. Simmer gently for 15 minutes.

2. Add the bonito flakes, turn off the heat, and allow to steep for 10 minutes.

3. Strain the dashi through a fine-mesh strainer. It will keep in an airtight container in the refrigerator for up to 3 weeks or in the freezer for up to 2 months.

What does confit mean?

→ **CONFIT IS ONE OF** those original and thoroughly old-school French preservation techniques that was widely used before refrigeration (if you can believe a time like that existed). The idea is to slowly poach salted meat in gently simmering fat, though you can also confit fruit in syrupy sweet sugar water to the same effect. If you cook something completely submerged in a saturated fat and then cool it, the fat will harden, acting like the tight lid on a jar to seal the food off, protecting what was cooked from the introduction of the harmful bacteria that would otherwise spoil it. But the technique is not simply for safe storage. Slow cooking this way tenderizes tougher cuts, and unlike braising in a water-based medium, the fat locks in moisture and concentrates flavors.

Confit has origins in southwestern France, where ducks and geese were simmered in their own fat to cook and preserve them, and the region is still known for the most famous example of the cooking technique: confit duck leg. In the old days, these preserved legs, cemented in fat, would be held in the root cellar and brought up, leg by leg, to feed the family through the long, lean months of winter (picture an ingenious cook for the Night's Watch in *Game of Thrones*). In more modern times, it's been repopularized as a go-to technique for restaurant chefs who have expanded the tradition to include other meats, fish, and vegetables simmered in different types of fats to flavor them.

Think of confit garlic in olive oil, or of potatoes long cooked in ghee. Tomatoes make another great confit, concentrating their flavor similarly to sun drying while preserving the integrity of the plump, moist fruit. An important element to keep in mind for confit is overseasoning. Unlike cooking with salt dissolved in water (where the salt water is discarded), whatever seasonings you add will be absorbed completely by the meat, so the flavors can be intense, and oversalting is a common mistake. ●

GARLIC CONFIT

Makes about 25 cloves plus oil

---

1 cup extra-virgin olive oil

2 heads garlic, cloves separated and peeled

Garlic confit is a great way to extend the life of those dying garlic cloves you have buried in a bowl on the kitchen counter or scattered at the bottom of your refrigerator drawer. Extremely versatile and easy to prepare, the preserved cloves will last for up to a month in the refrigerator. Daniel likes to smash them and use the paste to season roast vegetables, spread them on toast, or serve them whole with a grilled steak. The oil used to cook the confit makes a killer vinaigrette or a handy seasoning oil mixed with a few red chile flakes for drizzling on pizza or over a bowl of ramen.

1. Slowly heat the oil and garlic in a small saucepan over low heat. Cook gently, stirring from time to time and being careful not to let the cloves brown, until the garlic is soft and tender, about 35 minutes.

2. Let cool completely, then store the cloves in their oil in an airtight container in the refrigerator. The confit will keep for up to 1 month.

What is the difference between hot smoking and cold smoking?

→ **THESE VERSATILE COOKING TECHNIQUES** can be confusing to parse, so let's start with two simple definitions, then unpack their different uses. One of the oldest preservation techniques, hot smoking is the cooking of seasoned meat or fish in a smoky environment, typically using a low temperature over a long period of time. Hardwood is prized for this type of smoking because of the long cooking times (hardwood is denser and burns longer than softer wood). Wood fire is naturally moist, which helps steam the meat, breaking down tougher cuts and penetrating the flesh with smoky flavor. This is the foundation of America's legendary tradition of barbecue—the cooking of beef brisket, pork butt, and links over a long period until they are mouthwateringly tender. The wood of fruit and nut trees, like apple and hickory, is traditionally used, but local availability plays an important role in wood selection, which helps explain the subtle regional differences among smoked meats.

Cold smoking is smoking at a low temperature to flavor and preserve the food *without cooking*. Smoked salmon is the quintessential example of cold smoking, but the technique is also used around the globe with tofu, nuts, raw vegetables, grains, and oils. As the saying goes, "where there's smoke, there's fire," so the key is cooling the smoke so the flavor, but not the heat, is applied. The most common ways to do this are to route the smoke over a long distance (using an underground pipe) or to filter it through ice. In the case of salmon, the fish is cured with salt and then dried overnight to form a pellicle—a sticky and tacky layer of semidry meat that the smoke will stick to.

Smoke should be thought of as a uniquely delicious seasoning, similar to adding spices—something to be used with purpose and not applied haphazardly. For the home cook, smoking indoors can be troublesome, but there are different ways to produce smoke (or smoky flavor) in a relatively controlled fashion. The easiest way is to purchase a smoking gun, which is basically a vaporizer for wood pellets that shoots cold smoke with the press of a button. Daniel smokes on his stove top using a steamer basket filled with ice over a pan loaded with wood chips. The smoke rises through the ice, blanketing his fish (along with his carpets) in a cool, smoky cloud.

Matt's Brooklyn apartment is a no-smoking zone. He found out the hard way, which may have included a call to the Carroll Gardens ladder. He prefers to add smoky flavor without the ceremony of fire, opting instead to rely on products like smoked salt for their seasoning.

And then there's liquid smoke, which has gotten a bit of a bad reputation over the years—a rep Daniel thinks is pretty unfounded. Liquid smoke is made by scraping the walls of a smokehouse and dissolving the product (there are technically more steps in the process, but this is essentially what's going on). The smoky additive is maligned because it's considered cheating, and feels like a slap in the face for those who take the time (hours and hours for real pit barbecue) to season their meat with fiery perfume. While Daniel doesn't exactly endorse using it, in a pinch, liquid smoke ain't the devil. •

AMERICAN BARBECUE TRADITIONS

American barbecue is built around three main components: meat, smoke, and some kind of rub or sauce, and the different ways these components mingle throughout the country has created some very distinctive barbecue styles, particularly in the American South, which will be our focus. Here is Daniel and Matt's back-of-the-sauce-stained-napkin breakdown of some iconic examples of classic American barbecue.

In **North and South Carolina**, pork is king, and entire hogs are slowly smoked over hickory and then pulled or shredded. In eastern North Carolina, the sauce is uniformly vinegar based. In western North Carolina, mustard is added to the sauce, and the darker shoulder meat is prized.

Texas is all about the beef, with the most famous region located in the Hill Country outside Austin, where Czech and German immigrants long ago established large meat markets that remain today. Order your beef brisket and ribs by the pound, and they arrive wrapped in paper.

Memphis is all about pork ribs coated in a dry rub, which, as the name suggests, are not coated in a wet sauce, but instead a flavorful crust that is built by a low-and-slow cloud of hardwood smoke.

Finally, **Kansas City** may be America's most famous barbecue town, and its tradition works equally with both beef and pork. The meat is treated with a dry rub but also slathered with a table sauce that is thicker and more tomatoey than other sauces found in the barbecue belt. Most of the grocery store barbecue sauces, like Bull's-Eye and Open Pit, are based on a Kansas City style.

PROPER WHITEFISH SALAD

Makes 2 pounds

---

1 (2-pound) whole smoked whitefish, skin and bones picked clean and discarded

⅔ cup Hellmann's or Best Foods mayonnaise (or your favorite brand)

2 hard-boiled eggs, peeled and chopped

3 celery stalks, finely diced

Juice of 1 lemon

Kosher salt

Growing up in New York City, Daniel developed the tradition of walking across Central Park at Eightieth Street every Saturday, stopping in at Zabar's for a half pint of whitefish salad, and then crossing the street kitty-corner to H&H Bagels and asking for "two of whatever's hot." Those Saturdays sitting on the Broadway benches, digging into a warm, freshly baked bagel with an oversize scoop of smoked whitefish salad, is a memory to hold forever. It's as good as it gets. And you can make it at home–the whitefish, at least (fresh bagels are doable, too, but leaving them up to the pros will save you a day's work). Making the salad is quick and simple–just don't be tempted to skimp on the mayonnaise, which is integral to the recipe. Daniel advises keeping a whole ACME mail-order smoked whitefish, straight from Brooklyn, in the fridge at all times, but you can also find good-quality smoked fish in most local bagel shops.

1. Working with your fingers, gently break the whitefish chunks into small flakes, removing any errant bones.

2. In a bowl, combine the fish, mayonnaise, eggs, celery, and lemon juice and mix well. Depending on how salty the whitefish is, the salad may or may not need added salt. When seasoned properly, it should taste just a little bit too salty, as the seasoning will subside within an hour or two of mixing. The salad will keep in an airtight container in the refrigerator for up to 2 weeks.

Why are wild mushrooms like morels, chanterelles, and black trumpets so expensive?

→ **THERE ARE PLENTY OF** wild mushrooms hiding under rocks and at the base of trees deep in the forest. There are also mushrooms that arrive at the grocery store and specialty market from urban farms (more like warehouses on the edge of town) and "doubles" (the industry term for mushroom-specific houses) found in rural settings. The difference between wild mushrooms and their domesticated kin is that wild mushrooms are foraged by humans in the wild. Some of this foraging takes great effort, and often luck, causing a scarcity for many of the best 'shrooms, which is why honeycombed morels, aromatic golden chanterelles, and inky black trumpets regularly cost as much as thirty dollars per pound, with rarer varieties, such as matsutake, costing close to double that.

Each mushroom has a unique season, preferred growing medium, and region where they are likely to be found. But exactly when and where they appear is impossible to predict. The mushrooms we eat are the flowers of incredibly complex, enormous (sometimes miles in diameter), subterranean organisms feeding on dead leaves, trees, and insects. Ask a mushroom hunter and you'll be given enigmatic hints about where to look: "check in the northern shade of a white pine's trunk on a crisp spring morning" for morels, or "search under the maple leaves of a steep southerly slope, three days after an autumn rain" for black trumpets. Each species supports an equally mysterious network of cottage industries made up of foragers, buyers, aggregators, shippers, and sellers who bring their rarities from the forest to your local restaurant or supermarket. The industry is one of the few legitimately unregulated cash businesses remaining in food, and it supports thousands of artisans working with no more guarantee than last year's memory of where their bounty appeared.

Some mushrooms are bought and sold for medicinal purposes and others for their magically hallucinogenic mind-altering properties. Still others will kill you with just a touch of the tongue, and thousands upon thousands more are perfectly edible but simply don't taste good. You aren't getting any of this with the romaine lettuce trade, and the price per pound justifies the challenge, with experienced foragers collecting upward of $200 per hour or more.

For the home cook, mushrooms offer a great opportunity to introduce a meat-like element that soaks up the flavor of sauces and marinades and delivers a shot of umami from the high amount of glutamates packed into the caps. As for the genesis story of how mushrooms first ended up in a stainless-steel pan, Daniel and Matt like to think that some French chef pointed to the base of the tree and said, with a thick Lyonnaise patois, "Bring me that thing in the dirt; I have shallots and butter waiting." So thank you, old French guy. Mushrooms have an incredibly unique flavor, earthy and ancient, and a texture like nothing else. They are moist and low in calories, and even though they are mostly water, cooks can sauté them to caramelization. The authors are wild for working with mushrooms, whether cooked down with fat and acid or pickled. And raw you may ask? Not really fans, but this goes back to a salad they once shared in Los Angeles that proved to be an epic misfire—the crashing together of a chalky texture with a distinctly dusty flavor, topped with arugula. Be careful when serving mushrooms raw—but otherwise, it's all mushrooms, all the time. ●

SCRAMBLED EGGS WITH MOREL MUSHROOMS AND PECORINO

Serves 2

1 tablespoon extra-virgin olive oil

1 cup morel mushrooms, trimmed and washed

1 shallot, minced

2 tablespoons unsalted butter

Kosher salt

4 eggs, whisked with 2 tablespoons milk or water

2 teaspoons thinly sliced fresh chives or green onions

Freshly ground black pepper

¼ cup freshly grated pecorino romano cheese

For as long as he can remember, Daniel has been an avid mushroom hunter, searching for black trumpets, chanterelles, and porcini in the spring and fall. The first autumn after he moved to Los Angeles, he was surprised to find morel mushrooms, randomly and almost by fate, growing in his backyard in beachside Venice. The mushrooms were plump and plentiful, and he breakfasted on them well into December. This dish of buttery and soft scrambled eggs works perfectly well with any type of mushroom, but morels are especially delicious.

1. Heat the oil in a 10-inch nonstick frying pan over high heat until it just begins to smoke. Add the mushrooms, being careful not to let the oil spatter. Cook, without moving the mushrooms, until they begin to brown, about 1½ minutes, then give them one quick stir and continue cooking until they begin to lose their water and simmer in their own liquid, about 1 minute.

2. Add the shallot, 1 tablespoon of the butter, and ½ teaspoon salt and continue cooking until the liquid evaporates, about 2 minutes. Transfer the mushrooms to a plate and wipe the pan clean.

3. Return the pan to medium-low heat and melt the remaining 1 tablespoon butter. Add the eggs, chives, and a pinch of salt and cook slowly, stirring constantly, until the eggs are just beginning to set, about 3 minutes. Add the cooked mushrooms, stir once to incorporate, and serve immediately topped with a few grinds of pepper and the cheese.

I know pad thai and curry, but what single dish will help me truly appreciate Thai cuisine?

→ **MATT HAS SPENT SOME** time traveling around Thailand, and both Matt and Daniel have put in hundreds of highly enjoyable hours eating in the great Thai restaurants of San Francisco, New York, and Los Angeles (shout-out to Uncle Boons, Thai House Express, Sapp Coffee Shop, Ruen Pair, Mamu Thai Noodle, Pok Pok Ny, and the Elvis impersonator at Palms Thai). For their column in *Saveur*, they once reverse engineered a Thai sardine and lemongrass salad from their favorite New York City spot, Somtum Der, famous for its larb and scorching papaya salad. It was a relative success, but ultimately, Thai cooking has been more of a spectator sport for them. As deeply passionate fans of Thai cooking traditions, even the wonderful books by Leela Punyaratabandhu (*Simple Thai Food*) and David Thompson (*Thai Food*) couldn't get them over the hump to cooking Thai food more regularly. This was until the Thai curry entered the picture.

Daniel felt like he needed to crack the code, and he scoured YouTube to find an answer. There he found chefs pounding chiles with pestles in deep mortars. *Pok pok pok* goes the sound, which Portland chef Andy Ricker named his restaurants after. The two most common Thai curries are red and green. Red curry, kaeng phet, is made with dried red chile and such highly fragrant components as garlic, galangal, shallots, shrimp paste, makrut lime leaves, coriander seeds, cumin, and lemongrass. The well-pounded paste is cooked in a saucepan, first with oil, then with coconut milk. Red curries are made with beef, chicken, tofu, and vegetables. Green curry, kaeng khiao wan, is made with fresh green chile that is pounded and fortified with fish sauce, palm sugar, lemongrass, and coconut milk.

Thai curries are incredibly popular at Thai restaurants in the United States, as they should be. They are delicious. But there's another Thai dish that is refreshing, satisfying, and foundational in Thai cooking and possibly new to you: nam phrik. Some have described nam phrik as a chile dip, but it's closer to a relish. Every region of Thailand has its own version, and it's a prominent member of the Thai kitchen that is regularly added to rice or spread across raw or grilled vegetables as a side dish or main course. It's kind of like hummus in that way: it's both a side and a main (see page 302). "It's the most fundamental and the vastest group of dishes in Thai cuisine, and the one common thread that runs through every regional and subregional cuisine of Thailand," says Punyaratabandhu, adding that it's also quite opaque to those outside Thailand. According to Punyaratabandhu, there isn't a Western equivalent. "Sauces or relishes are the closest things, but they don't function in a meal in the same way a nam phrik does."

Nam phrik is truly one of the most powerful, fragrant, and absolutely delicious bites you will ever eat in the world. The base is a union of onion, shallots, garlic, lime juice, shrimp paste (or fish sauce), and typically chiles (but not always). Textures can vary from a liquid to a paste. "It's almost like a sauce, but it's more than a sauce," Punyaratabandhu observes. "Nam phrik is not a sidekick ever—it's never been. It's a prominent part of a multicourse meal, as prominent as a stir-fry or soup or meat dish." The bottom line is that boat noodles can be pretty great, but you should also seek out the heroic nam phrik when ordering from your favorite Thai spot. ●

LON PLA ROM KHWAN
SMOKED TROUT RELISH

Serves 4 to 6

4 ounces smoked
trout fillet

2 cups unsweetened
full-fat coconut
cream

4 ounces peeled and
deveined medium
shrimp, finely
chopped

4 ounces 70 percent
lean ground pork

¼ cup packed light
brown sugar

¼ cup Thai or
Vietnamese tamarind
paste

Kosher salt

2 ounces shallots,
thinly sliced
lengthwise

1 red jalapeño
or Fresno chile,
stemmed and cut
crosswise into
¼-inch-thick slices

1 green jalapeño
or serrano chile,
stemmed and cut
crosswise into
¼-inch-thick slices

Sliced raw vegetables
(such as cucumber,
radish, carrot, and/
or green pepper) for
serving

Warm cooked jasmine
rice for serving

"Dishes categorized as nam phrik are sometimes awkwardly rendered 'relishes' and 'dips'—probably the best English words for them mostly due to a lack of better alternatives," says Leela Punyaratabandhu, who provided this recipe. Most Thai restaurants in the United States don't even put dishes in this family on the menu, perhaps because they're afraid their diners won't know how they fit into a traditional Thai meal ensemble. In Punyaratabandhu's household, this incredibly flavorful dish of coconut cream, tamarind, and pork takes commonly found smoked trout in an exciting direction for Western cooks. It's best served as a dip with raw vegetables, such as cucumbers, radishes, and green peppers, and with rice.

1. Remove and discard the trout skin. Using a fork, break up the flesh into flakes about the size of M&M's.

2. In a 2-quart saucepan, combine the flaked trout and coconut cream and bring to a boil over medium heat. Stir in the shrimp, pork, sugar, and tamarind paste and cook, stirring constantly and breaking up the trout and pork into small crumbles, until the shrimp is opaque and the pork is no longer pink, about 5 minutes.

3. Check the consistency. At this point, the relish should be slightly thinner than Bolognese sauce. If it's too thick, thin with a little water. Season to taste with salt. The relish should be equally sweet, sour, and salty. Remove the pan from the heat, stir in the shallots and chiles, and cover the pan to wilt them, about 2 minutes.

4. Let rest, covered, until lukewarm. Serve with the raw vegetables and rice as part of a larger meal.

friend of FOOD IQ

LEELA PUNYARATABANDHU **is the author of three cookbooks, including** *Bangkok* **and** *Flavors of the Southeast Asian Grill***, and is one of the most respected Thai food experts in the game.**

Thai cuisine has grown in popularity over the years, with many people seeking out cooking that stretches well beyond pad thai. That said, misperceptions persist. Name one.

That the best Thai food is street food. Or, worse, that all Thai food is street food. I don't know where the idea came from, but it never seems to go away. Do you need to go sit next to a stinky canal to eat the best food in a large country? No. Have you heard of home cooking? Where do you think cooking originated from? Not dragging a stove onto the street.

But Thai street food can still be pretty good, no?

I mean, 90 percent of what you find on the street is better than what you can order from the suburban Thai restaurant. But the other word that comes with "street" is "cheap," which is a mischaracterization of how Thais eat in general.

How do you describe the difference between northern and southern Thai cooking?

This is like asking how southern and southwestern American food differs. It's impossible [to summarize]. People have tried to say that the [food of the] central parts of Thailand are sweeter and not as spicy. Not true [laughing]. You have sweet things in the north and the south, and less sweet things in the northeast, but they have some.

What is dry braising? I thought braising meant liquid was required.

→ **"DRY BRAISING" IS ONE** of Daniel's favorite ways to cook meat, even if it's a little obscure to the home cook. That's because the words *dry* and *braise* seem contradictory. After all, braising almost universally involves liquid—red wine or vegetable stock or soy sauce—in which a cut of meat or some vegetables are slowly cooked in a wet environment over a long period of time. But what makes pit-smoked barbecue so delicious (in both texture and flavor) is dry braising, and the same low-and-slow technique can be used without the smoke.

You've probably dry braised yourself without even knowing it. A rack of ribs wrapped in foil and placed in an oven at 250°F for several hours is a form of dry braising. What's happening is the meat is braising in its own moisture, which slowly breaks down the connective tissue, leaving a richly moist flavor and fork-tender texture. Take a tough lamb neck, place it in a lidded cast-iron pot, and cook it for three hours on low. It doesn't sound like it should work, but the meat will be outrageously tender.

Dry braising doesn't work with all meat. The cut needs to be tough and flavorful, rich with fat and sinew. Short ribs, lamb shoulder, brisket, veal breast, and pork belly all are good candidates. Dry braising whole fish can also work well. To dry braise, Daniel likes to put the meat into a heavy pot (though porous clay works really well, too) and then seal the top first with plastic wrap, then a layer of aluminum foil, and finally the pot lid. It may feel weird to be cooking with plastic wrap in this way, but it creates a seal that promotes steaming within. Just be careful the plastic isn't exposed to the outside of the pot, as it will melt, and that's a real pain to clean up.

This technique is used by Daniel and Matt's friend Justin Smillie, the crazy-talented chef behind the Obama family's favorite beef short rib, which he created for New York's Il Buco Alimentari e Vineria and served at his popular restaurant Upland. Dry braising can also be used with inherently tender meats, like chicken thighs, for ninety minutes, or with larger, tougher cuts, like lamb shoulder, for six hours or more. ●

DRY-BRAISED LAMB SHOULDER WITH ANCHOVY AND GARLIC

Serves 6 to 8

---

1 (6- to 8-pound) bone-in lamb shoulder

Kosher salt

20 cloves garlic (from about 2 heads)

20 anchovy fillets

1 bunch sage

1 bunch thyme

1 bunch rosemary

2 tablespoons extra-virgin olive oil

Daniel developed this recipe while working as the chef of the Inn of the Seventh Ray, a long-standing romantic creek-side restaurant in Topanga Canyon, just north of Los Angeles, and it's one of the best lamb dishes around. Dry braising (which is basically slow roasting a cut of meat in a tightly sealed pot to create steam) cooks lamb with its own juices, breaking down the tough sinew and leaving the meat moist and fall off the bone tender. The long cooking process renders the fat, basting the meat as it cooks and mellowing the gamy flavor. Rosemary, sage, and thyme are rich in terpenes (aromatic plant compounds), which perfume the meat with an earthy, coniferous fragrance. At the restaurant, Daniel would roast the lamb shoulders overnight, pulling them out of the oven first thing in the morning, when the breakfast cooks arrived. The pulled shoulder was served warm with a rotating seasonal salad as an accompaniment.

1. The night before cooking, season the lamb heavily with salt (aim for 1 percent by weight, or roughly 4 to 5 tablespoons), rubbing it on all sides. Store, covered, in the refrigerator.

2. About 5 hours before serving, preheat the oven to 230°F. Using a paring knife, stab the meat all over, making twenty incisions each about 2 inches deep. Insert a garlic clove and an anchovy fillet into each incision.

3. In a Dutch oven, toss the sage, thyme, and rosemary with the oil, coating the herbs evenly. Nuzzle the lamb into the pot, surrounding and covering it with the herbs. Cover the pot with plastic wrap, then with aluminum foil, and finally with the lid. Place in the oven and dry braise for 5 hours, resisting the urge to open the lid. The meat will be fork-tender and falling off the bone.

What is chicken adobo?

→ **THE TERM** *ADOBO* **MEANS** different things to different people: a seasoning blend in a plastic jar found in the Caribbean and South and Central America; a recipe (or cooking technique) spread by the colonial Spanish around the globe; or a bottled pepper sauce used to marinate meat for preservation and flavor favored by Mexican cooks. Adobo has a place in kitchens all around the world, from Puerto Rico to Spain to the Philippines, where it serves as the island nation's official dish. It works as both a noun and a verb, and it can be made with virtually every protein—fish, pork, chicken, shellfish, or even vegetables. While there are many ways to make adobo, the one constant is the presence of vinegar, which serves as a marinade, tenderizer, preservative, and the leading flavor profile of this dish.

The Filipino origin story is up for serious academic debate, but most food scholars fall on the side that says a version of what we know today as adobo existed well before the Spanish colonized the region. "It seems clear that it was a precolonial dish, which makes sense because, in a hot climate, you have to be able to preserve food," says journalist Ligaya Mishan. "So when the Spanish arrived and saw that vinegar was being used, they used the verb that made the most sense." That would be *adobar*, meaning "to marinate."

But whether the Spanish brought adobo to the Philippines during their three-hundred-plus years of colonial rule, or learned the technique on any of the more than seven thousand islands and took it elsewhere, it's clear that adobo became a popular dish everywhere the Spaniards made shore. And, as the dish proliferated, each culture appropriated it as their own, changing the recipe to favor local tastes and work with available ingredients.

Vinegar (acid) and soy sauce are the key ingredients that define a Filipino adobo. Pork or chicken is marinated and stewed in the salty, acidic sauce with ginger and garlic until it's emphatically tender, then served with white rice and vegetables. In Latin America, salt and roasted chiles replace the soy sauce, adding an element of heat to the technique.

The magic trick that adobo plays comes from the balance of acid and salt, opposites on the palate that fool the tongue, canceling each other out and creating that mouth-puckering flavor any adobo fan can recognize. The combination of ingredients makes an exceptional preservation technique, allowing vats of chicken and pork to make long voyages, circumnavigating the globe below deck during the colonial era. Nowadays, adobo has grown beyond its seafaring origins, and the word itself is synonymous with a flavor profile, labeling sauces and spice mixes and signifying that an intense, salty, and acidic vibe lies within. ●

friend of FOOD IQ

LIGAYA MISHAN writes extensively about food and culture for the *New York Times* and is the coauthor of *Filipinx: Heritage Recipes from the Diaspora* written with the chef Angela Dimayuga.

How big is the universe of Filipino adobos?

There are a million adobos. The novelist Gina Apostol has said that, of all Filipino dishes, adobo "has the most leeway for a cook's imagination, hubris, art or bigoted sense of one's own mother's love-and-greatness."

And how does the flavor of vinegar run through Filipino cooking?

Vinegar is a constant, and I would argue that sour is the dominant flavor of Filipino cooking. Throughout Southeast Asia, there are many flavors, but sweetness persists. But it's the sourness in the Philippines that makes it unique.

You are writing a book about the wide world of Filipino food. What dishes should we seek out?

Laing is taro leaves stewed with coconut milk and chiles. Chiles are not a common ingredient in Filipino cooking, and it's a real test for the book because taro leaves are not that easy to cook. It's a really simple dish, where every ingredient counts, and I just love it. There's also sisig, which is pork jowls crisped up with onion and calamansi [lime] and an egg. It's such a crowd-pleaser. I also love kalderetang kambing, which is a goat stew. I can't explain why I love it, but it's got this mineral taste. It's so good.

TITA BABY'S CHICKEN ADOBO

Serves 2

1¼ cups water

¾ cup white distilled vinegar

¾ cup dark soy sauce

½ teaspoon black peppercorns

8 cloves garlic, smashed

1 bay leaf

2 whole chicken legs, each split into thigh and drumstick

2 cups warm cooked white rice

3 green onions, white and green parts, thinly sliced

Chicken adobo is one of the most popular recipe searches on the Internet, and for good reason. It's universally loved, easy to prepare, and after being cooked, it lasts for a week in the refrigerator and reheats perfectly. This recipe comes from Daniel's sister-in-law Stephanie, a first-generation Filipina American who learned to make the dish from her mom, Susan Aquino (Tita Baby). Dark drumstick and thigh meat will yield the juiciest results, so they're always the first choice, but if you prefer breast meat, you can follow the same recipe. Make sure to marinate adobo for at least twelve hours before cooking to ensure the flavor penetrates. This recipe also works well with pork belly, but you'll need to increase the cooking time to an hour.

1. In a bowl, stir together the water, vinegar, soy sauce, peppercorns, garlic, and bay leaf. Add the chicken pieces, cover, and marinate in the refrigerator for at least 12 hours or ideally overnight.

2. Pour the chicken along with the marinade into a pot and bring to a simmer over medium heat. Turn down the heat to low and simmer gently for 30 minutes.

3. Transfer the chicken to a plate. Raise the heat to high, bring the cooking liquid to a boil, and boil until reduced by three-fourths, about 8 minutes. Strain the liquid through a fine-mesh strainer set over a heatproof bowl. The braising liquid will thicken slightly into a sauce that you will use to glaze the chicken. (It will thicken as it cools, so don't be worried if it seems thin at this point.)

4. Preheat the broiler. Position an oven rack about 8 inches from the heat source. Arrange the chicken, skin side up, on an oven-safe pan, and broil to caramelize and crisp the skin, about 4 minutes (be careful not to burn the skin).

5. Divide the rice between two individual plates. Place the chicken on the rice and top with the warm braising liquid. Garnish with the green onions.

What is a gastrique?

→ **DANIEL ONCE WORKED AS** a young cook under the legendary nouvelle cuisine chef Jean-Louis Palladin, and the memory of Palladin's gravelly voice, pitched low by his appetite for Marlboro Reds, will forever be seared in Daniel's brain. So this question is answered in the Palladin voice—and if you see Daniel, ask him for a Palladin story, or three. They are very good.

Most every cuisine has a foundational sweet-and-sour sauce, and gastrique is the fancy-sounding French version. Gastrique is all about balance—the more sweet you add, the more you need to counter it with sour. This concept is used throughout cooking, and it's why you add, for example, acidic lime juice to sweet corn in Mexican elote. The balancing act can be a little counterintuitive, but you experience flavors relative to the last thing you tasted (remember as a child brushing your teeth and then drinking sour orange juice for breakfast), so if you want something to taste sweeter, you can either mix in a whole bunch of sugar, or you can add a little something sour, which will alert your tongue to the inherent sweetness of the initial ingredient. If you keep adding sweet and sour, you trick your tongue, creating a vibrant puckering sensation, and this is where gastrique comes into play. Although the technique has been around since the days of Auguste Escoffier scribbling in his notebook, the term wasn't crystallized until the 1980s, when the French nouvelle movement aimed to eschew the heavy, flour-based mother sauces for lighter and brighter sauces—using, you guessed it, the balance of sugar and acid.

To make a gastrique, start with a dry pan or one lacquered with fond from meat cooking, add sugar or honey, and toast it until it's caramel. Next, deglaze the pan (see page 120) using vinegar, white wine, or citrus juice—the latter for the famous dish duck à l'orange. The extremely flavorful gastrique can be used to top roasted poultry, fish, pork, vegetables, and even desserts like baked apples or poached pears. The balanced sauce amplifies all of the surrounding flavors, and it's a great addition to your sauce arsenal. ●

A CLASSIC GASTRIQUE

Makes ½ cup

⅓ cup honey

⅔ cup apple cider vinegar

Pinch of kosher salt

This is the most basic gastrique recipe around, and it makes a delicious sauce for pork, chicken, or baked apples. That said, the formula is meant to be a jumping-off point for experimentation. Swapping out the cider vinegar for a different type or using citrus juice will drastically change the flavor of the sauce, while trading out the honey for white or brown sugar, brought to different levels of caramelization, will add a nutty, toasted note of molasses. In addition to the base honey or sugar and acid, you can add berries or other fruits, wine, or spices as additional flavorings. Try adding ¼ cup basic gastrique to your next pan-roasted chicken gravy, and you'll be amazed by how it brightens the sauce.

1. In a small, heavy saucepan, toast the honey over medium-low heat until the color begins to darken, about 4 minutes.

2. Add the vinegar and salt and continue cooking, stirring from time to time to dissolve the honey, until the mixture thickens to nappe consistency (coats the back of a spoon, and when you trace a trail with your fingertip across the back, the trail holds its shape without dripping). The total cooking time is about 10 minutes.

What is the difference between curry powder and garam masala?

→ **DANIEL AND MATT HAVE** long been major fans of Indian cuisine and culture, and they wanted to dive a little deeper into these two popular spice blends that may or may not have been sitting on your spice rack uninterrupted for longer than they should. Linguistically, both curry powder and garam masala pose a bit of a riddle. The word *curry* refers to an Indian dish—not a spice blend—that is cooked with a myriad of spices, including but not limited to coriander, cumin, fenugreek, black pepper, and turmeric. The word is also used for the leaves from the curry tree, which are a popular ingredient in southern Indian cooking.

In India, curry powder doesn't technically exist. Cracking into a bottle of curry powder purchased in the United States will likely reveal a slightly sweet spice blend that includes a whole bunch of turmeric, appearing in different shades of yellow depending on the brand, as well as cinnamon, fennel, and black pepper. This is the spice blend that the British framed as curry powder, but in actuality, the turmeric-heavy blend is a type of Madras curry powder back in India. Madras is the old English name of the port city of Chennai, the capital of the southern Indian state of Tamil Nadu.

The French version of curry powder is called vadouvan. It is based on the original Madras blend, but with way more dried garlic. "It's become a bit of a fashionable thing in food media to say that colonizers like the British have invented these things that cannot be found in India, but it's more like the British popularized one type of spice blend and by default made it a monolithic aspect of the cuisine," says Meherwan Irani, chef and owner of the spice retailer Spicewalla. Madras is also the root of the slightly sweeter Japanese curry, which was introduced to Japan by the British Navy in the late 1800s.

The term *garam masala* translates to "spice mix," and it's also difficult to define, with recipes varying from city to city and family to family. It's one of the few pre-ground spice mixes used in India, where the practice of grinding whole spices for cooking is common. Garam masala serves as a foundation of not just Indian dishes. It is also found in nearby Bangladesh and Sri Lanka and in Nepal, where it's used as an aromatic and mostly rubbed over meat before it hits the grill. It is added to roasted vegetables and dal as well, though with a very light hand. While it is difficult to summarize the flavor profile of garam masala in a word, one thing is pretty obvious when you taste it alongside Whole Foods curry powder: it's stronger and more savory, often favoring cumin over turmeric for its base. Although generally not spicy in the sense of chile heat, some versions lean into the warming spices of nutmeg, clove, and green cardamom, including a version sold at Spicewalla. "While in Western culture, garam masala or curry powder was applied to everything and considered a catchall, in India, there are eight or nine types of masala, some with dried coconut, some with Kashmiri chile, and all are used with specific dishes," says Irani.

Spices have a shelf life, around six months to a year max, and making your own garam masala is a great way to use up spices that might otherwise sit around and become stale. Daniel likes to blend his own, preferring to make a small dish-specific blend rather than a generic mixture. When Daniel worked in French restaurants, he fell hard for vadouvan, and there was no going back. ●

friend of FOOD IQ

MEHERWAN IRANI is the James Beard Award-nominated chef-owner of the restaurants Chai Pani and Botiwalla in Decatur, Georgia, and Asheville, North Carolina.

What's the most underrated spice?

Smoked paprika is underrated and underappreciated. It's a remarkable product–here you have the pimentón, sun dried, then smoked over oak. So if you stop and think about it, if you grill a lot but don't have a wood-fired grill, why don't you substitute smoked paprika as a heat source–instead of chile flakes–or to add sweetness and smoke to ketchup, mayonnaise, or a barbecue rub? It's not just for classic Spanish dishes like paella or patatas bravas.

What's a masala dabba, and how is it fundamental in an Indian home kitchen?

It's your handy spice kit where you store ten to twelve spices in a metal container that can be easily accessed, instead of in a cluttered spice drawer. The spices in the dabba will cover 70 percent of what you are cooking, no matter your region or religion. And if you look at a family's dabba, you can tell where they come from.

What's a high-impact spice that can change a dish–for better or for worse?

Turmeric. I am the most careful when I use it, and I start with the least amount possible and go from there. If you are not careful with it, it can take a French or Chinese dish and make it Indian. Also cumin powder. It will instantly muddy or make a dish earthy. It will take a dish and make it taste like it was made by an American who just spent six months living at a yoga ashram and thinks he knows something about Indian food.

FOOD IQ

GRILLED CHICKEN TIKKA MASALA SKEWERS

Makes 4 skewers

Kosher salt

2 tablespoons fresh lemon juice

4 cloves garlic, smashed

1-inch knob fresh ginger, peeled and minced

2 tablespoons garam masala

1 tablespoon ground turmeric

½ cup whole-milk plain yogurt, plus 4 tablespoons for serving

1 pound boneless chicken thighs, cut into 1-inch cubes

1 red onion, quartered and layers separated

Warm cooked white rice for serving

2 tablespoons chopped fresh cilantro

1 lemon, cut into wedges

Daniel will go to the mat to argue that chicken tikka masala, perhaps the most quintessential example of Indian Mughlai cuisine, is his absolute favorite (and possibly the absolute best) way to cook chicken. Considering that there are hundreds, maybe even thousands, of methods on the chicken recipe Internet, this is quite the statement. The best version he had was from a charcoal grill at Karim's in Delhi, which was pretty close to an out-of-body experience. And here's the adaptation. Marinating the chicken in yogurt tenderizes the meat and allows the salt to penetrate deep into the flesh. One word of warning: There's no substitute for time when marinating. This chicken is best when marinated for at least twenty-four hours and up to three days.

1. At least 1 day and up to 3 days before you plan to serve the dish, marinate the chicken. Start by stirring together 2 teaspoons salt and the lemon juice in a bowl and let sit for 5 minutes. Add the garlic, ginger, garam masala, turmeric, and yogurt and mix thoroughly. Then add the chicken and turn to coat evenly. Cover and refrigerate until ready to cook. (Or transfer the contents of the bowl to a plastic freezer bag and refrigerate.)

2. When you are ready to cook, light your charcoal grill. (In the absence of a grill, preheat the broiler, position an oven rack about 8 inches from the heat source, and preheat a grill pan on the rack. The cooking time will be about the same.) If using wooden skewers, soak them in water for 10 minutes to prevent them from burning over the fire.

3. Remove the chicken from the marinade. To ready the skewers, alternate pieces of the chicken and onion, dividing them evenly among four skewers.

4. Grill the skewers directly over the fire, turning often, until the chicken is just cooked through and ideally charred on the outside and the onion is tender and lightly charred, about 5 minutes.

5. Serve the skewers over rice. Garnish with the cilantro and accompany with the lemon wedges and yogurt.

What is escabeche?

→ **NEARLY EVERY COUNTRY IN** the world has a version of cooked meat, poultry, fish, or vegetables marinated in an acidic sauce of vinegar or citrus. The technique, widely called escabeche, is so popular that pinpointing its exact origin would prove difficult, but early recipes can be traced back to Byzantine-era North Africa, when the dish traveled northward to Gibraltar and was given its name. Through Spanish colonization, the acidic preservation technique found its way around the world, and by the 1600s, a mention of marinating cooked fish in vinegar is found as far away as Japan (called nanbanzuke, the dish was introduced by the Portuguese and is still popular to this day).

As the dish traveled, so it evolved, with spelling, pronunciation, and ingredients bent to suit each locale. In the Virgin Islands, the dish is a colorful affair, with thinly sliced carrots and peppers draped over crispy fried pompano marinated in locally available citrus juice. In Italy, the fish (often sardines) is breaded before it's fried and marinated, stretching the portion size of the dish and offering an extra absorbent layer to soak up the acidulated sauce. Shellfish such as crabs, oysters, and mussels are marinated in Portugal under the escabeche banner. The list goes on in countries from Peru to the Philippines, and the possibilities are endless, making the technique hard to encapsulate. But no matter the iteration, the fundamental technique remains the same.

Daniel was first introduced to escabeche while working at Le Bernardin in New York City, where the dish has been served for the past twenty years, its preparation evolving along with the seasonal menus, including examples from Spanish mackerel with portobello mushrooms and tomatoes to oysters with fennel, shallots, and cilantro. Escabeche is extremely versatile, and it travels well, fitting in as perfectly as a fancy appetizer as it does at a beachside picnic. It's especially useful when cooking for large parties because you can prepare it in advance without the quality eroding. Next time you have friends over, try having the escabeche plated as a first course, ready and waiting before your guests arrive, so you can concentrate on hosting. ●

SWORDFISH ESCABECHE

Rich and oily fish like swordfish, with its meaty texture, stand up particularly well to the sharp and flavorful marinade of escabeche. Make sure to pick the freshest fish available, and use whatever seasonal vegetables you can find. For balance, Daniel always includes onions, which soak up the vinegar and add a much-needed touch of sweetness. The trick is not to overcook the fish, or it will fall apart. The dish needs to marinate for at least four hours before serving, but it lasts for up to a week in the fridge, and it's at its best after twenty-four hours or more in the marinade. Once you've got the hang of it, try adding the additional step of breading and lightly frying the fish—the breading absorbs the sauce, seasoning the fish even more intensely.

Serves 2

2 (6-ounce) swordfish steaks, ideally ¾ inch thick

1 teaspoon kosher salt

¼ cup extra-virgin olive oil

2 cloves garlic, thinly sliced

1 small red onion, cut into ½-inch-thick slices and separated into rings

1 red bell pepper, stemmed, seeded, and cut into ½-inch-wide rings

2 thyme sprigs

¼ cup white wine vinegar

2 thin lemon slices

1 teaspoon freshly chopped fresh flat-leaf parsley

1. Season each swordfish steak on both sides with ½ teaspoon of the salt.

2. Gently heat the oil and garlic in a sauté pan over medium-low heat until the oil just begins to bubble and the garlic cloves soften, about 3 minutes.

3. Add the onion and bell pepper and continue cooking, stirring frequently, until the vegetables just begin to soften, about 3 minutes. You want the onions and peppers to retain some of their crunch.

4. Add the thyme and swordfish steaks, pushing the vegetables aside so the fish is touching the bottom of the pan. Scoop the vegetables over the top, then cover and continue cooking until the fish is just cooked through, about 4 minutes. Add the vinegar and lemon slices, and turn off the heat.

5. Transfer the fish to a tightly sealed container and let it rest in the refrigerator until completely cool before serving.

6. Serve garnished with the parsley.

What is Kobe beef, and is it really better?

→ **THERE'S A LOT OF** confusion surrounding Kobe beef. The name "Kobe" was co-opted by American marketing firms in the early 2000s to help sell "Japanese-style" beef produced from a few imported Japanese cows (Wagyu) crossbred with American Angus cattle. With this, American Wagyu was created. But the name was deemed overly complicated in the end, so any Japanese-style beef produced in America was designated "Kobe beef." True Japanese beef didn't find its way onto US soil until late in 2012, when the USDA lifted its years long ban on foreign cattle inspired by foot-and-mouth disease. That's not to say that American Kobe beef isn't special or delicious, but the meat you've tasted likely has little in common with the traditionally raised Japanese specialty that shares its name.

Another important thing to clarify is that Kobe beef, even in Japan, is a branding designation for a conglomerate of beef producers located in the Hyōgo Prefecture, one of Japan's popular beef-producing regions. The history of beef in Japan dates back to the second century, when cattle (called "Wagyu," from Wa, or "Japanese," and gyu, or "cow") were introduced as plough animals. Japan's relative isolation until the mid-1800s maintained the animals' pure lineage, setting them apart from other cattle. When beef consumption was popularized after World War II, Japanese farmers worked to tenderize their tough and muscular indigenous beasts of burden, feeding them grain-rich diets and limiting their physical activity. Thus, Japan's famously hyper-marbleized and meltingly tender beef was born, along with a swelling legend.

In general, beef is graded on its marbling, or how much intramuscular fat is present in the meat. The more fat, the more tender—and the higher the grade, and the more expensive. True Japanese beef is graded on an alphanumeric scale, where anything with an A designation must be 100 percent purebred Wagyu. To simplify things, Japanese A2 is relatively equivalent to American prime beef, and anything higher is extraordinarily rich and extremely expensive. Small portions of A4- and A5-grade Wagyu are griddled (teppanyaki), grilled (yakiniku), poached (shabu shabu), or braised (sukiyaki) on special occasions as a celebratory treat.

So what about all those Kobe sliders? Don't get Daniel started on the craze, which Anthony Bourdain summed up pretty perfectly in a 2016 interview with *First We Feast*. "There's a certain douche tone that's detectable to me," he said of the restaurant trend that popped off in the 2010s, adding that there's no way you could appreciate the things that make Kobe interesting and expensive in a little burger or a meatball drowned in sauce. "You're just selling status there and bragging rights, and the last thing they care about is, 'Is this the best?'" ●

SHABU SHABU

Serves 4

1 pound frozen udon noodles

6 shiitake mushrooms, stemmed and caps cut in half

1 bunch beech mushrooms, stem ends trimmed

1 (14-ounce) package firm tofu, cut into ¾-inch cubes

¼ head napa cabbage, cut crosswise into 2-inch-wide strips

1 negi (Japanese green onion), white part only, cut into 1-inch-wide rings (or substitute the white part of leek or green onion)

1 carrot, peeled and cut diagonally into ½-inch-thick slices

4 cups dashi (page 197) or water

10 ounces Wagyu rib-eye steak, thinly sliced

1½ cups yuzu ponzu for dipping (see Japanese Yuzu Ponzu Crudo, page 165)

Shabu shabu, the incredible technique of boiling thinly sliced beef in a communal pot of boiling water, may seem like a complicated ordeal, and it's true that it involves some specialty equipment (a portable burner, for example) and requires prep time. But once you get the hang of the setup, it's quite fast, and the cooking happens while you're eating, so it can actually be quite efficient. Plus, it's a fun and festive way to share a one-pot communal meal, with multiple courses served from the same vessel (meat, vegetables, and noodles). If you want to go above and beyond, you can add more than one dipping sauce and dried spices to the mix. Sweet soy sauce, spicy sesame Sriracha, and shichimi togarashi work well, to name a few.

1. Bring a large pot of water to a rolling boil over high heat. Add the noodles and blanch for 1 minute, then drain, rinse under cold running water, and set aside in a bowl.

2. Place a portable gas burner in the center of the table and top with a donabe (see page 62) or Dutch oven. Arrange the shiitake and beech mushrooms, tofu, cabbage, negi, and carrot in the pot. Add the dashi until the vegetables are three-fourths of the way submerged. They will shrink as they cook. Arrange the meat on a plate and place the plate and the bowl holding the noodles near the burner. Divide the yuzu ponzu between two small bowls for dipping.

3. Heat the pot slowly over medium heat until the dashi just begins to simmer. Using chopsticks, take turns dipping pieces of the meat into the simmering broth until just barely cooked (about 40 seconds), then dip into the ponzu and eat immediately. As the vegetables cook, remove them from the broth and eat them, dipping them in the sauce to season.

4. When the meat and vegetables are finished, add the noodles to the pot to heat them, then ladle them into serving bowls along with the broth to finish the meal.

What is nixtamalization?

→ **OVER THIRTY-FIVE HUNDRED YEARS** ago, nixtamalization was discovered by Mesoamericans, and its legacy is still felt today when you bite into a lengua taco from your favorite taco truck. It's a foundational process for releasing nutrients from the partially indigestible corn kernel, allowing the plentiful grain to sustain life around the world. As a culinary process, nixtamalization is relatively simple: dried corn kernels are cooked in an alkaline solution and then hulled. Today, calcium hydroxide, also called slaked lime, has replaced the traditional use of wood ash. This loosens the hard outer hull and extracts beneficial nutrients like niacin and calcium, making the corn a complete food source. While the modern process remains the same as the ancient one, the end result is as much about nutrition as it is about elevating flavor and preserving a culturally defining way of life. Like so many of the world's great culinary traditions that were once born of necessity—pickling, fermenting, curing, and smoking among them—nixtamalization leads to incredibly delicious results.

The most famous example of a product in the United States that relies on nixtamalization is the corn tortilla—that subtly tangy, tongue-puckering astringency is the noticeable effect an alkali has on your palate. To make tortillas, the cooked corn is ground through a grain mill (molino) to create flour (masa harina), which is then mixed with a little water to form a pasty dough called masa. The dough is then shaped into small balls, which are pressed into flattened disks and cooked dry on a griddle called a comal. Masa is also the central ingredient in sopes, tamales, empanadas, and pupusas, to name just a few foods that crop up throughout the Americas. But freshly made masa, ground on small cast-steel mills or large industrial lava-stone wheels, has, in large part, been replaced by Maseca, an instant, just-add-water masa product.

"Nixtamalization was dying as a product of industrialization, which is triggered by the need to feed more people at a cheaper price point," says José R. Ralat, the taco editor of *Texas Monthly* (yes, this is a real and glorious job) and one of the world's great authorities on the taco. He says that while cooking with instant masa is not inherently wrong, due to NAFTA, the corn used in the product was primarily trucked in from US farms, hurting small Mexican farmers along the way. Making your own masa can be a fun and enriching weekend project, but for most people, it's not a reality for day-to-day life. Luckily, many Mexican markets sell refrigerated fresh masa, so there's no excuse not to use the fresh stuff next time a recipe calls for it.

For the taco fan, the flavor and texture of a corn tortilla made with fresh masa is unmistakable, and seeking out taqueros (taco chefs) who work with these ingredients is highly advised. This may cost you a few extra shekels, but put it in perspective. At two dollars or three dollars apiece, tacos are inherently inexpensive, so spending a little extra for good quality isn't going to break the bank. Tacos are a "perfect food," according to Ralat . . . and Daniel and Matt could not agree more, or think of many better ways to spend their money. •

friend of FOOD IQ

JOSÉ R. RALAT **is the author of *American Tacos* and the taco editor of *Texas Monthly*, where he regularly writes about Mexican American food and culture.**

Gun to your head: corn or flour tortillas?

It depends! It depends on the filling, and on what region the taquero is trying to evoke, because flour is the default tortilla for most of the northern states of Mexico and the borderlands of the US. So, if this person is offering me a breakfast taco, I'm going to go for flour. Is this person offering me tacos al pastor? I want corn. But always go for the tortilla that is made in-house.

What has Taco Bell meant for the American taco?

Everything. Its significance and influence cannot be understated. Whether you like it or not, historically, it's done more for Mexican food than any other large corporate entity or restaurant. I wouldn't have my job without it.

How do I find great tacos in my town?

Look for a full parking lot. Lines. There are code words on the outside of the building or on the menu. For example, if the restaurant takes its name from a town or region, I want it to specialize in that particular food.

TAMALES DE RAJAS
CHEESE AND PEPPER TAMALES

Makes 24 tamales

---

24 dried corn husks

4 poblano chiles

2 pounds fresh tamale masa

½ cup (1 stick) unsalted butter, melted

Kernels from 6 ears corn, roughly chopped, or 3 cups frozen corn

Kosher salt

1½ pounds queso Oaxaca, cut into ¼-inch cubes

Making tamales is a labor of love, with an emphasis on the labor, and some of the ingredients you'll need can only be found in a Mexican supermarket, including fresh masa, which is critical. But once you taste freshly steamed tamales made with your own two hands, you'll realize they're completely worth the effort. Plus, they last for a week in the refrigerator and for up to two months in the freezer when tightly wrapped, so making a big batch is the way to go. This recipe is for Daniel's favorite tamale, stuffed with spicy roasted chile strips (rajas) and stringy cheese, but you can stuff your tamales with any number of ingredients, from red chile pork to chicken mole to refried black beans—or even just wrap the plain masa. A final word: You can make tamale masa with Maseca brand corn masa flour, lard, and baking soda, but the whole point here is to taste the difference the freshly ground corn makes.

1. Rehydrate the corn husks by soaking them in boiling water for 10 minutes.

2. Meanwhile, begin fire-roasting the poblanos. To fire-roast the chiles on a gas stove top, turn on a burner to high. Then, one at a time, place the chiles directly on the metal grate of the burner and roast, rotating with tongs as needed, until completely blackened and blistered, about 6 minutes. As the chiles are ready, transfer them to a bowl, cover the bowl with plastic wrap, and allow the chiles to steam and cool for about 10 minutes. If you don't have a gas stove top, preheat the broiler. Position an oven rack about 8 inches from the heat source and broil the chiles on an oven-safe tray, turning them as necessary to char the chiles completely on all sides, then place them in the bowl and cover. Once the chiles have steamed and cooled, cut them open, remove the stems and seeds, and scrape and wipe away the charred skin. It's okay if a few burnt bits remain. Cut the flesh into ¼-inch dice and season with a pinch of salt.

3. In a large bowl, combine the masa, butter, corn kernels, and 2 tablespoons salt and mix well.

4. Place a steamer basket in the bottom of a large pot with a tightly fitting lid. Add water to a depth of about 2 inches to the pot (the water should not touch the bottom of the steamer basket).

5. Make the tamales, working with one husk at a time. Spread 2 heaping tablespoons masa on the center of the corn husk, then top the masa with 1 tablespoon each of the roasted chiles and the cheese. Close the tamales by folding the narrow top end of the husk onto the masa and rolling the sides to create a small, masa-filled envelope with an open top. The masa will expand as it cooks, so don't tighten the husks too much, or the filling will ooze out.

6. Arrange the wrapped tamales, open side up, in the steamer basket. This can be a bit tricky, as you need them all standing upright. You can use aluminum foil to help prop them up and to fill the extra space if your pot is too big.

7. Cover the pot and bring the water to a boil over high heat. Lower the heat to a simmer and simmer the tamales for 1 hour. The tamales will steam, cooking the inside and basting them from their open upward end, keeping them moist throughout the long cooking process. Check the water level from time to time, adding more water as necessary to ensure that the pot doesn't boil dry and burn.

8. Turn off the heat and allow the pot to cool on the stove for 30 minutes before opening the top and removing the tamales for serving. Reheat leftovers in a small steamer for 7 minutes or microwave them for 90 seconds on high power.

What is jamón ibérico?

→ **SPAIN HAS A BEAUTIFUL** tradition of curing the hind legs of pigs, and jamón ibérico is widely considered the highest form of that art. Similar to prosciutto or American country ham, Spanish jamón takes time and extreme levels of dedication to produce. The pigs' hindquarters are first salted and left for a few weeks, then they are hung for (literally) years to slowly dry, concentrating their flavor and tenderizing the muscle in the process. The technique of salt curing was developed as a form of preserving meat before the era of refrigeration, but nowadays, jamón prepared in this manner is sought after for its unique flavor: deep and nutty, with a near cheese-like texture.

Jamón serrano, hung for six to eighteen months, is widely available around the world, making up most of Spain's enormous ham production (Spain produces more cured ham than any other country in the world). Jamón ibérico, on the other hand, has a more limited availability. It's hung for twenty-four months or longer, and the hams are produced from Spain's famed black Ibérico pigs, which roam freely in the country's vast southern forests. The most prized type feeds solely on acorns (jamón ibérico de bellota). The meat has a deep mahogany hue and is heavily marbled with bright white veins of rich intramuscular fat. The limited availability and long curing process make jamón ibérico a prohibitively expensive delicacy, costing upward of $80 a pound and up to $1,000 for a whole leg.

When you visit Barcelona or Madrid, or anywhere else in Spain for that matter, chances are that one of the first foods you'll seek out is jamón, because nothing says Spanish holiday like eating an outrageous amount of paper-thin sliced pork washed down with a gently effervescent white wine or fino sherry. For decades, American diners back home sought to repeat these experiences by searching for jamón stateside, only to be stymied by the product's limited distribution. Most Spanish meatpacking facilities do not conform to the United States Department of Agriculture's specifications, and the nature of jamón's production method makes it difficult to pass USDA guidelines for importation. If you're thinking about bringing a leg back in your suitcase, think again. It's illegal to cross the border with meat, and there's a risk of heavy fines and even jail time for offenders. With limited availability, as well as a surging demand from a proliferation of Spanish tapas-style restaurants around the country (and world), the popularity of jamón continues to grow. •

WHEN PEOPLE FINALLY GOT HIP TO AN AMERICAN NATIONAL TREASURE: COUNTRY HAM

The great irony of the jamón ibérico boom, especially during the rise of tapas in the 2000s, was the simultaneous disinterest in the great American ham tradition dating back hundreds of years. It wasn't until David Chang started putting the name Allan Benton (of Benton's Smoky Mountain Country Hams in Madisonville, Tennessee) on his menu at Momofuku Ssäm Bar, along with farms from Kentucky and Virginia, that domestic ham plates became fashionable. Granted, these US traditions were originally inspired by Italian, French, and Spanish immigrants landing in the mountains of America's Midwest and South. It's interesting to see how coveting imported ham has led to American diners looking inward.

THE BEST MEAT LOAF: BEEF, PORK, AND JAMÓN

Makes two 4-inch square meat loafs

Meat Loaves

1¼ pounds ground beef, 80 percent lean (chuck is ideal)

12 ounces ground pork (shoulder is ideal)

4 ounces jamón scrap meat, minced

2 ounces jamón fat, minced

1 cup chopped fresh flat-leaf parsley

3 cloves garlic, minced

2 teaspoons kosher salt

2 teaspoons smoked paprika

Pinch of red chile flakes

1 cup whole-milk ricotta cheese

1 cup plain Italian fine dried bread crumbs

2 eggs

For Serving (Optional)

1 cup ketchup (preferably Heinz)

½ cup salt-roasted almonds, chopped

8 cloves garlic, finely chopped and fried golden brown in extra-virgin olive oil

When you slice jamón, you're left with bits and pieces—extra fat, skin, and scraps of meat that can't be served. The trick is to collect all of this for a rainy day—or a cloudy day with a chance of the best meatballs, or in this case meat loaf, you'll ever make. (Daniel keeps a pint container in the refrigerator for saving cured meat scraps.) The skin and bones make an excellent broth, similar to this book's recipe for Parmesan Broth (page 29), and the meat and fat are packed with flavor that you can incorporate into meatballs, burgers, or any other ground meat preparation. It goes without saying that this recipe works just as well with any cut of jamón. In other words, you don't need to wait for the scraps, but when you pay upward of $1,000 for a leg of ham, you damn well want to make sure you're using every last bit of it.

1. Preheat the oven to 325°F. Line a deep 9-by-13-inch baking dish with parchment paper.

2. In a large bowl, combine all of the ingredients for the meat loaves and mix well.

3. Divide the meat mixture in half and form each half into a 4-inch square loaf. Place the loaves in the prepared baking dish.

4. Bake the loaves until an instant-read thermometer inserted into the center registers 145°F, about 1 hour. Let cool for 5 minutes before serving.

5. If serving with the optional sauce, in a small bowl, stir together the ketchup, almonds, and garlic. Slice the meat loaves and accompany with the sauce, if using.

What is emulsification, and why is it so French?

→ **EMULSIFICATION IS ONE OF** the fundamental concepts of French cooking, and it's a technique that helps define French food's unique identity. France has long respected the work of chefs as artists and praised culinary advancement in the same breath as the arts and sciences. Long before chefs became the "new rock stars"—a groan-inducing term that was introduced in the United States in the mid-aughts— French chefs were indeed celebrated like the Rolling Stones. They've competed in their own restaurant kitchens (for critical praise and Michelin stars) as well as publicly in organized competitions. The world can thank the French for many culinary innovations, not least of which is emulsification.

The concept of emulsification is a little sciency even for us. It's slightly elusive, and it's difficult to explain without breaking out the cellular diagrams, so please excuse the forthcoming analogies. Imagine dropping a handful of dirt into a bucket of water and mixing it up. The water would stay cloudy for some time because the smaller particles of dirt would remain "suspended" in the water. Over time, however, the dust would settle, and the water would clear up again.

In science (and in cooking), this temporary condition of suspended particles is called a suspension. Now imagine mixing a handful of salt into the bucket of water. The salt would dissolve and remain mixed with the water for the foreseeable future, just like in the ocean; this is called a solution. An emulsification is the third, more complicated concept, whereby a protein is added into the equation, allowing otherwise immiscible liquids (like oil and water) to stick together. The protein (often egg yolks or reduced stock or mustard) acts like glue, allowing water molecules to stick to tiny fat droplets, such as oil or melted butter.

A classic example is mayonnaise, in which oil is emulsified with the water in lemon juice by slowly whisking both into protein-rich egg yolks. It's a magical concept that yields a smooth and viscous texture unachievable by any other means. Other examples of emulsifications include mustardy vinaigrettes, beurre blanc (butter and wine), béarnaise sauce (butter, egg, and vinegar), hollandaise sauce (butter, egg, and lemon juice), and sabayon (egg yolks and wine). Notice the Francophile theme here?

The more fat you add, the thicker the emulsification becomes, thus the high calorie count on that jar of Hellmann's. Once thickened, the emulsification can hold other ingredients, which makes the technique a great building block for various recipes (two of the best-known French sauces, mayonnaise and hollandaise, are emulsifications) and well worth learning. Mayonnaise is the base for many popular creamy dressings, such as Caesar (mixed with anchovies, garlic, and Parmesan cheese), ranch (mixed with buttermilk, garlic powder, and tarragon), and—well—French (mixed with ketchup), as well as countless relishes and sauces, from aioli to rémoulade.

But before you start blending away, beware the dangers of moving too fast. Starting an emulsification can be frustratingly difficult, and it takes practice and patience to perfect. For mayonnaise, start by thinning the egg yolks with lemon juice and a little water, then slowly drizzle the slightest stream of oil into the mixture while whisking vigorously. The oil should immediately disappear, clouding the liquid to a flat, opaque white and thickening it as you go. If, at any time, droplets of oil appear or the liquid acquires a glossy sheen, then something's gone wrong. In the kitchen, this is called "breaking" the emulsification, and it usually happens if the oil is added too quickly. If you catch the break early, you can whisk in a few drops of warm water and reverse the effect. But if it goes too far, the only fix is to start all over again. All is not lost, however, as once you've gotten a new emulsification started, you can slowly add in your broken mess and bring it back together. There's one more thing: emulsifications with butter and other saturated fats like lard that are solid at room temperature must be held warm enough to remain liquefied but not so hot as to cook the egg yolks, adding a further challenge to the formidable technique. We, along with our naked and boring steamed asparagus spears, thank you old French chefs for spreading the gospel of your fatty sauces. ●

ASPARAGUS BÉARNAISE

Makes 1½ cups
sauce; enough for 2
bunches asparagus

Kosher salt

2 bunches thick
asparagus spears

3 tablespoons minced
shallots

¼ cup white wine
vinegar

1 teaspoon freshly
cracked black pepper

1 cup (2 sticks)
unsalted butter

2 tablespoons finely
chopped fresh
tarragon leaves

2 egg yolks

1 tablespoon water

1 tablespoon fresh
lemon juice

Béarnaise sauce is one of the most challenging emulsions to make, but Daniel knows you are up for it. The challenge lies in the difficulty of maintaining the sauce at a constant temperature while mixing. There are a hundred techniques to accomplish this goal, and every chef has his or her own "foolproof trick." But to truly master the technique, you need to learn to identify and control the temperature and adjust as you go. No book can fully accomplish a béarnaise tutorial, and you should certainly check out YouTube for some examples before tackling it. One important factor to keep in mind is the butter temperature. Many a béarnaise has been broken because the butter was too hot, cooking the eggs on contact. Traditionally, the sauce is made with clarified butter, but Daniel prefers the subtly nutty flavor (and ease) provided by skipping the clarifying step.

1. Bring a large pot of extra salty water (½ cup salt per 4 quarts water) to a rolling boil over high heat. Prepare an ice-water bath for the asparagus.

2. Trim off and discard the tough lower asparagus stems, then peel the tender stalks to just below the tip to reveal their pale green interior.

3. Add the trimmed asparagus to the boiling water and blanch until just cooked through, about 2 minutes. Immediately transfer the asparagus to the ice-water bath to stop the cooking, submerging them until completely cool. Drain and reserve at room temperature on a serving plate.

4. To make the béarnaise sauce, in a small saucepan, combine the shallots, vinegar, and pepper and bring to a boil over medium heat. Cook until the vinegar has reduced to 1 tablespoon, about 2 minutes.

5. Meanwhile, in a separate small saucepan, melt the butter over low heat, then turn off the heat.

6. To create a double boiler, pour water to a depth of 1 inch into a medium saucepan and bring to a simmer. Rest a stainless-steel bowl in the rim of the pan over (not touching) the simmering water. Add the shallot-vinegar mixture, all but 1 teaspoon of the tarragon, the egg yolks, water, and a pinch of salt to the bowl and cook, continuously

whisking vigorously, until the yolks begin to expand, thicken, and lighten in color, about 6 minutes. This step takes longer than you think it should, and it's important not to heat the eggs too quickly—even a few seconds over an open flame and the eggs will scramble, ruining your béarnaise.

7. Turn off the heat under the double boiler and slowly whisk in the lukewarm butter, 1 tablespoon at a time. The béarnaise sauce should have a matte finish. If the sauce takes on a shiny glaze, chances are that it's gotten too hot. In that case, remove the bowl from atop the pot and whisk the mixture slowly until it cools slightly. If the sauce thickens to a stiff consistency, add a few tablespoons warm water to thin it. When all of the butter has been incorporated, whisk in the lemon juice, season to taste with salt, and then stir in the remaining tarragon.

8. Serve immediately, spooned over the asparagus spears. Béarnaise sauce needs to be held between 110° and 130°F, otherwise the sauce will break. If you need to delay, cover the bowl with plastic wrap and set it atop a pot of 150°F water to maintain the temperature.

What's the difference between tequila and mezcal?

→ **THERE'S A POPULAR DRUNKARD'S** tale told by lively bartenders and impassioned brand ambassadors (and more calmly by bottle shop employees), and it describes humble Jaliscan farmers pooling their blue agave with the other farmers from their pueblo and boiling vats of brew over outdoor fires to distill their local spirit. Once upon a time, that tale was true, but today, the tequila business is a multibillion-dollar industry dominated by multinational corporations working out of world-class, highly technical distilleries and exporting their liquid around the globe. The story still pervades—only now the tale has shifted south to the state of Oaxaca, the distant land of smoky mezcal (also long famous for its distinct and delicious cuisine).

Tequila and mezcal share a lot in common. Both are agave spirits produced in much the same way, but mezcal is a wider category from a taxonomy perspective: mezcal is any agave spirit produced in nine regions, while tequila has to be made from the blue agave and is produced in five much smaller regions (and mostly in the state of Jalisco, where the town of Tequila is located). Both are made by harvesting the core of the agave plant (called the piña), but while tequila uses a process of steaming and distilling, mezcal is cooked in large vats lined with wood and charcoal, which produces a sharp and often smoky flavor (though some are smooth and mild).

Tequila has had a marketing head start, popularized as a spring break elixir in the 1990s and later embraced by cocktail-focused bartenders, who integrated the spirit into cocktails that realized its potential well beyond the margarita. In the late 2000s, "tequila" was broken into several categories, among them blanco (young), reposado (rested), and añejo (aged in oak for one to three years), to help codify the different aging techniques and better communicate their flavor profiles.

And mezcal is following suit. While some are still produced by smaller operations, the vast majority of what is exported to the United States is controlled by the same large conglomerates producing tequila today. This isn't to say that large companies don't make excellent products; on the contrary, the consistency and quality of currently available mezcal and tequila far exceeds that of the bygone mom-and-pop era. These are great spirits, rightfully holding their own alongside the whiskeys, rums, and brandies of the world—drinks to enjoy responsibly . . . or less responsibly while among friends. But beware the marketing dollar, and beware the bartender's tale: the evocative story of nostalgia about that small farm outside Tapalpa might not be representative of the whole truth. •

MEZCAL PALOMA

Serves 1

---

2 ounces mezcal

2 ounces grapefruit juice

½ ounce fresh lime juice

1 ounce simple syrup (equal parts sugar and water, dissolved)

2 ounces sparkling water, chilled

There's nothing more refreshing on a hot, dry day than a cold paloma, an easy-drinking combination of tequila, lime juice, and grapefruit soda. Mezcal is often served with a grapefruit slice, a traditional pairing, making the grapefruit soda a natural bedfellow. Be careful, however. The combination is fast flowing like lemonade, so don't forget the delayed punch the mezcal will deliver. For a fancy presentation, mix a few tablespoons kosher salt with a pinch each of sugar, lime zest, and árbol chile powder, then, rubbing the rim of a glass with a lime wedge so the mixture will stick, coat the rim of the glass.

1. Fill a cocktail shaker half full with ice, add the mezcal, grapefruit juice, lime juice, and simple syrup, and shake vigorously.

2. Strain into an ice-filled tumbler, top off with the sparkling water, and stir to incorporate.

friend of FOOD IQ

CHANTAL MARTINEAU is a journalist and author of *How the Gringos Stole Tequila*, detailing the rise of Mexico's iconic liquid export, and coauthor of 2018's *Finding Mezcal*.

Why is mezcal always thought of as smoky?

It comes down to logistics. Most of the entry-level mezcals focus on smoke, and most drinkers are introduced to mezcal through cocktails, so, ipso facto, the first thing you are probably going to taste is a smoke-forward mezcal, and not the more nuanced ones.

What else can be there in terms of the flavors?

Once you press beyond forty dollars a bottle, you can taste so much. Mezcal is made in almost every state of Mexico, so there's tropical fruit in some, and green vegetables or chocolate in others. Minerality shows itself in cool ways, too. It's really endless.

Is mezcal here to stay in terms of Americans drinking it on the regular?

While all of these stories have been written in the media, it's not the new kid on the block anymore. It's cooler than tequila in many ways [laughing].

12 Favorite (Essential, Life-Changing) Things to Cook Forever

There are several classic recipes that every home cook should have ready in her or his back pocket, and here are Daniel and Matt's top twelve, along with some tips for making them in the best possible way. Are there more than twelve favorite dishes to cook forever? Of course. Was it difficult for the authors to narrow these down to a dozen? Of course. But at the end of this chapter, you'll have a better understanding of some of the foundational dishes that make the authors tick (in the kitchen), and hopefully you'll pick up a few forever recipes of your own along the way.

How do I learn to love the pancake as an adult?

→ **EVERYBODY LOVES PANCAKES ONCE** in a while. No? It's one of those foods that is the opposite of polarizing. Eating pancakes is often a way to pretend you're not eating dessert for breakfast, especially with a hangover—and, let's face it, sometimes even eggs Benedict or avocado toast feels a little too adventurous for those desperate times. Luckily, there's the short stack with syrup and seasonal fruit, or the Dutch baby (sometimes called "Dutch boy"). Pancakes come in many forms: sweet and savory, dense and fluffy, thin and puffy, and made to celebrate the eight days of oil (see Daniel and Matt's pancake power rankings below).

Daniel has a bit of a history with pancakes, and with one recipe in particular that has stuck with him like Grade B maple syrup on a silver dollar flapjack. (Fun fact: Until only recently, Grade B was actually a preferable rating to Grade A. Grade B is now called Grade A Dark Color, Robust taste, clearing up some confusion.) In 2005, Daniel was the chef at Axe, an organic restaurant in Venice, California, responsible for making one of the most popular pancakes to be served in Los Angeles at the time: a multigrain mélange of barley, millet, brown rice, oats, rye, and a large amount of poppy seeds (legend has it that Dennis Hopper once failed a drug test after consuming these pancakes). The genius recipe came from his boss, Joanna Moore, who closed Axe in 2014 but is still selling the frozen mix at farmers' markets around California.

When Daniel first tasted the iconic pancake at Axe, it was like nothing he'd ever had. It was hearty, crunchy, and with a batter thick like wet cement that came alive on the griddle, sizzling in a healthy pool of vegetable oil. For many of its fans, it is the gold standard against which all breakfast pancakes are judged. The anticlimactic secret is that it's quite easy to make: it's essentially a classic whole-grain pancake recipe mixed with store-bought ten-grain cereal (Bob's Red Mill sells a good one), cooked brown rice, and millet. Daniel estimates he's made five thousand (or was it ten thousand?) of them. His recipe below is a close approximation of the original Axe pancake, but it's adapted slightly out of respect for Joanna's secrecy and tweaked with his own decades of pancake love in mind. ●

A PANCAKE POWER RANKING

While working on this question, Daniel and Matt spoke for nearly an hour, debating their favorite pancakes from around the world. Why did it take so much time? Because the pancake comes in many packages, and when you start comparing Korean pajeon to Danish Æbleskiver, things get a little heated. In the end, they found room for compromise, and with that in mind, here's a ranking counting down to number one of their five favorite pancakes anywhere.

5. Made popular in Hiroshima and Osaka, **okonomiyaki** is a savory pancake and near-perfect drinking food made with flour, dashi, grated yam, seafood, and topped with bonito flakes and a thick sauce made with Worcestershire.

4. Yorkshire pudding is actually a pancake, if you think about it: it's a savory batter cooked in hot beef tallow to accompany a steak or boiled beef dinner.

3. Korean pajeon is made with rice and wheat flour, eggs, and green onions, and mixed with many different fillings, including kimchi, seafood, and beef.

2. The **blueberry buttermilk short stack**, topped with Grade B Vermont maple syrup, almost gets top billing.

1. The **latke**. Daniel and Matt grew up with Jewish delis and annual Hanukkah parties serving up both good and bad latkes. But it's the homemade versions turned out every December—the potatoes hand shredded and the water properly squeezed out, the onions and potatoes fried to a golden crisp—that take the top spot.

MULTIGRAIN ADULT PANCAKES

Makes three 8-inch pancakes

1 cup 10-grain hot cereal mix (preferably Bob's Red Mill brand)

¼ cup millet

6 cups water

¾ cup whole wheat flour

½ cup all-purpose flour

2 tablespoons light brown sugar

1 teaspoon baking powder

2 teaspoons kosher salt

1½ cups whole milk

1 egg

¼ cup vegetable oil, plus 3 tablespoons for cooking

1 cup cooked brown rice

1 tablespoon poppy seeds

Butter and maple syrup for serving

Pancakes are delicious–we all agree on that. But they also don't have to be unhealthy carb bombs. Adding whole grains sets this recipe apart from your run-of-the-mill breakfast cake, giving these cakes a uniquely toothsome texture that eats more like a meal than a sweet side dish served with eggs.

1. The night before cooking, combine the cereal mix, millet, and water in a bowl, cover, and refrigerate.

2. When ready to cook, in a bowl, stir together the whole wheat and all-purpose flours, sugar, baking powder, and salt. Add the milk, egg, and the ¼ cup oil and gently mix to incorporate. Drain the cereal-millet mixture and add it along with the rice and poppy seeds, then gently mix until just combined.

3. Heat 1 tablespoon of the remaining oil in a 10-inch nonstick frying pan over medium-high heat until the oil is sizzling hot. Add 1½ cups of the pancake batter to the pan, using the back of a spoon to spread it evenly to the edges. Lower the heat to medium and cook until the edges begin to brown and small bubbles begin to appear on the surface, about 3 minutes.

4. To flip the pancake, slide it out of the pan onto a dinner plate, then invert the pan over the top of the plate. Holding the plate from underneath in the palm of one hand, the frying pan handle in the other hand, and applying pressure to ensure the plate and pan remain connected, quickly flip them over so the pancake, uncooked side down, falls back into the pan.

5. Continue cooking the pancake until it is cooked through, about 2 minutes. A toothpick or cake tester inserted into the center should emerge without any raw batter stuck to it. Slide the pancake out onto a dinner plate.

6. Repeat with the remaining batter and 2 tablespoons oil to cook two more pancakes. You can hold the finished ones in a low oven until ready to eat. Serve with butter and maple syrup.

Italians, Germans, Israelis, Popeyes: who makes the best chicken cutlet?

→ **THE CUTLET QUESTION IS** one the authors tackled in a *TASTE* column, and after its publication in 2018, there were some letters! This is not a bad thing. It's important from the jump to set some ground rules. First off, what is a cutlet—or better yet, what makes a cutlet a cutlet? Broadly speaking, the definition changes based on where you are from, with examples found in nearly half the world's cultures. An English person might tell you a cutlet is simply a grilled, bone-in rib eye, while a Ukrainian would say it's a panfried minced meat croquette. As New Yorkers, Daniel and Matt define a cutlet as a thinly sliced and pounded piece of meat, usually chicken or veal (but sometimes pork), that has been breaded and fried. To simplify things, for our purposes here, that's the definition of cutlet we're going to explore.

New York City–style breaded cutlets are ubiquitous worldwide, although their name changes depending on their point of origin. That said, the two dominant names in the game are the Italian Milanese and the Austrian schnitzel. Schnitzel has the widest reach globally, with examples on all five continents, and preeminence in the kitchens of Africa, the Middle East (it could be argued that this is the national dish of Israel), and Oceania—the latter dating back to the Austro-German colonial era. Milanese is a close second, stretching beyond its northern Italian home to South and Central America. Here in the United States, we refer to the preparation as a cutlet (derived from the French côtelette) or, in God's country (that is, the American South), chicken fried, which refers to it being breaded and cooked in the style of fried chicken.

Breaded cutlets are less commonly found in East Asia, although one of our favorite examples is the Japanese tonkatsu, made from a thicker cut of pork (ton means "pig" and katsu is shortened from katsuretsu, the Japanese transliteration for cutlet). Tonkatsu is dredged in flour, dipped in egg, and breaded with panko, super-crispy crumbs ground from bread baked with an electric current that yields an ultra-fluffy, crustless loaf that is perfect for crumbing.

While each of these preparations has its own delicious merit, the Italian Milanese is Daniel and Matt's personal favorite because it's the cutlet of their childhood. As with so many of Italy's great culinary techniques, the Milanese was developed in poor villages as a means to stretch and make palatable a small amount of tough meat in an attempt to feed the whole family. Slicing the cutlets thinly across the grain and then pounding them with a blunt object (a wooden mallet) helps to tenderize the well-worked muscles. Breading can double the weight, and triple the volume, while retaining the moisture from the little fat that renders out. You may have your own personal favorite, and the lines are open for debate on this favorite dish from around the world. ●

friend of FOOD IQ

SHERRY HOLZMAN is Daniel's mom—his first chef instructor, his biggest fan, his fiercest critic, and his most tireless advocate. Sherry is a fine artist by trade, with a focus on oil painting, paper crafting, and decorative weaving. She is a passionate self-taught cook who has been collecting favorite recipes for over half a century. Daniel conducted this interview.

When did I first start calling them "kickin' chutlets"?

Shama Merry's kickin' chutlets came about when you and your dad inadvertently said my name wrong. "Mama Sherry" became "Shama Merry," and it just stuck. Chicken cutlets were everybody's favorite. I would use that wooden pounder to flatten the breasts between Saran wrap so they wouldn't get all goopy, then I dredged them in eggs and bread crumbs, and there you have it. You have to use very fine bread crumbs, like the Progresso ones—that was the base for the chicken parmesan.

My grandma was a great cook. You didn't learn anything from her?

I watched my mom, but I didn't learn how to cook from her like you did, stirring mushrooms from my hip when you were two years old. I did learn how to make kasha and bow ties from her—kasha varnishkes. You have to cook the kasha; first you roast it in the pan to bring out the nutty flavor, then you add the water, which would sputter and boil over, so you have to be careful. You sauté mushrooms and onions in butter, then mix it all with cooked bow ties—that was my favorite.

What did we like to eat as kids?

You liked every single thing that I made. Chicken parm was number one, and lasagna was another favorite, although that was time-consuming. Meat loaf. Every day I would go to the market with you kids, and we'd pick what to make for dinner—whatever looked good. Always vegetables, sometimes noodles. You and your brother loved noodles with ketchup and cottage cheese.

FOOD IQ

CHICKEN PARMESAN

Serves 4

Two (5-ounce) Classic Chicken Cutlets (page 168)

1½ cups Forty-Minute Red Sauce (page 143)

6 ounces fresh mozzarella cheese, sliced ¼ inch thick

3 tablespoons freshly grated Parmesan cheese

Chicken parmesan was Daniel's father, John Holzman's, favorite meal. And chicken parmesan is Daniel's favorite meal. Daniel prides himself on making what he believes to be the best chicken parmesan around, and the key is nailing all of the important ratios. Too little sauce, and your dish will be dry; too much cheese, and it's a gooey mess (though that's a far cry better than too little cheese). To start, pound the chicken thin. You will need to shallow fry the chicken in good olive oil. Then you need to bake the fried chicken cutlets with the sauce, which allows the breading to absorb the flavor of the tomatoes. It's not enough to simply ladle tomato sauce over your cutlet and melt some cheese on top, contrary to what many red sauce joints tend to do. Have a little patience, and you will eat like a king—like Daniel and his father, John.

1. Preheat the oven to 375°F.

2. Place the chicken cutlets in a 9-by-13-inch baking dish. Cover them with the tomato sauce, then arrange the mozzarella slices over them, covering them entirely.

3. Bake until the sauce is bubbling hot and the cheese begins to brown, about 20 minutes.

4. Let rest for 10 minutes, then scatter the Parmesan over the top before serving.

How do I make the best chicken soup like Grandma used to make?

→ **IF THERE WERE A** single dish that crossed cultures around the meat-consuming world more fluidly than any other and that held important roles in both home and restaurant kitchens, it would most likely be chicken soup. Nearly every country on earth has a version. And unlike other widespread dishes whose origins can be traced and similarities codified, variations of chicken soup are genuinely unique to each culture. In China and Korea, ginseng and jujubes are added for both their flavor and their medicinal properties. Ashkenazic Jews have their bubbe's matzo ball soup. Greeks have avgolemono. In Thailand, home cooks incorporate coconut milk and lemongrass, while Mexicans have caldo de pollo, with cilantro often playing a starring role. In the Philippines, moringa leaves are presented in tinola, a fragrant chicken soup made with green papaya. In the Yucatán Peninsula, sopa de lima is tart with a dose of vitamin C.

Daniel and Matt have their own family memories of chicken soup. Matt's dad, Rick, made a pretty classic French Provençal version pulled from the Julia Child playbook (sweet carrots, bracing onion, and celery rounding it out). Speaking of playbooks, Rick's soup, made on Sunday afternoons, often followed a crushing Detroit Lions loss. At least there was soup. Daniel's mom, Sherry, made chicken soup for her boys whenever they got sick, following her mom's recipe but with the addition of alphabet noodles and dill.

But how do you make the best chicken soup? The question had been in the back of Matt's head for some time, especially since writing a Korean cookbook, a cuisine in which soups are foundational, so he posed it to Daniel. Do you need to cook your chicken soup for hours and hours, or can you make a simple broth in forty-five minutes? Does time really extract flavor? The answer is yes and no. Good chicken soup cannot really be made in half an hour. Many Vietnamese *pho gà* recipes stipulate several hours—up to twenty-four—on the stove. Jewish matzo ball soup can be made in an hour or less. Then there is a decision to make: Are you using the chicken you are cooking in the soup (say, for pulled chicken and dumplings), or is this more of a bone broth, enriched with collagen that has been melted away over time, giving the broth its body? Korean samgyetang comes to mind. Collagen is the melted connective tissue, prevalent in sinewy cuts and ligaments, that gives chicken soup its body, and it is the reason rich chicken broths congeal when they're chilled. Chicken feet are the key to adding collagen; add enough, and your soup will take on a lip-smacking tacky texture.

In the United States, chicken soup is more of a frontier food—originally made by dropping whole raw birds into a cast-iron pot filled with water and cooking it over the hearth. But in other countries, it's more of an extrapolation of making stock (see page 80), using the bones to form a flavorful broth. There is no single way that is definitively better or worse, and there are no certainties. Well, there is one: Matt eating Rick's soup ladled out after a Lions defeat—you can count on that. ●

MEXICAN CHICKEN AND RICE SOUP

Serves 8

1 whole chicken,
about 4 pounds

1 white onion, halved

1 jalapeño chile,
stemmed

1 large tomato, cored

1 bunch cilantro,
stems and leaves
separated

Kosher salt

2 teaspoons freshly
ground black pepper

4 cups warm cooked
white rice

2 limes, quartered

Daniel learned this recipe working his first executive chef job in California, at Axe restaurant in Venice, where the cooks would make spicy chicken and rice soup for their dinner. The recipe was so good that Daniel put it on the menu and has been cooking it ever since. The spice in hot chiles is concentrated in their seeds and their pithy white interior, so if you prefer your soup on the milder side, remove the seeds and pith before adding the chile to cook.

1. Put the chicken into an 8-quart stockpot and add water to cover by about 2 inches. Add the onion, jalapeño, tomato, cilantro stems, and ¼ cup salt and bring to a boil over high heat, then lower the heat to a simmer and simmer uncovered for 1 hour.

2. Remove the pot from the heat and transfer the chicken to a large plate. Set a fine-mesh strainer over a bowl and pour the broth into the strainer. Transfer the solids in the strainer to a blender, add a ladleful of the strained broth, and blend on high speed to create a smooth puree. Return the strained broth to the stockpot, add the pureed vegetables and pepper, and season with salt to taste.

3. When the chicken is cool enough to handle, pull the meat from the carcass and tear it into bite-size pieces. Discard the bones, gristle, and skin. Add the pulled meat to the soup pot.

4. Reheat the soup until piping hot. Scoop ½ cup of the rice into each of eight individual bowls and ladle the soup over the rice. Garnish with the cilantro leaves and serve a lime wedge alongside each bowl.

How do I scramble eggs like a chef?

→ **"COOK ME AN EGG!"** It's the request many young cooks are given when trying out for a job in the finest kitchens around the world—a make-or-break moment in every young toque's life. Executing a perfectly cooked egg, on the spot, is more than the sign of a skilled line cook who has the chops to navigate an omelet, a poach, or an over easy. It's an opportunity to assess the candidate's behavior under pressure—to see how the cook performs in the literal heat of the kitchen. And eggs are delicious, so there's always the promise of a good snack at the test's completion.

The focus here is on the scrambled egg, a big favorite of Daniel and Matt's. Unlike the folded omelet, the scramble—while requiring patience—doesn't need any special pan or spatula skills. Scrambled eggs are about texture and flavor, not perfect edges and angles, which can send even the most slightly neurotic home cook into a spiral.

The first thing to keep in mind for perfect scrambled eggs is that you need much more butter than you think—like a teaspoon or more per egg. Yes, more than you think. Butter adds flavor and richness, and it keeps the eggs from sticking to the pan. The second important factor is heat. Soft scrambled eggs require very low heat for a longer amount of time than you think—in fact, properly scrambled eggs take upward of twelve minutes for the best results. Cook them too quickly and you'll get big, hard chunks of cooked egg mixed with a raw runny mess or, worse yet, crunchy browned bits throughout. The goal is to slowly heat the eggs, mixing them constantly until they just set, then voilà.

A French omelet is simply scrambled eggs that have been allowed to cook for a final extra moment to set the outside into a shell. For a reference, check out the Jacques Pépin omelet video on YouTube, one of Daniel and Matt's favorite food things on the Internet. "It is difficult to make a real good omelet," Pépin confirms in a silky Franco-American accent that reminds of his upbringing in Bourg-en-Bresse, before making two versions (the country omelet and the classic French omelet) in less than five minutes in the least difficult manner. Pépin is the sun all egg cooks revolve around. Long live the scrambled egg.

SCRAMBLED EGGS WITH AMERICAN CHEESE

Serves 1 generously

3 eggs

1 teaspoon kosher salt

2 tablespoons water

1 tablespoon unsalted butter

2 slices American cheese, cut into 1-inch squares

There is no dish taken for granted more often than scrambled eggs, and it makes sense. Most Americans grow up eating aggressively cooked supermarket eggs for breakfast at home, or late at night with hash browns at the diner. The technique with which those eggs were cooked before landing on the plate can often be an afterthought. But gently scramble a farm-fresh egg, and the dish is a completely different experience. Rich and flavorful. Creamy and satisfying. So take advantage of the opportunity to eat better eggs when you do eat them—fresh from the farmers' market is the best option (and the option Daniel and Matt strive for). And a word on butter: Buy good-quality European-style butter, and use it to cook your scrambled eggs. It's an integral ingredient, not just a coating to stop the eggs from sticking to the pan.

1. Crack the eggs into a bowl, add the salt and water, and whisk together until blended.

2. Melt the butter in a 10-inch nonstick frying pan over medium-low heat. Add the eggs, scraping them out of the bowl with a rubber spatula. Cook, stirring continuously as they begin to heat. Avoid the temptation to accelerate the process. When the eggs begin to set, fold them so that no cooked eggs remain in contact with the pan long enough to set completely. The cooking process should take about 10 minutes.

3. When the eggs start to set, stir in the cheese and continue cooking until the cheese melts and disappears, about 2 minutes.

4. When the eggs resemble loose and wet cottage cheese, remove them from the heat and plate immediately. The eggs will continue to cook after you remove them from the pan, so stop a little earlier than you think you should.

How do I bake chocolate chip cookies with an extreme level of confidence?

→ **EVERYONE HAS A HOT** and chewy take on what makes a chocolate chip cookie one of the most iconic American foods, beloved around the world. Each manifestation has its fan base, whether it's Mrs. Fields cookie cakes; the recipe pressed into your palm by Ruth Graves Wakefield, the guardian of the Toll House cookie; or the many boutique chocolate chip cookie sellers appearing in the listicles of your favorite city publication. Should the cookie be thick or thin? Cakey or crispy? What about the chocolate ratio? How big should it be? Wheat flour or rye flour or a blend? Extra salty? All of these factors are up for debate, and Daniel and Matt are not here to say which one is the best.

The best chocolate chip cookie is a matter of personal preference, but it's also a matter of trend. In 2020, Matt's *TASTE* colleague Kaitlin Bray wrote a fascinating article titled "Did Instagram Ruin the Chocolate Chip Cookie?" Bray's contention was that the cookie had lost its way. "If your Instagram feed is anything like mine, I suspect many of the cookies racking up likes are deeply flawed. These oozing blobs are woefully imbalanced, often too bitter, too salty, and not structurally sound," she wrote of the cookies popular at the time for having a disproportionate chocolate-to-cookie ratio that would make even Jacques Torres blush. Back in 1936, when Wakefield, a Massachusetts chef and owner of the Toll House Inn, dropped chopped pieces of a chocolate bar into a butter drop cookie recipe, altering the cookie world forever, twelve ounces was considered the correct amount of chocolate for sixty cookies. Today, that is suitable for twenty. The reason for the chocolate arms race by recipe writers of all backgrounds (Martha, Ina, Dorie, and Kenji have all increased their chocolate amounts in recent cookie recipes) is the prevailing attitude in food media that more is often better. And as our tastes shift from ultrasweet to more bitter, pressing the cacao gas pedal and leaning in to dark chocolate has become the road ahead.

We're here to offer some suggestions, with a handy chart that breaks down the different ways to make the chocolate chip cookie match your taste. If you want it crispy, granulated sugar is the key. If you want it cakey, brown sugar will get you there. Follow this chart and choose your own adventure. ●

friend of
FOOD IQ

CLAIRE SAFFITZ is a chef, cookbook author, and prodigious baker. You may know Claire from her ridiculously cool videos on the *Bon Appétit* video series *Gourmet Makes*. We know her from her best-selling debut cookbook, *Dessert Person*—and now for besmirching the reputation of the cookie.

Please rank the following: pies, cakes, cookies.

Pies are number one because I am a pie person. Pies are, for me, a primary mode of doing justice to the seasons. You can always take what's seasonal and beautiful and enhance it and honor it in a pie, I think. That said, I think a lot of pies are pretty terrible.

Wait, so pies are bad?

I'm not talking about the tabletop pies you buy from the grocery store; I'm talking about a beautifully done, seasonal pie with fresh produce and an all-butter crust. My number two is cake. And, of course, we're talking about vast categories here. Cakes fall on a spectrum, and there are so many different varieties. But I would then say cake because I always enjoy that cakey texture—something light, with that little bit of sponginess and hints of vanilla and all that. Plus, cake is just so celebratory.

What about cookies?

While chocolate chip cookies, and especially *warm* chocolate chip cookies, would be one of my favorite things to eat in the world, I think I generally derive less pleasure and can express less creativity through cookies because it's sort of a stricter format, and there aren't as many opportunities to use fresh ingredients. Cookies aren't really my forte, but I realize how important they are for portability and ease.

And is there a wild card category we've forgotten?

Tarts and anything in the puff pastry category. Tarts, to me, are just the epitome of elegance and simplicity. Especially a galette. You get that better ratio of crust to filling, and it's just so elegant. I love making them.

CHOOSE-YOUR-OWN-ADVENTURE CHOCOLATE CHIP COOKIES

Most savory-inclined cooks (read: non-bakers) lack the confidence to bake with creative abandon like they do when cooking a back-pocket Tuesday night primavera, or throwing together an after-work snack with fridge scraps. That's because they know small ingredient changes can have a big impact when baking, and there's no way to taste and adjust a brown butter blondie along the way. But with a basic understanding of each ingredient's impact on the whole recipe, and a base ratio to work from, learning to bake creatively is within everyone's reach. Take a look at the chart on pages 256 to 257, which breaks down chocolate chip cookie recipes by ingredients as a percentage of the flour weight. You'll see how the cookie's evolution from extra crispy to ooey-gooey chewy is accomplished by shifting the fat, sugar, and egg ratios. Technique plays a significant role in the outcome as well: Cooking at a lower temperature gives the butter a chance to melt before the eggs set, producing a thinner, wider cookie. Creaming the butter and sugar together both helps jump-start the caramelization process, giving your cookies a deeper flavor, and makes their texture more uniform throughout. Play with the recipes below to create your personal ultimate chocolate chip cookie recipe.

1. Using a stand mixer fitted with the paddle attachment, cream the butter on high speed until soft and malleable, about 3 minutes. Add half each of the white sugar and brown sugar, the salt, and vanilla and continue beating on high speed until the sugars have dissolved, about 4 minutes.

2. Stop the mixer and scrape down the sides of the bowl. On low speed, add the remaining white and brown sugar and the eggs, and mix just until incorporated, about 1 minute.

3. Stop the mixer and scrape down the sides of the bowl. In a bowl, stir together the flour and baking soda. On low speed, add the flour mixture and mix just until incorporated, about 3 minutes. Add the chocolate chips and mix until just incorporated. Baking your chocolate chip cookies from room temperature will yield thinner disks, while chilling the dough will help keep them thick and chewy.

4. If you want a thin, crisp cookie, preheat your oven to 325°F. Scoop the dough into 1-inch balls and arrange the balls on a sheet pan, spacing them at least 6 inches apart. Bake the cookies, rotating the pan front to back halfway through baking, until deeply browned, thin, and bubbling, 14 to 16 minutes. Let cool on the pan on a wire rack for 5 minutes, then transfer the cookies to the rack to cool completely.

5. If you want a thicker, chewier cookie, cover the bowl and chill the dough in the refrigerator for at least 1 hour or up to 2 days. Preheat the oven to 400°F. Scoop the dough into 1-inch balls and arrange the balls on a sheet pan, spacing them at least 6 inches apart. Bake the cookies, rotating the pan front to back halfway through baking, until lightly browned, 11 to 13 minutes. Let cool on the pan on a wire rack for 5 minutes, then transfer the cookies to the rack to cool completely.

**Makes thirty-six
4-inch cookies**

extra crispy   crispy

	%	GRAMS	CUPS	%	GRAMS	CUPS
Flour	100%	190	1.5 cups	100%	210	1.75 cups
White Sugar	105%	200	1 cup	95%	200	1 cup
Brown Sugar	149%	283	1.25 cups	107%	225	1 cup
Butter	139%	264	18 tbsp	107%	225	2 sticks
Eggs	53%	101	2	24%	51	1 ea
Vanilla	5%	9	2 tsp	7%	14	1 tbsp
Salt	3%	5	1 tsp	4%	8	2 tsp
Baking Soda	2%	3	.5 tsp	4%	8	1½ tsp
Chocolate	179%	340	12 oz	162%	340	12 oz
Total Weight		1395			1281	

average			thick 'n' cakey			soft 'n' chewy		
%	GRAMS	CUPS	%	GRAMS	CUPS	%	GRAMS	CUPS
100%	286	2.25 cups	100%	286	2.25 cup	100%	318	2.66 cups
87%	248	1.25 cups	52%	149	.75 cup	0%		
19%	53	.25 cup	19%	53	.25 cup	100%	318	1.5 cups
79%	227	2 sticks	69%	198	14 tbsp	71%	227	2 sticks
18%	51	1 ea	36%	102	2 ea	32%	102	2 ea
5%	14	1 tbsp	3%	10	2 tsp	4%	14	1 tbs
2%	5	1 tsp	2%	5	1 tsp	2%	5	1 tsp
2%	7	1 tsp	1%	4	.5 tsp	2%	7	1 tsp
119%	340	12 oz	119%	340	12 oz	107%	340	12 oz
	1231			1147			1331	

Why is my whole roast chicken always dry?

→ **WHAT CAN BE SAID** that hasn't been said about roasting a chicken? It is, by the authors' estimates, one of the most written about, discussed, debated (and sometimes actually cooked) recipes of all time. Almost everybody has some connection to roasting a chicken at home—including the chicken-adjacent turkey on Thanksgiving. So we all know the approximate benchmarks for when a roast chicken is done right (moist, juicy, flavorful, crispy) and when it's done the opposite of right. Therefore, the strategy behind this question is to dissect what is happening when a chicken is not properly cooked, with the hope that pointing out these errors will steer you in the right direction.

First, and most critical, is that chicken is summarily underseasoned and overcooked. Also, and very much related, is the fact that home cooks often underestimate the time it takes to properly season chicken in advance of cooking. If you've read the question about properly seasoning meat (see page 108), these lines will act as a bit of an echo, but they are worth repeating. Salt takes time to penetrate the meat—an hour or more per pound. And adding salt isn't just about adding flavor. It also raises the boiling point of the water molecules within the protein, allowing the meat to cook at a higher temperature without breaking down the cells, which is what causes the meat to dry out. A well-salted piece of chicken essentially prevents itself from overcooking. If you season a whole chicken, inside and out, and then pop it directly into the oven, only the outer layer will be seasoned, and you won't benefit from the protective properties of salt.

Second, different parts of the chicken cook differently, and for different amounts of time. For example, a breast may react better to dry-heat roasting, while fattier thighs may take better to braising. When you roast the entire bird in one go, you are attempting to get the best of both worlds. You are compromising. But you cannot have it all. The most important thing to keep in mind is that the breast always cooks faster than the dark meat (we're looking at you, drumsticks and thighs). Adding to this conundrum is that the breast has less fat and is therefore inherently drier, so you risk overcooking an already dry cut of meat.

There are a couple of ways to mitigate this risk. You can spatchcock, which is a way of butterflying and flattening the bird, allowing for maximum exposure to heat and more even cooking. The downside is that the presentation of the whole chicken is lost, which is arguably the primary reason you chose to roast a whole bird in the first place. The other option is to roast the chicken at a lower temperature. By roasting it at 225°F for 1¼ hours, instead of 350°F for 40 minutes, you are slowly heating all of the meat consistently, which cooks the breast and dark meat more evenly. But what say you regarding that crispy skin? Surely your slowly roasted bird will be pale and soggy? There's a second crucial step that you can add a little bit later.

Which brings us to the subject of nap time. This point cannot be written enough in this book, or spoken on podcasts, or tattooed on one's forearm (send us the pics): all meat needs to rest. When a chicken is pulled from the oven, the outside begins to cool while the heat continues to migrate inward, allowing the inner dark meat to reach doneness and the outer breast to cool and stop cooking. You should think about resting your meat for several minutes a pound. For example, a five-pound chicken should sit out for at least twenty minutes, if not more. In fact, an hour is ideal. This is why chicken that's rested and reheated (or served at room temperature) is often so moist and delicious. Hello, rotisserie chicken from Costco.

Finally, what about that crispy skin? If you are thinking that crispy skin is only the product of high-heat cooking, you're right! The trick to turning out moist chicken with crispy skin is to heat your oven to 500°F while the chicken is resting, then pop the bird back in to blast the skin and reheat the flesh for an additional ten minutes. The skin will be deeply browned, the breast will be moist and tender, and all will be right with the world. ●

MARINATED ROAST CHICKEN WITH SUMAC, LEMON, AND SALT

Serves 4

1 (3½-pound) whole chicken

Kosher salt

2 tablespoons sumac powder

Juice of 1 lemon

2 tablespoons extra-virgin olive oil

This recipe was inspired by a roast chicken recipe in *Moro East* by Sam and Sam Clark, the book that first introduced Daniel to Lebanese cuisine. Sumac is a red berry that is high in vitamin C and has a brightly tart flavor, and using it is a great way to add acidity to a dish without the moisture that comes with lemon juice or vinegar. If you're up for a little foraging adventure, sumac grows wild all over the northeastern United States, fruiting in the late summer and early fall. The foot-long, velvet-textured, blood-red fruits are easy to spot growing alongside highways. To harvest, you simply cut the fruit from the shrub, rub the small red berries off into a bowl, whirl them in a blender, and then sift through a medium-fine strainer, separating the small, inedible black seeds from the tart red powder. You can also find sumac powder in most spice shops and online.

1. Rub the chicken inside and out generously with salt (aim for 1.5 percent by weight, or about 2 tablespoons). Season inside and out with the sumac and lemon juice, cover with plastic wrap, and refrigerate for at least 24 hours or up to 4 days.

2. An hour before cooking, pull the chicken out of the refrigerator and rub it all over with the oil.

3. Preheat the oven to 325°F.

4. Place the chicken, breast side up, on a rack in a baking dish or pan. Roast until an instant-read thermometer inserted into the breast away from bone registers 125°F, about 1¼ hours.

5. Remove the chicken from the oven, cover it with foil, and let rest for 30 minutes.

6. Increase the oven temperature to 500°F. Uncover the chicken and return it to the oven to reheat, cooking until the skin is a deep golden brown, about 25 minutes. Let rest uncovered for 10 minutes before carving to serve.

FOOD IQ

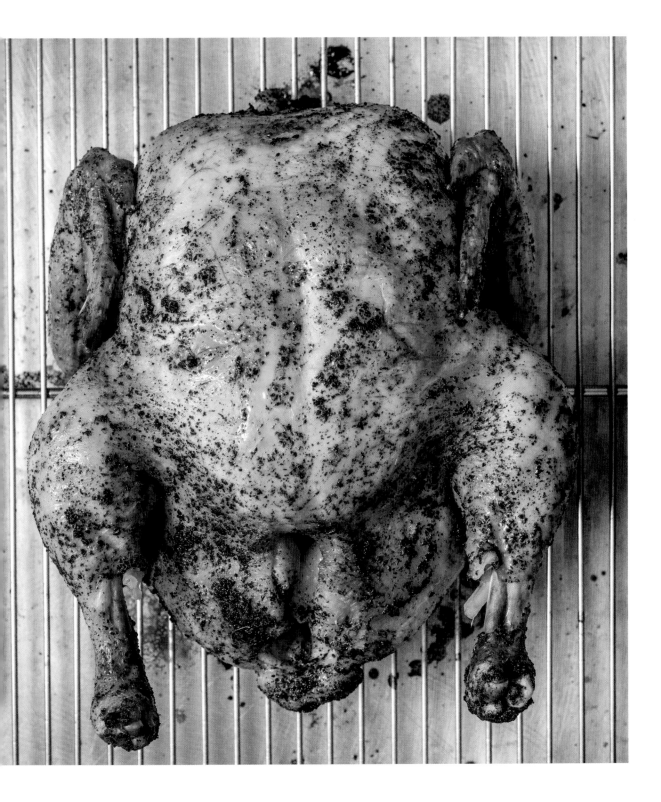

How do I make a truly exceptional hamburger?

→ **GOOD QUESTION! (DID YOU** just say that aloud?) But most of us love hamburgers for different reasons. This is because there are many different hamburgers to love. Some like them thick and juicy with the metallic kiss of ultra-rare meat. Others like a sloppy mess of melted cheese and condiments, the patty playing second fiddle. Some prefer them smashed, and others favor them grilled over an open flame. Most of us like a fast-food burger, but we'll debate the merits of In-N-Out Burger versus Shake Shack for three rounds at the bar. Our personal tastes typically align with a great restaurant burger experience. Indeed, rarely will you hear folks at the office remark on how their buddy's backyard burger blew them away last weekend. Daniel and Matt must acknowledge that recommending "the best" burger method is hardly the best for everyone. But this is as close as it comes.

It all starts with the meat, and the understanding that not all ground beef is created equal. Simply put, the more fat you have in the ground beef, the more flavorful the burger will be. A pretty standard baseline is beef labeled 80–20, which describes the ratio of meat (80 percent) to fat (20 percent) and is often simply labeled "80 percent lean ground beef." Reaching for a 90–10 will likely yield a dry, hockey puck–style burger, and anything lower than 70 percent lean beef will tend to shrink as the fat renders out or, worse yet, drip and ignite if you're cooking over an open-flame grill. The good news is that ground beef is priced according to the percentage of lean meat, so the higher the fat percentage, the lower the cost (within the same grade of beef)—a win-win for you.

Which brings you to the meat itself. Cheap supermarket meat is often a conglomerate of scraps from multiple sources (and sometimes many animals). This isn't necessarily a bad thing, but beware the ground beef sale sign: the cheapest meat can be pretty funky stuff (there have been reports of bleaching scraps for the ground beef market). Great burgers start with whole muscles, ground chuck being the most typical. But many cuts are used for grinding, each with subtle differences of flavor, texture, and fat content. If you're really getting into it (and good for you for asking this question!), you can also select your grind size, with a larger grind offering a more toothsome bite. Ask your butcher to help you with that.

With the beef selected, all that's left to do is form and season it. Daniel is firm in his opinion that burgers should be formed first, then seasoned a few minutes before cooking—long enough for the salt to partially penetrate but not long enough for the beef to begin to cure. There are, however, plenty of chefs who would argue for seasoning the mix before forming in order to salt the entire burger evenly. Daniel is staunchly against adding other ingredients to the meat, with the exception of the cheesy pride of Minneapolis, the Juicy Lucy, of course.

Next, there's the cooking surface, which can be broken into two camps: the flat-top griddle (hi, McDonald's) and the open-flame grill (helllllllo, Burger King). Cast-iron pans, or any frying pan for that matter, would technically fall into the flat-top category. Arguments exist on either side of the griddle versus grill debate, and Daniel is not going to die on this hill. But each has a clear benefit. Chargrilled meat is flavor forward and wins in the ease of cleanup category. Flat tops are easier to manage, offering a clean flavor with the distinct advantage of indoor cooking. Matt is, hands down, a fan of the flat top. Char equals bitter and masks some of the inherent flavors of the ground beef. Let the beef speak! Daniel thinks that arguing against a grilled burger is an extremely weak position. But you, the home cook, should make your own decision and live with it.

Finally, some words about condiments and buns. A perfect burger is all about balance; no single component should overpower another. Most would define the "special" sauce as a casual mixture of ketchup, mustard, and mayonnaise—and maybe a little relish, plus a dash of Worcestershire sauce or Tabasco. Do burgers require a sauce? No. Buns come down to texture and should be chosen based on the type of burger. The thicker and juicier the burger, the stronger the bun needs to be. Potato or Hawaiian rolls are perfect for thin-patty smash burgers, while kaiser rolls or soft baguettes are a better choice for rare bistro burgers. What you put on top is your preference. Grilled onions and Swiss? Bacon and Cheddar? Classic American cheese with lettuce, tomato, and raw onion?

In general, both Daniel and Matt fall into the "less is more" camp. Matt prefers his burgers austere and always topped with American or Cheddar cheese—there is no such thing as a plain hamburger in his world. Daniel isn't a precious hamburger guy, so he likes it however the chef is serving them up.

Did this answer the hamburger question, or simply complicate things further? Burgers are highly subjective beasts, but if you follow the recipe below, you'll be on the right track. ●

DANIEL AND MATT'S TOP FIVE BURGERS

Daniel: **Au Cheval** (Chicago), **In-N-Out** (all over the American West), **Diner** (NYC), **Corner Bistro** (NYC), **McDonald's** Big Mac (that's right, all you haters).

Matt: **Cassell's** (Los Angeles), **Veselka** (NYC), **Shake Shack** (NYC; this is 2005 Matt speaking, when the burgers were served at a humble stand in a Manhattan park), **White Castle** (everywhere, but mostly the Midwest), **Superiority Burger** (NYC; the best vegetable burger on the planet).

OKLAHOMA FRIED ONION BURGERS

Makes 2 double-double burgers

1 sweet onion, sliced as thinly as possible on a mandoline (see page 60)

Kosher salt

1 tablespoon vegetable oil

10 ounces 80 percent lean ground beef, portioned into 4 balls

4 slices American cheese

2 potato rolls, split (Matt recommends Martin's, but any will do)

Few people remember that White Castle was the original fast-food burger joint. Closing in on a hundred years ago, Billy Ingram started frying his mini patties over thinly sliced grilled onions in Wichita, Kansas, and the White Castle slider was born. Say what you will about fast-food restaurants and their effect on the American food system (there aren't many good things to say), but there's no denying their influence on American gastronomy. The fried onion smash burger has fallen from fashion (though burger scholar George Motz might disagree), but Daniel swears that it's the best burger he's ever made at home. The trick to making a great one is slicing your onions ultrathin and salting them so they lose their moisture and fry up faster—you want the onions crispy brown, on the verge of burnt black.

1. In a bowl, mix the onion slices with 1 tablespoon salt and let rest for 20 minutes. Drain the onion slices, squeezing out any excess water, then mix them with the oil.

2. Heat a large cast-iron griddle or 12-inch frying pan over medium-high heat until smoking hot. Make four piles of sliced onion in the pan, then nestle a beef ball on top of each pile. Using a stiff metal spatula, smash each ball down into the frying onion slices to flatten it. Cook them on high until the onions are deeply browned around the edges, about 4 minutes.

3. Then flip the burgers and onion over and lay a slice of cheese on top of each. Arrange the roll halves, cut side down, over the top to steam and cook the burgers for 2 minutes longer. Transfer the rolls, cut side up, to two plates and scoop two patties, with all of the crispy melted cheese and onions, onto the warmed roll bottoms, cover with the roll tops, and serve immediately.

What is the best way to braise chicken?

→ **MATT'S WIFE, TAMAR ANITAI,** pulled up a chair when Daniel and Matt started talking about braising chicken—specifically discussing the trio's mutual appreciation for and mild obsession with a style that originates in the Basque region, an autonomous community that encompasses the western Pyrenees Mountains bordering the Bay of Biscay in northern Spain. While the people living in the region are proudly independent—and speak a language that has no ties to any other language in the world—anyone who has traveled around the region has no doubt that the cuisine is influenced by both Spain and France. Sausages, cheese (hi, Idiazábal), pintxos, percebes, and wine (hello, txakoli) from the region are all considered world class, and for years, the region has been home to some of the most celebrated restaurants in the world, including Arzak, El Bulli (RIP), Mugaritz, and Asador Etxebarri, Daniel's favorite grill restaurant in the world. Amazing food abounds in the region, but when the three got to talking, the conversation centered on chicken, and specifically the best braised chicken known to man: chicken Basquaise.

Basque cuisine is informed by its mountainous terrain, dry heat, and proximity to the sea. Spicy peppers are grown and celebrated throughout the region and, along with dried chorizo, onions, garlic, and tomatoes, play an important role in building the flavor profile of this incredible and classic chicken braise. The precise ingredients vary, with as many specific recipes as there are households in the region, and each family priding itself on its own iteration. Daniel fell in love with the dish and developed his recipe while working for chef Laurent Manrique in San Francisco. Tamar fell hard for the stewy dish while waiting to board a flight east at the Delta terminal at LAX, where she stumbled upon Basque chicken at Lemonade, a quick-serve chainlet popular in Southern California. A recipe from Lemonade's 2013 cookbook includes artichoke hearts and olives, and it's now her gospel.

Overall, this is a serious chicken dish for a less serious weeknight dinner—a great fridge cleaner that works well with most vegetables and can be served over rice or potatoes. The cooked dish will last for up to five or so days in the refrigerator, making it an ideal recipe for a week's worth of quick lunches and dinners. Once mastered, chicken Basquaise will quickly become one of your go-to suppers, inspired by the authors' love for regional Spanish foodways and by another person's memorable time at the Los Angeles International Airport food court. ●

CHICKEN BASQUAISE

Daniel has honed this recipe over the years and landed on a real winner. The chorizo works with the tomatoes to give the dish a mildly spicy, rich, and acidic balance that creates a remarkable flavor combination. You can add more vegetables to the braise if you prefer a heartier stew. Daniel often pitches in red potatoes, which soak up the flavor from the sauce.

Serves 4

4 whole chicken legs (thigh and drumstick)

4 teaspoons kosher salt

3 tablespoons extra-virgin olive oil

6 cloves garlic, smashed

4 ounces Spanish dry chorizo (ideally Palacios brand), sliced into thin rounds

½ red onion, cut into ¾-inch dice

1 red bell pepper, stemmed, seeded, and cut into ¾-inch dice

1 teaspoon sweet paprika

½ cup dry red wine

1 (14-ounce) can chopped tomatoes with their juice

1½ cups chicken stock (or substitute bouillon)

2 bay leaves

4 cups warm cooked white rice

1. Season the chicken legs with the salt, rubbing it all over, and then set them aside for at least an hour or for up to overnight in the refrigerator.

2. When ready to cook, heat the oil in an 8-quart Dutch oven or other heavy-bottomed pot over high heat until it just begins to smoke. Add the chicken legs, skin side down, and cook until well browned, about 6 minutes. Then flip the legs to brown the second side, about 5 minutes. Transfer the chicken to a plate.

3. Lower the heat to medium-high and add the garlic, chorizo, onion, and bell pepper and cook, stirring frequently, until the onion is soft and translucent, about 8 minutes.

4. Add the paprika and stir to incorporate. Then deglaze the pot, adding the wine and raising the heat to high to bring it to a boil. Scrape up any caramelized bits (fond) that have built up on the bottom of the pot, then cook until the wine is almost completely evaporated, about 5 minutes.

5. Add the tomatoes, stock, and bay leaves and bring to a simmer. Adjust the heat to medium-low, nestle the chicken legs into the pot, cover partially, and simmer for 1 hour. The chicken should be tender but not falling off the bone.

6. Scoop 1 cup of the rice onto each of four individual plates. Serve the chicken and sauce over the rice.

How do I make great pizza?

→ **ASK ANY PROUD NEW** Yorker, and they'll tell you THE RULES of pizza. How do you properly eat a slice? Fold it in half and dodge the dripping pepperoni oil before rushing to a meeting, an off Broadway play, or home to pass out at four-thirty in the morning. Which toppings are allowed? Cheese (called a "regular slice") or silver-dollar-size pepperoni is preferred. Sausage, peppers, mushrooms, and onions are all allowed. Never pineapple. Buffalo chicken passes modern-day muster. New York City is proud of its pizza. After all, pizza by the slice was invented there when Gennaro Lombardi came up with the idea to serve his pies piecemeal at Lombardi's, the first pizzeria planted in American soil, opened on Spring Street in 1905 and still baking pies out of its original coal oven.

Lombardi's pizza was adapted from the pies of Naples, Italy, where modern-day pizza was invented in the late eighteenth century by adding tomato and cheese to flatbread (focaccia). The popularity of pizza exploded in the United States following the Italian migration, with each region developing its own nuanced idiosyncrasies to suit local tastes using available local ingredients. Think Chicago deep dish, Detroit cheese crust, and Connecticut clam pie.

Daniel has been making pizza for many years now. His first job, at the age of fourteen, was delivering pies for Gino's, across from his childhood apartment on Eighty-Third Street in Manhattan. He learned to make Neapolitan-style pizza in his early twenties at a pizza-pasta wine bar in San Francisco, then later worked with a master pizza maker named John Arena to hone his craft before opening his own slice joint—Danny Boy's Famous Original—in downtown Los Angeles. All this is to say that he knows what he's talking about when it comes to melting cheese on round tomato bread. Matt has been along for the ride and is proud of his partner for embarking on a journey to becoming a legit pizzaiolo.

The number-one rule for home pizza making is to acknowledge that the final outcome is not determined mere minutes before the pie is served. Pizza is made (or seriously messed up) by the many decisions throughout the process, starting way ahead of time with your selection of style and ingredients. Depending on the equipment you have on hand, your first choice is whether to make a pan pie (square slices baked in a pan) or a regular slice pie (round pie baked on a stone). If you have both a stone and a pan, the choice is yours (without a proper stone, you're relegated to panned pizza for the time being). From there, preparation is everything, and this begins with the dough, which has a near-infinite number of outcomes determined by the type of flour, the amount of olive oil and salt, the fermentation time and style, and, most important, the hydration—that is to say, the amount of water added to the dough. How much water is added is important with pizza. Those slices with giant air bubbles? There's lots of water in there. The classic NYC slice cooked in a gas-fired Bakers Pride bread oven is thin, crisp, and has way less water.

Delicious and, frankly, noticeable dough flavor takes time to develop and is best started the night before by kneading high-protein wheat flour with water, yeast, salt, and olive oil. Yeast is a living organism, and the warmer the environment, the faster it works. So if you want a longer fermentation time, your best bet is to keep it cool, storing the dough in the refrigerator overnight. The longer the fermentation, the more flavor will develop. But there's a critical balance to observe: wait too long and the yeast will run out of food, imploding on itself and resulting in a flat pizza that doesn't rise, with a blanket of sadness all around. It takes time to learn the small idiosyncrasies that help you navigate the process, and there's no real shortcut other than experience, so be patient and feel your dough at every stage to help familiarize yourself with its different symptoms.

The next day, you'll want to portion and ball your dough, stretching it around itself to create a tightly packed sphere about the size of a softball. The last stage in the dough-making process is the final rise, or proofing. This is where you let your dough warm up, waking the yeast before baking. You'll know you're ready to bake when a finger gently pressed into the dough ball leaves an indentation rather than bouncing back—this happens around 55°F.

If you're using a pizza stone, make sure to heat it for at least an hour before baking your first pie. Investing in a heavy pizza stone—one that holds heat—is pretty critical to achieving an evenly cooked pie with a crisp crust. Beware that many stones sold at kitchen stores are way too thin to retain enough heat for multiple pies, so you'll want to give the stone time to recover its heat between pies. Ideally, your stone is one inch thick—a little pricier than most, but the investment will be well worth it.

When the dough is ready, it's time to stretch it (being careful not to press down on the outside crust), top it with toppings (less is more when it comes to toppings, so don't overload your pie), and bake it. About those toppings: Wet toppings are pizza's number-one enemy; add too much moisture, and your crust will never crisp up properly. Your best bet for an excellent pie is to precook the toppings to dry them out a bit—sautéed mushrooms or spinach, roasted peppers or onions, cooked and crumbled sausage.

Making pizza at home is a lifetime journey of trial and error, and many books have been written about the process, the best of which is *The Pizza Bible* by Tony Gemignani. To get you started, here's a great home recipe for making a classic New York–style pie. •

NEW YORK-STYLE PIZZA DOUGH AND SAUCE

Great dough starts with great ingredients, and you'll want to get your hands on high-protein bread flour for the best results (look for brands like King Arthur or General Mills). For the classic New York pie, you'll want to source Grande or Polly-O mozzarella cheese, which is semidry and formed in plastic-covered loaves—not the fresh stuff that comes packed in water. Daniel's tomato sauce is always made from Stanislaus canned tomatoes, the pride of Modesto, California, so get yourself a can of chopped tomatoes in their juice, and mix it with a little olive oil, salt, garlic powder, and oregano, then water it down to pourable applesauce consistency. Can't find Stanislaus? San Marzano brand, Bianco DiNapoli or your favorite brand will work well too. And while the great majority of these recipes in *Food IQ* use volumetric measurements (that is, cups and teaspoons), using weight to calculate the ingredient amounts for the dough is critical here. It's yet another example of why you should invest in a digital scale (see page 56).

Makes four 11-ounce dough balls for 13-inch pies

750 grams bread flour

4 grams active dry yeast (about ½ packet)

465 grams ice-cold water

15 grams extra-virgin olive oil

17 grams kosher salt

For the Dough

1. Put the flour into the bowl of a stand mixer fitted with the dough hook. Sprinkle the yeast over the top, then add the water and mix on the lowest speed for 2 minutes.

2. Stop the mixer, cover the bowl with a damp kitchen towel, and let rest for 20 minutes.

3. Increase the speed to medium-high and continue mixing while slowly adding the oil and salt until completely combined, about 2 minutes. Reduce the speed to low and continue mixing for 6 minutes. If your mixer is struggling, remove the dough from the bowl and knead by hand on a lightly floured surface until silky smooth and elastic, about 10 minutes. This is your workout!

4. Transfer the dough to a large bowl, cover the bowl tightly with plastic wrap, and refrigerate overnight. (The dough will double in size, so make sure the bowl is big enough.)

5. About 2 hours before baking, remove the dough from the fridge, divide it into four equal portions, and ball it, stretching it around itself to form a taut sphere.

6. Allow the dough to warm to 55°F before stretching.

Makes about 2 cups;
enough for eight 13-
inch pizzas

2 cloves garlic, chopped

¼ cup extra-virgin
olive oil

1 (28-ounce) can
crushed tomatoes

1 teaspoon dried or
fresh oregano

1 teaspoon garlic
powder

Small pinch of red chile
flakes

2 teaspoons kosher
salt

For the Sauce

1. In a heavy-bottomed 4-quart pot, combine the chopped garlic and oil over low heat and cook, stirring occasionally, until the garlic is soft and fragrant, about 8 minutes. Do not allow it to brown.

2. Add the tomatoes, oregano, garlic powder, chiles flakes, and salt, raise the heat to high, and bring the sauce to a boil. Lower the heat to a simmer and simmer uncovered, stirring frequently, for 35 minutes. Remove from the heat and let cool before using. Leftover sauce can be stored in an airtight container in the refrigerator for up to 1 week and in the freezer for up to 2 months.

Makes 1 pizza

1 proofed dough ball
at 55°F

1 cup bread flour, for
stretching and dusting

¼ cup pizza sauce
(recipe above)

4 ounces firm (not
fresh) mozzarella
cheese, shredded

For the Pizza

1. Place your pizza stone on the center rack of your oven, then preheat the oven to 500°F for 1 hour before baking.

2. Pour the flour onto the large, flat work surface where you intend to stretch your dough. Using a bench scraper, gently lift the dough ball from its proofing bowl and place it in the flour. Then, using your hands, scoop some flour over the ball, covering it completely.

3. Working from the center outward, gently press the dough into a rough round, then, working slowly, stretch it with your knuckles until it reaches 13 inches in diameter. Do not touch the outermost rim.

4. Gently lift the dough round and shake off the excess flour onto a wooden paddle (aka a pizza peel; a thin wooden cutting board will work as a substitute). Place the flattened dough on the paddle and stretch the edges into a circle. Spoon on the tomato sauce, using the back of the spoon to distribute it evenly up to the edge of the crust. Distribute the cheese evenly over the top.

5. Slide the pizza onto the pizza stone by gently shaking the peel at a 45-dgree angle to the stone and pulling backward as the pizza slides off. Bake the pie, rotating it 180 degrees halfway through baking, until the edge of the crust is deeply browned, about 8 minutes. Use the paddle to retrieve the pie from the oven, then cool for 1 minute on a wire rack before serving.

Do I need a smoker and a southern drawl to make great barbecue ribs?

→ **YES ON THE DRAWL,** no on the smoker. Wait, no, the other way around! It's an unfortunate necessity that the smoked and seasoned ribs, the ones with the pinkish-gray flesh that make your hands smell like smoke in the most enjoyable way for hours after the meal, require smoking to get that way. You'll need a barbecue setup where meat is smoked (and cooked at a low temperature) with hardwood to properly barbecue ribs. This is because "barbecue" is a defined term. It's not grilling (that's cooking over an open flame, often involving charcoal). Grilling is not barbecuing—even though barbecuing is what some people wrongfully refer to anytime there's meat cooked over fire. So the barbecue ribs people rave about are, by definition, the product of smoking with hardwood and cooked in a smoker.

But back to the original question, which, for the record, is placed in this section because barbecued ribs are Matt's singular, all-time favorite, ride-or-die food. You will hear from his mother below about his early love of ribs. If you remove the barbecue from the title, do you really need a smoker to make great ribs at home? It certainly helps, but no, amazing slow-cooked ribs don't require smoke. Great ribs, juicy and falling-off-the-bone ribs, do need to be cooked slowly (over three hours) at a consistent 225°F in a moist environment. And you can create this environment in your oven at home. Will you get that smoky flavor? No, but you will get tender ribs that will be the second-best thing to real Memphis or Texas or Kansas City barbecue.

The thing that makes ribs so singularly unique and delicious is their combination of fat, protein, and connective tissue, all packed tightly together between the bones. When they're slowly cooked, the sinew melts, giving the meat an especially rich mouthfeel, while the fat renders out, basting the flavorful, well-worked meat as it slowly breaks down and tenderizes. The trick to cooking ribs properly is keeping them from drying out (see more in the dry-braising question on page 210). The best way to do this in a conventional oven is to season the ribs, then wrap them in plastic wrap, then in foil, and then bake them. The plastic locks in the moisture while the foil keeps the plastic from burning. Adding sauce to the mix is at your discretion, but beware that rich and fatty cuts of meat need more seasoning than leaner cuts. Whether that sauce is from a bottle (Bull's-Eye was a longtime favorite in Matt's west Michigan household) or homemade, acid is the key to cutting through the fat, so be generous with the vinegar.

It's fair to conclude that Daniel and Matt are not faulting the spareribs from your local Chinese take-out spot or the riblets at Applebee's. There are plenty of traditions where smoke is not present, and they are all really delicious—falling just short of those pulled from a fifty-five-gallon drum smoker. ●

friend of
FOOD IQ

CHERYL RODBARD is a former record store owner and waterbed saleswoman, and later taught kindergarten at Mattawan Early Elementary School for nineteen years. She is also Matt's mom.

Why did Matt love ribs so much?

It was always his preferred vacation food, especially during road trips. Walt's Hitching Post in Kentucky, across the bridge from Cincinnati, was a place we visited when driving to Florida. He also liked local places in Kalamazoo, like Damon's and Fricano's. That boy was never afraid of a messy meal.

You always boil the ribs before roasting them in the oven. Why the boiling step?

We were rendering out the fat that created this chewiness off the bone. The flavor of the meat right next to the bone is best. And we were also dealing with a different kind of rib back then. Now, baby back ribs are not so fatty and overly meaty.

What was your recipe at home?

Once you boil the ribs, dry them off and place them in an oven with a little bit of sauce, and roast them at just over 300°F. We tented [them] with foil and roasted them for a couple of hours on low, then removed the foil for the last bit of time—slathering on sauce at the end.

Matt remembers Open Pit was the family barbecue sauce brand of choice, right?

Yuck, no. Bull's-Eye is what we liked to use. We never really cared for Open Pit. It was too vinegary for ribs.

FOOD IQ

TECHNICALLY-NOT-BARBECUE OVEN RIBS

**Makes 2 racks;
serves 4**

2 full racks baby
back pork ribs

1 tablespoon
kosher salt

1 tablespoon sugar

1 teaspoon chili
powder

1 teaspoon onion
powder

½ teaspoon ground
cumin

½ teaspoon garlic
powder

½ teaspoon black
pepper

1 cup barbecue
sauce, plus more
for serving

This recipe for ribs in the oven, the Rodbard way, comes from Matt's mom, Cheryl. With the absence of a smoker, the oven is the next best bet for preparing moist, succulent ribs. These ribs utilize a dry rub that adds flavor to the meat before a low-and-slow steam roast, thanks to plastic wrap, that gets the meat to fall-off-the-bone status. This recipe calls for the use of your favorite barbecue sauce, be it homemade or a bottle pulled from the grocery store shelf. Bulls-Eye is the Rodbard family favorite.

1. Boil the ribs in salted water to cover for 15 minutes, occasionally skimming off the fat. Remove the racks from the water, let cool, and pat dry. If you don't have a pot large enough to hold whole racks, a roasting pan spanning two burners on the stove top works well.

2. While the ribs boil, make the dry rub. In a small bowl, stir together the salt, sugar, chili powder, onion powder, cumin, garlic powder, and pepper, mixing well.

3. Once the ribs are cooled and dry, rub them all over with the dry rub, then wrap them tightly with plastic wrap and then again with aluminum foil. The ribs can be cooked immediately, but for the best results, allow them to cure for 2 to 3 hours or up overnight in the refrigerator.

4. Preheat the oven to 225°F. Place the wrapped rib racks in a roasting pan, slip the pan into the oven, and bake until the meat is extremely tender and the racks bend when "waved" (think of waving a hankie at a departing ship).

5. To finish, remove the pan from the oven and raise the oven temperature to 400°F. Unwrap the rib racks and coat them with the barbecue sauce. Return the pan to the oven and bake until browned and crusted, about 20 minutes. Let rest for 5 minutes before cutting the racks into individual ribs and serving.

What's the greatest dumpling in the world?

→ **FOR DANIEL, THE ANSWER** is obvious. The greatest dumpling in the world is the matzo ball. Wait, the matzo ball is a dumpling? Daniel believes pretty firmly that the dumpling does not need to have a wrapper. (He and Matt debated this for a good ten minutes before Matt was worn out and steered the conversation to calmer waters.) The truth is that every culture on the planet has a dumpling. It's hard to argue against a Chinese pot sticker (jiān jiǎo) stuffed with sautéed cabbage and fatty ground pork. But, ohhhh . . . what about the Japanese gyoza, smaller than the pot sticker and punching hard with the garlic? But, ohh . . . what about a swing through Russia to taste the pelmeni in Siberia, or the pierogi in Poland, or the vareniki in Ukraine, or the Ashkenazi kreplach in some corner of Eastern Europe?

You see what's happening here? Dumplings are really hard to rank because they span many different flavors and base starches. In the American South, chicken with dumplings rules the land, and in Korea, it's the steamed mandu packed with pork, garlic, ginger, and sometimes simply made with butter and pork. If you've ever seen Park Chan-wook's movie *Oldboy*, mandu will never look the same to you. So, what is the greatest dumpling in the world? It's the one you're making for dinner tonight, or the one you're ordering at your favorite restaurant tomorrow afternoon. It's the dumpling your grandmother makes for you on visits to the Old World (or just a Chicago suburb), and it's one of the greatest foods around. ●

BUTTER MANDU

Makes around 90 dumplings

2 cups roughly chopped green cabbage

2-inch knob fresh ginger, peeled and thinly sliced across the fibers

4 cloves garlic, chopped

2 pounds 80 percent lean ground pork

1 tablespoon kosher salt

1 pound (4 sticks) unsalted butter, cut into chunks and softened to room temperature

90 fresh refrigerated or thawed frozen round Asian dumpling wrappers

Cabbage kimchi, homemade (page 294) or store-bought, for serving

Light soy sauce for serving

Vegetable oil for panfrying (optional)

This recipe originally comes from *Koreatown*, a book Matt wrote with his friend Deuki Hong. This is Deuki's father's mandu recipe, with origins in North Korea, the ancestral home of mandu. (Sharing a border with China, it's no coincidence that mandu sounds a lot like mantou, the Chinese word for steamed bread.) Unlike versions stuffed with finely chopped kimchi, Deuki grew up eating his mandu with kimchi served on the side. The star in this recipe is the very generous quantity of butter, which is mixed in with the pork, garlic, and ginger, adding a real-deal richness to every bite. Not typically used in East Asian cooking, butter is a fully Americanized, fully awesome way to rethink the mandu.

1. Place the cabbage, ginger, and garlic in a food processor and pulse until finely chopped. Transfer the cabbage mixture to a large bowl.

2. Using your hands, fold the pork into the cabbage mixture just enough to combine. Sprinkle in the salt and then gently fold the butter into the mixture until thoroughly combined.

3. To assemble the mandu, set the filling, the dumpling wrappers, and a small glass of water on your work surface. Work with one wrapper at a time so the wrappers don't dry out. Place about 2 tablespoons filling in the center of a wrapper. Be careful not to overfill them, or the wrapper will burst and the filling will leak out during cooking. (If your wrappers are small, decrease the amount of filling per dumpling; the mandu should be full but not difficult to close.) Dip your fingertip into the water and paint the edge of the wrapper, then fold the wrapper over to form a half-moon and pinch the edges together to seal. Mandu can be cooked right away or frozen for later.

TO STEAM: Pour water to a depth of a few inches into a large pot and bring to a boil over high heat. Lightly oil the bottom of a steaming basket with vegetable oil and set the basket over (not touching) the boiling water in the pot. Arrange the mandu in a single layer, not touching, in the basket. Cover the basket and steam until the wrappers appear a little translucent and the filling feels firm to the touch, 5 to 7 minutes. Serve immediately with the kimchi and the soy sauce for dipping.

TO FRY: Coat a sauté pan with vegetable oil and place it over medium heat. When the oil is shimmering hot, place the fresh or thawed mandu in a single layer, not touching, in the pan, and fry, turning once, until golden brown on both sides and cooked through, 3 to 4 minutes on each side if freshly made and 5 to 6 minutes if frozen.

What's the secret to making restaurant-good mac and cheese?

→ **ADDRESSING THIS QUESTION STARTS** with the simple declaration that Kraft mac and cheese from the box is a pretty fine example of mac and cheese. While it's sometimes a little runny if you splash it with too much milk, the radiant yellow hue and the closed-fist punch of powdered cheese is something that nobody should take for granted. Matt had a friend living in Yunnan, China, and twenty-four boxes of Kraft Macaroni & Cheese was his single request from back home. That said, mac and cheese doesn't always have to be easy. In fact, when you think of mac and cheese—with roots going back to Thomas Jefferson's love for the Mornay sauce brought back from France to Monticello by his personal chef, a pioneering and deeply important African American man named James Hemings—it's a pretty impressive dish and a true classic. "Monticello became this hub, and really the first American culinary school, and people would send their cooks to learn from James and then go back to their plantations to cook," says Thérèse Nelson, a chef and founder of Black Culinary History. And a version of mac and cheese was certainly one of those dishes.

In the book of Daniel, the pasta of choice for unbaked mac is elbow macaroni. The small size and thin tube allow for the right amount of melty cheese to fill the inside and coat the outside. This is to say that he's not a big fan of the fancy pasta shapes mixed with squeeze cheese—save your rigatoni, shells, and radiatori for a more subtle cheese sauce that won't overwhelm the palate with oozing Wisconsin lava. If you opt to step it up a notch and get into the big-dog shapes, you'll want to swap out the American cheese for something drier, like Cheddar or Swiss. To build a typical mac and cheese, you start with béchamel sauce, made by whisking seasoned milk into flour cooked with melted butter to thicken it. Once your béchamel is thick and stable, you melt in your cheese. The process is fairly simple, unless, of course, you intend to bake it, which complicates matters a bit further.

Daniel and Matt agree that the ideal mac and cheese is the crispy-edged cube cut from a baking tray at a fried chicken joint or a southern meat and three restaurant. Baked mac is truly an art form, crispy on top and creamy in the center, with either a coating of bread crumbs or a righteous amount of cheese crowning the brick. This outcome is challenging because cheese doesn't like to rise above its boiling temperature. At 180°F, cheese starts to denature and break, and the milk protein and fat separate, turning your creamy sauce into an oily pool.

To make mac and cheese work requires twice cooking. After the cheese sauce is made and mixed with the cooked pasta, the dish is molded and cooled. Once set, the pan is baked in an oven hot enough to brown the top and crisp the sides before the center can overheat, breaking the cheese sauce. Daniel has laid out a plan with the recipe that follows to get you there. ●

friend of FOOD IQ

THÉRÈSE NELSON **is a New York City chef, food scholar, lecturer, and founder of Black Culinary History, an online resource tracking Black food history, past and present.**

How is mac and cheese a Black food in America?

I would consider it a huge part of the soul food tradition, which is a very particular distinction to make. Soul food refers to migration and cross-cultural influence, and what people found when they left their origins, in this case the South. The mac and cheese you are talking about is specifically the mac and cheese from the 1940s to the 1960s, a period when soul food became important in American cities.

Is soul food southern, then?

I have many debates about this, but soul food is really formed outside the South. It's about how you figured out home. It's the taste of home.

So why is this mac and cheese so delicious?

The recipe shouldn't really be right [laughing]. You are talking about a cream-based sauce, like Mornay sauce, with all this cheese and fat that only exists when it's hot. All the magic exists in that moment. It's like risotto in that way. But the code has been broken in the Black kitchen. People used evaporated milk and eggs and cream and created a new version.

Mac and cheese with eggs?

The egg is meant to stabilize, and it's used as a thickener, and the sauce in this version is an uncooked sauce that is combined with the cooked noodles and then baked. The egg serves almost like a custard and comes together in this Harold McGee-type alchemy.

And what's your favorite mac and cheese from a restaurant?

One of my favorite places ever was in Newark, New Jersey, where I grew up. It was called Je's, and [its mac and cheese] was creamier than any other restaurant's. It was less eggy, and it was made to order on the line. It wasn't cubed, and it was really creamy, but you always got a little crust on top. It was amazing.

CREAMY *AND* CRUSTY MAC AND CHEESE

Serves 8 generously

1 pound elbow macaroni

2 cups whole milk

2 eggs

2 tablespoons all-purpose flour

2 teaspoons kosher salt

½ teaspoon sweet paprika

½ teaspoon garlic powder

½ cup whole milk cottage cheese

10 ounces mixed grated cheese such as Cheddar, jack, mozzarella, and American

Mac and cheese is America's ultimate comfort food. Loved by children and adults alike, the rich and creamy texture is an unparalleled food feat. Baking the mac to get a browned, crispy, crusty outside requires some care. If the center heats past 180°F, the cheese sauce can break, and if that happens your mac will be a greasy mess.

1. Preheat the oven to 350°F.

2. Bring a large pot of water to a rolling boil over high heat. Add the macaroni and cook, stirring frequently, until fully cooked according to the directions on the package. Drain and reserve.

3. In a blender, mix the milk, eggs, flour, salt, paprika, garlic powder, cottage cheese, and mixed grated cheese and blend on high until completely incorporated (about 2 minutes).

4. In a large bowl, mix the cooked macaroni with the cheese sauce.

5. Pour the macaroni and cheese mixture into a 9-by-13-inch baking dish, spreading it evenly, then bake for 35 minutes.

6. Rest at room temperature for 15 minutes before serving.

Weekend Cooking Projects: Is the Juice Worth the Squeeze?

An all-day, or all-weekend, or even all-month cooking project can be a ton of fun. Without the correct preparation and planning, though, it can also turn out to be a frustrating and ultimately miserable waste of time. And, sure, sometimes cooking is more about the journey than the end result (said nobody!). In this final chapter, Daniel and Matt offer several slightly more complicated recipes and explain why they are actually worth the effort.

Is it worth making my own yogurt?

→ **HAVE YOU EVER SAT** around and thought about yogurt? How that carton of milk transforms into the thick (and, depending on your preference, much thicker!) morning (or afternoon or evening) hit of protein, sometimes dolloped over granola, sometimes spiked with cucumber and coriander for a raita, and sometimes blended with fruit into a smoothie or something baked. Yogurt is one of the most ancient and versatile dairy products around, and yes, you should make it at home, but you should also reach for it in the ever-expanding yogurt aisle in your local grocery store.

Yogurt is milk that has been fermented with specific bacteria (yogurt cultures) in a controlled environment. The process of making yogurt at home is actually quite simple and rewarding, and if you eat it daily, it can save you a fair bit of coin. Freshly made yogurt can be extremely delicious, but, as with anything made from milk, the quality of your outcome will rely directly on the quality of its underlying base ingredient: the milk. Whether you're souring cream for crème fraîche, coddling milk for cottage cheese, or making overnight yogurt for breakfast, you'll first want to find yourself a good-quality dairy to source from.

To start the process, you'll need a yogurt culture to ensure the correct bacteria are working on your dairy; there are a number of ways to get your hands on some. If you're the scientific type, you can source the pure stuff in either liquid or powdered form on the Internet or from a local brewing supply shop, and if you're the courageous type, you can make your own by curdling milk with a lemon slice, cardamom seeds, or chile stems overnight. But if you're the Daniel-and-Matt type, the easiest source of yogurt bacteria is yogurt itself. A tablespoon of plain cultured yogurt from the supermarket is enough to produce two quarts of homemade stuff overnight. And once you've made a batch, you can use it to make subsequent batches. It's a virtuous cycle indeed.

There are plenty of tools sold that claim to help make the process foolproof, and most will simplify the system to some extent. But before you reach for Amazon Prime, know that you can make yogurt with nothing more than a stainless-steel pot on your stove top. A thermometer will save you a lot of stress and guesswork (and, at this point in the book, you should probably already have one of those), so procuring one is highly recommended.

Once you've chosen your milk (be it sheep, cow, goat, or otherwise), you'll want to heat it up to cook off any harmful bacteria that will compete with the good bacteria you're trying to cultivate (in the dairy biz, they call this pasteurization). All you need to do is bring the milk to a boil and then simmer it for 15 minutes. Once done simmering, you'll cool the milk to 115°F, add your starter bacteria, cover the pot, and keep it warm (around 100°F)—and 8 to 10 hours later, you'll be rewarded with a truly delicious, thick and creamy batch of fresh yogurt. If you like extra-thick Greek-style yogurt, you can drain the yogurt in a colander lined with cheesecloth in the fridge overnight. So, you were wondering what makes Greek yogurt thick like that? Just draining regular yogurt—that's all.

The tricky part with making yogurt at home is keeping the batch consistently warm while the bacteria work their magic. You can usually find a good spot on top of the fridge, in the base of an old-school gas oven with the pilot light lit, or on or around the stove top. Place cups of water in a few choice spots, and check their temperature after a few hours to see if any work out. And if all else fails, this is where the specialty equipment can come in handy (which is certainly worth the cost if you're planning on making yogurt regularly). A few common cooking gadgets, like slow cookers and Instant Pots, have a yogurt setting that will hold temperature for you. •

friend of FOOD IQ

PRIYA KRISHNA is a prolific reporter, writing frequently for the *New York Times*, and the author of the cookbook *Indian-ish*.

You wrote a great column for *TASTE* called "The Country's Best Yogurt Column." Why write exclusively about yogurt?

It is my favorite food. Ever. Of all time. And it's one of the most interesting and underutilized foods in the United States today. I grew up with my dad making homemade yogurt for me, and I took it upon myself to be this yogurt researcher and go to the store and try all of these different brands, logging whether one had different creaminess, or one had different fat content, or one was made with cow's or goat's milk. I was always looking for the best.

How is yogurt used differently in India?

In Indian cuisine, you'll find yogurt in hot and cold dishes, desserts, and mains. It's used in a variety of ways. In the United States, you are seeing it as just yogurt and granola. Yet that is not to say things aren't changing. I wrote a piece about dairy-free yogurts that was really interesting. They actually taste good! I've also written about the tart frozen yogurt boom—and bust—that America imported from South Korea.

And you wrote a pretty amazing rant against nonfat yogurt. What's wrong with it?

I have a lot of strong feelings, but basically, unless I am in need of a substitute for spackling paste, you are not going to find me buying nonfat yogurt. It's like an Italian suggesting fat-free mozzarella.

HOMEMADE SHALLOT LABNEH

Makes 1½ cups

2 cups plain whole-milk yogurt

½ shallot, minced (about 3 tablespoons)

1 teaspoon kosher salt

Homemade labneh, a thick form of double-drained yogurt popular in Middle Eastern cooking, is actually one of the easiest recipes to prepare. It makes for a delicious snack served on its own with pita bread, works as a spreadable condiment for sandwiches or a creamy enricher dolloped in soups or over salads, and can be served alongside proteins like chicken or fish. If hanging the yogurt ball proves tricky in your modern, glass-shelved refrigerator, try putting the ball in a colander over a bowl. Once you feel comfortable with the technique, try substituting crushed garlic, spicy chiles, or honey for the shallots. You may be thinking, "This sounds a lot like Greek-style yogurt." You would be right and wrong. Labneh is thicker and creamier than the Greek yogurt found in supermarkets, plus the enzymes in the yogurt work to change the flavor profile of the shallots over time, creating a flavor that can't be accomplished otherwise.

1. In a bowl, mix together the yogurt, shallots, and salt.

2. To hang the yogurt to drain, drape four sheets of cheesecloth, stacked on top of one another, over a bowl. Pour the yogurt into the center of the cheesecloth, gather the corners, twist together, and tie with butcher's twine, closing the cloth around the yogurt to form a tight ball the size of a softball or a large orange.

3. Hang the ball of yogurt in the refrigerator, placing a container beneath it to catch the drippings, and leave it overnight. Once the labneh is ready, it will keep in a covered container in the refrigerator for up to 3 weeks.

What is sourdough, and what more is there to say about it?

→ **DANIEL AND MATT STARTED** working on this question early in the process of writing this book, before the world was shut down during a global pandemic that confined many to their homes to shelter in place, Zoom into the reality of working remotely, and, apparently, make sourdough. The spring of 2020 will be remembered for a lot of things, and one of them is "that time when America ran out of flour and active dry yeast, and everybody learned how to make sourdough bread." Books like Ken Forkish's seminal *Flour Water Salt Yeast* flew off the shelves, helping shepherd in the great sourdough expansion, with home cooks leaning in to naturally yeasted (for some, the only yeast available) breads. As this book is being wrapped up in late 2020, it's clear that sourdough had a moment, and that that moment may have shifted, for some, from expansion to exhaustion. But in the end, sourdough is, of course, here to stay.

Let's back up a few thousand years. Sourdough has been around for a very long time, with evidence of its existence dating back to 5,000 BCE. So it's safe to say that sourdough came before most foods we eat today, and that its current discovery is very much a rediscovery, not unlike the recent "discovery" of organic farming practices (see page 184). Sourdough isn't some new, hippie invention, and it certainly isn't centered in the region around San Francisco, where it's been promoted and celebrated dating back to the 1840s. Sourdough bread exists in one form or another in every corner of the world, from France's pain au levain to Mexico's birote and Ethiopia's injera. The explanation for its ubiquity is simple. Yeast exists everywhere (yes, literally everywhere), and if you leave a bowl of wet flour (or any moist organic matter) out at room temperature, it will begin to ferment. That is to say, the natural yeast in the air will settle on it and start feasting, converting sugars to gases and alcohol. When you add concentrated yeast, like the active dry variety from those supermarket packets, the process moves quickly, beating out any other bacterial growth. But natural yeast takes time, and during this time, other bacteria work in concert with the yeast, adding additional flavors, most notably lactic acid bacteria, which produce—wait for it—lactic (and acetic) acid. Thus, you have the sour flavor of naturally leavened (or, as we call it in the United States, sourdough) bread.

When given a second to catch your breath and think all this through, the process is absolutely mind-blowing. It's as close to alchemy as humankind has ever come. You, the home baker, are harnessing nature's elves, transforming boring flour and ever-present water into deliciously leavened bread. To begin making sourdough, you need to collect, concentrate, and grow yeast. You do this by leaving a simple dough of flour and water on your countertop, which collects and feeds the natural bacteria from the air. Each day, you add more flour and water to the bowl, feeding and growing the bacteria. Over time, a strong enough concentration of yeast will grow so the yeasty flour (by then called a "starter" or christened with a name that you give it) begins to expand and contract in a daily cycle. The whole process takes about two weeks before you can start baking bread.

Once you have your starter bubbling away, you can add it to recipes in much the same way you would include active dry yeast. It's really that simple—until it isn't. Because, of course, as with all artisan crafts, the more you learn, the more complicated things become. For the professional baker, naturally leavened bread can become a true art form. The Internet is littered with "crumb porn"—images of the photogenic gas pockets profiled in the cross section when the loaf is sliced. These pockets fill with gas and solidify, revealing themselves when cut. (Checking back through the authors' Instagram feed may or may not reveal a crumby post or two.) There's been a lot written about sourdough bread, and yes, it's one of the more challenging techniques to master. But don't be fooled by the complicated procedures and all those words spilled about the practice. Sourdough is fundamentally simple. •

FIVE-MINUTE ROSEMARY SOURDOUGH CRACKERS

Makes 24 crackers

100 grams sourdough starter

30 grams all-purpose flour

30 grams whole wheat flour

6 grams dark rye flour

2 grams kosher salt

18 grams extra-virgin olive oil

15 grams water

2 tablespoons chopped fresh rosemary leaves

1 tablespoon Maldon salt, caraway seeds, or poppy seeds for topping

Maintaining a sourdough starter is a virtuous circle. Each day (god willing), you use your starter to make bread, reserving a little bit of the starter to feed the next day's batch. On days when you don't intend to bake, you simply discard the portion of starter that would have been used to make dough for bread. Anyone who has grown and cared for a starter knows the deep pain associated with throwing away this brilliantly yeasty, flavorful concoction, so Daniel set out to develop a quick sourdough cracker recipe (with some help from his friend and colleague Erin Euser) to utilize the discard.

This recipe takes less than five minutes to prepare (plus fifteen minutes baking time), and it makes delicious, crunchy, whole-grain crackers worthy of your best cheese board or perfect for snacking. Matt originally pushed back on this recipe's inclusion. Why spend the time to bake a cracker when so many great crackers are sold in stores? Does making a cracker result in the same feeling as making homemade sriracha? That is, admitting that the big companies make it so much better that it's futile to attempt your own. But Matt realized he was so wrong about crackers after watching Daniel recipe test this one into the ground over several attempts, only to eventually rise from the ashes like a crispy, crunchy phoenix slathered with a soft tomme de Savoie.

1. In a bowl, combine the starter, the three flours, kosher salt, oil, water, and rosemary and mix to bring everything together into a rough dough.

2. Knead the dough in the bowl between your hands until smooth and homogeneous, about 2 minutes. Gather the dough into a ball, wrap in plastic wrap, and refrigerate for at least 4 hours or ideally overnight.

3. When ready to bake, preheat the oven to 350°F.

4. Lay a sheet of parchment paper on your work surface. Dust the chilled dough with all-purpose flour, place it on the parchment, and roll it out as thinly as possible into a rectangle. Dock the dough (punch little holes all over the dough with a fork or a special roller docker—like matzoh—to prevent it from rising). Using a fluted pastry wheel, cut the dough sheet into cracker-size pieces, each about 2 inches square. If you don't have a pastry wheel, a sharp knife or pizza cutter will work.

5. Mist the dough with water (if you don't have a mister, a pastry brush will work) and sprinkle evenly with the Maldon salt.

6. Carefully slide the parchment paper with the dough directly onto the rack of the preheated oven (it's easier to remove the rack with oven mitts and bring it to the crackers than attempt to bring the parchment with the dough to the oven). Using your fingers, encourage the paper and dough to sag between the bars of the oven rack, which will create a subtle vertical wave-like pattern in the crackers as they bake.

7. Bake the crackers, rotating the parchment back to front halfway through baking, until they turn golden brown, about 15 minutes. The timing will depend on how thinly you rolled them. Let cool completely on the parchment before packing them away in an airtight container (freezer bags work perfectly).

How do I make kimchi?

→ **THIS QUESTION TAKES MATT** back to a farm in rural Gangwon-do, a region of South Korea's extreme northeast where mountains meet the ocean. It was November, and Matt was there traveling with the chef Edward Lee, reporting a story as well as absorbing all things Korean that would end up in *Koreatown*. It was fall, which meant kimjang (kimchi-making season) was in full swing, and he and Edward (and, somewhat randomly, *The Hills* star Audrina Patridge—long story) were invited to a farm to see kimchi made in the most traditional way, which included more than seventy-five heads of brined napa cabbage being mixed and stuffed into a large kiddie pool by a crew of amazingly talented—and seriously rubber-gloved— women. It was an extremely badass way of making baechu kimchi, and the bar was set for all of his future autumnal kimchi making.

As Deuki and Matt wrote in their book nearly a decade ago (and have been preaching ever since), kimchi can be thought of more as a verb than a food item. It's a culinary technique that involves taking a vegetable, brining it, mixing it with spices (and sometimes other vegetables), and fermenting it for days, weeks, or even months in order to preserve it, extending the vegetable's shelf life while unlocking otherwise indigestible nutrients. The most common example, called khakdugi, is made with cabbage (배추) and white radish (무), but the uninitiated often refer to it by the name for the technique from which it is derived, kimchi.

To answer your other question: yes, you should make your own kimchi. Much of the stuff you find in glass jars at the grocery store, and in plastic containers at bodegas and vegetable markets, is pretty great—and if you find a source you love, stick with it. But making your own kimchi is a really fun project that allows you to witness a real transformation, harnessing the natural power of good bacteria to create something that can be valued well beyond the sum of its parts. Plus, next time you're at a Korean BBQ restaurant, you'll appreciate the hard work that went into that spicy and bracingly funky side dish you might have taken for granted in the past. Here are the key steps in the kimchi-making game.

Buying the cabbage

Look for napa cabbage that appears healthy and fresh, and remove the outer few layers of leaves if anything is browned. At Korean markets, the peeling away of blighted leaves is often done right in the store. The remaining leaves should be tightly packed. Kimjang aligns with napa cabbage season, which runs from October through December and is when the cabbage is fresh and packed with the most flavor. Cabbage is salted ahead of time using an overnight brine solution.

Paste and marinade

In kimchi making, rice flour paste is an important binder for the marinade, which includes an essential ingredient: salted fermented shrimp called saeu-jeot. While some recipes call for fish sauce, salted shrimp adds a pronounced flavor that is just too good to omit. Once combined with the cabbage (don't forget to wear gloves!) and stuffed into glass jars or plastic containers of varying sizes, the waiting game begins.

Kimchi is alive!

Kimchi is all about personal taste, and some like their kimchi fresh, while others like it older and funkier. A general suggestion is to make a large batch (use six to eight heads of cabbage) and store it in several jars to sample after different resting periods. But if you're new to the kimchi-making process, start small with this recipe and scale up later. After five days, pull out a small jar of kimchi and eat it wrapped in lettuce with some grilled marinated short rib (kalbi). After ten days, pull out another jar, and place it on the table to serve with bulgogi (grilled thin beef slices) or broiled mackerel (a Korean classic). Keep one jar in the back of your refrigerator for two months and then stew it down in a kimchi jjigae. ●

friend of FOOD IQ

ROY CHOI is a Los Angeles-based chef, cookbook author, and television host and producer. His Korean-Mexican taco truck Kogi is credited (by the authors and many others) with putting the Korean taco on the map.

How did we get to this point, with Korean food becoming so popular in America?

David Chang ripped the seams, forcing Korean food into popular culture. Good Korean food has always been here for people who knew food. Chefs in New York were eating at Korean restaurants in the 1990s, but you can't deny the impact of Momofuku. There were no American chefs serving kimchi, and it just wasn't cool. Dave cracked the door, then I stepped through it, and completely by accident. My goal wasn't to make Korean food cool. It was just to cook LA food. Trying to sell kimchi by intellectualizing it, with Korean ambassadors touting the health aspects, just didn't work. But give someone a kimchi quesadilla, and that's something they can get behind.

What is kimchi to you?

You can make kimchi out of anything. The cabbage version is the most famous, but there are hundreds of fruit and vegetable kimchis: strawberries, apples, radish, shiso, chives, onions, carrots.

How do I choose which Korean restaurant to try in my town?

Ninety percent of Korean restaurants are at least good, and a good way to judge is if they are storing stuff in the dining room, like boxes of ingredients in plain sight. It means they're too busy to put them away or find storage. That's a good sign. Then there's the first bite. If it's stale or old, it's not getting better from there. The first bite should be vibrant and delicious.

Where's Korean food going from here?

The first wave was straight immigrant food, then came the second wave of popularization with guys like David Chang. Then the third wave really legitimized Korean food, with Deuki Hong and restaurants like Cote and Atoboy educating people's palates. Who knows where the fourth wave will take us, but there is still a lot to learn. Korean food is very regional. If you want to taste Chungju bibimbap, you need to go there to taste the dish.

BAECHU KIMCHI

Napa cabbage is the king of all kimchi, and it will very likely be the kimchi emoji when that is eventually introduced. There are literally thousands of different kimchi recipes and combinations, all tied to the seasons. That said, this recipe from Matt's friend Deuki Hong (a version of which ran in *Koreatown*) is special. The less common ingredients, including the sweet rice flour, finely ground red chile flakes (gochugaru), and fermented shrimp, can be found at your local Korean market.

**Makes three
1-quart jars**

Cabbage

3 quarts water

1 cup coarse sea salt

1 large napa cabbage (2 to 3 pounds), quartered lengthwise

Rice Flour Paste

1 tablespoon sweet rice flour

½ cup water

Marinade

1 small white onion, roughly chopped

½ cup roughly chopped Asian pear

2-inch knob fresh ginger, peeled and roughly chopped

6 cloves garlic, finely chopped

4 fresh red Korean chiles, stemmed and halved lengthwise

¼ cup water

¼ cup salted fermented shrimp (saeu-jeot)

¼ cup sugar

½ cup rice flour paste (recipe above)

1 cup finely ground gochugaru

1. To brine the cabbage, in a large container, combine the water and salt and stir to disolve. Add the cabbage quarters and let sit at room temperature for 6 hours. This brining step both adds flavor and opens the pores of the cabbage, allowing the marinade to soak in. Remove the cabbage from the brine, rinse with cold water, and taste for seasoning. If you prefer it saltier, return it to the brine for another 6 hours or up to overnight. The saltiness is a matter of personal preference.

2. Once the cabbage is brined, make the rice flour paste. In a small saucepan, combine the rice flour and water, place over medium-high heat, and whisk continuously until the mixture comes to a boil. Then continue whisking until the mixture develops a pudding-like consistency, about 2 minutes. Remove from the heat, transfer to a heatproof container, let cool for a few minutes, and then cover and refrigerate until cold.

3. To make the marinade, in a blender, combine the onion, pear, ginger, garlic, chiles, and water and blend until smooth. Transfer to a bowl, add the salted shrimp, sugar, rice flour paste, gochugaru, green onions, carrot, and daikon, and mix well.

4. Drain the brined cabbage, rinse well with cold water, and place in a very large bowl. Using latex gloves, toss the cabbage with the marinade, coating it thoroughly. Transfer to clean, large glass jars or plastic containers with tight-fitting lids. You can cut the cabbage so it will fit more easily in the jars or plastic containers, or you can keep the leaves whole and pack them tightly. Affix the lids loosely so the fermenting gases can escape, and place the jars in a cool, dark, dry space and let them ferment for 1 day. Heads up: the fermentation process may cause some kimchi juice to bubble over, so place the jars on a sheet pan or in plastic bags.

1 bunch green onions,
green tops only, thinly
sliced

1 carrot, peeled and
grated on the large
holes of a box grater

½ cup coarsely grated
daikon radish

5. Refrigerate for 5 to 7 days, until the kimchi has reached your desired
level of funk. Kimchi will keep for up to 6 months in the refrigerator,
getting progressively funkier as it ages.

Is DIY canning really as scary as it sounds?

→ **CANNING** **IS THE CATCHALL** term used to describe the preservation of cooked food in a sterile environment. But canning is not relegated to the canned vegetable aisle. It encompasses tins of tuna, jars of tomato sauce, and jugs of shelf-stable juice (meaning they don't need to be stored in the refrigerator). While canning plays an incredibly important role in the commercial food world, the emotion built around canning at home is usually one of apprehension, and even a little fear. Are you going to kill your grandma with that ill-advised kitchen experiment? Possibly—although hopefully not after reading this.

Of course, canning sounds much scarier than it is. The process has been around for more than a hundred years, and you probably don't know too many people who have died from improperly canned food. That's not to say there aren't safety precautions to adhere to, but if you follow directions, there's a truly exhilarating hobby to discover. Daniel and Matt enjoy a solid weekend canning project, and you might, too.

The basic, back-of-the-napkin science around canning is this. Food goes bad when bacteria are given the opportunity to reproduce in it. When you cook food, you kill bacteria. If you cook food in a sealed can, you kill the bacteria inside, and no new bacteria can get in, so the food won't go bad. There's a little bit more science involved to ensure you're cooking the food long enough and at a hot enough temperature to actually kill the bacteria, but there's nothing so complicated that your great-great-uncle couldn't do it with a fireplace and a mercury thermometer—because he likely did.

The only other thing to keep in mind when considering canning is that acidity really matters. In case you don't remember high-school science class, here's a refresher. Everything has a different level of acidity on a scale from 0 to 14, called a pH scale, with 7 being neutral (water has a pH of 7). The more acidic something is, the lower its pH. Tomatoes are a little acidic, so they have a pH of 4, while lemon juice is more acidic and scores a 2. Anything lower, and you get into the caustic territory—the stuff they use to dissolve bodies in *Breaking Bad*. Traveling north of 7 on the pH scale, you get into your basic ingredients, like eggs and baking soda, but those don't really play a role in the world of canning.

Bacteria have a hard time living in acidic environments, so the lower the pH, the less time and the lower the temperature you need to cook things in order to ensure you've killed the bacteria. This matters to the home canner because, unless you intend to pressure can, which is an advanced technique mostly used for industrial applications, the highest your water temperature will get is 212°F (after which it boils and evaporates). And if you intend to can at 212°F, you'll need to keep the ingredients you're canning below a pH of 4.5—roughly the acidity of a tomato. Anything higher on the pH scale and the cooking temperature won't kill the bacteria. This is the reason why home canners tend to lean toward more acidic creations, like pickles and tomatoes, and less sweet and savory stuff. It's easy to lower the pH—you can drop green beans into vinegar or add a hit of lemon juice to your strawberry jam—but adding acid to meats will often ruin their flavor, so home canning lives in the fruit and vegetable kingdom.

One word—well, one scary word—of additional warning: botulism. This is the one type of bacteria that home canners are most concerned about, and the reason botulism is most associated with canning is that it's an anaerobic bacteria, meaning it doesn't require air to grow and can live in a sterile canned environment. That's why a bloated can is an immediate red flag and should be discarded, though in our modern times, there are thankfully very few cases of botulism.

So, what's the motivation for canning? We all know there are exceptional examples of canned foods available at a very low cost. Daniel and Matt have brought up canning in questions in the past, all the while acknowledging the amazing canned tomatoes, jams and jellies, and pickles available in the grocery store. Canning is like any other cooking habit. If you do it enough times, the process becomes more of a routine, so it's less an ordeal and more a fun afternoon distraction. You spot some amazing late-season strawberries at the farmers' market, and you decide to take them home for jam. ●

CANNED BRANDIED CHERRIES

Makes six ½-pint jars

4 quarts plus 1 cup water

1 cup water

1 star anise pod

1 cinnamon stick

1 teaspoon kosher salt

2½ pounds ripe cherries, stemmed and pitted

2 tablespoons fresh lemon juice

¾ cup brandy

Making brandied cherries is a great way to extend the tiny stone fruit's fleeting spring season, and the process is a quick and simple entry into the world of canning. The cherries are perfect for cocktails and adult dessert toppers; there's nothing that makes ice cream scream like a cherry on top. Daniel makes a big batch every spring and gives them out as gifts throughout the year. This recipe does call for patience, however. The cherries need to rest in their jars for at least two months before they reach their full, flavorful potential. After that, they will last for up to two years.

1. Pour 4 quarts of the water into an 8-quart stockpot and bring to a boil over high heat.

2. Meanwhile, in a 4-quart saucepan, combine the remaining 1 cup water, the sugar, star anise, cinnamon, and salt and bring to a simmer over medium-low heat, stirring until the sugar has dissolved, about 4 minutes.

3. Add the cherries, lemon juice, and brandy to the sugar mixture, turn off the heat, and let sit for 10 minutes. Then ladle the cherries and their cooking liquid into six ½-pint canning jars, leaving ½ inch headspace at the top of each jar. Following the manufacturer's instructions, close the jars with their lids.

4. Carefully lower the filled jars into the boiling water (a pair of canning tongs is an invaluable tool for this task). The water should cover the jars by at least 1 inch.

5. Return the water to a full rolling boil and boil the jars for 10 minutes. Then carefully remove the jars to a countertop and let them cool. If your jars have two-part lids, press against the center of the lid with a fingertip; if it remains depressed, the seal is good and the jars can be stored away in your pantry, where they will keep for up to 2 years. If the seal is not good, clean the rim of the jar, close the jar with a new lid, and repeat the cooking process to seal properly.

How do I make a delicious duck like the ones from the windows in Chinatown?

→ **DANIEL HAS BEEN VISITING** New York's Chinatown since he was very young, taking the 6 train down to Canal Street for Jewish Christmas banquets and knocking down a dozen char siu bao (steamed pork buns) with his brother and their dad. One of his favorite Chinatown dishes then, and to this day, is the lacquered duck often displayed in windows for all the passersby to see. It's a thing of beauty—the crisp, glazed crispy skin, dripping fat, and sweet dark meat all coming together in one bite. In New York, Wu's Wonton King and Peking Duck House offer some of the city's best versions, and with a generous BYOB policy, they have become a place for sommeliers and wine fans to bring their favorite bottles of Pinot Neros and Alsatian blancs to swap while snacking on duck skin. Daniel and Matt are here to say that, while the Peking Duck Restaurant Experience® can't be beat—served with the traditional steamed pancakes and sweet-tart hoisin sauce—there's also a great opportunity to make your own delicious duck at home for a dinner party or just for your family.

The dish dates back centuries to the royal court of China, and today, the breed of duck typically used for the dish is the American Pekin (sometimes called the White Pekin). Note that the name of the dish and the breed are unrelated, which is often a misconception. In a restaurant setting, the first stage of preparation is to blanch the duck for thirty seconds in a pot of boiling water seasoned with maltose syrup. The malt imbues the skin with a subtle sweetness and adds the necessary sugars to facilitate the deep caramelization for which the dish is known. Next, the duck is "blown," which is an essential step for achieving shatteringly crispy skin. In restaurants, using an air compressor and a hose, compressed air is blown through the cavity of the bird to separate the flesh from the skin so the thick layer of fat can render and drain.

The ducks are then hung overnight in the refrigerator to dry before being steam roasted, which melts the fat in their skin. The final step is basting the duck with hot oil to crisp the skin. In a home oven, dry roasting at a high temperature simulates this process of basting with hot oil. Daniel has made Peking duck at home many times, and while it's time-consuming, it is always worth the work. Five ingredients, an hour or so of prep time, and three days of waiting is all you'll need. But talk about a serious dinner party flex! ●

HOME-COOKED PEKING DUCK

Serves 3 or 4

4 quarts plus ¼ cup water

1 whole duck (preferably Pekin) with the head attached, about 5 pounds

⅓ cup maltose syrup or honey

¼ cup soy sauce

2 tablespoons kosher salt

¼ cup hoisin sauce

1 tablespoon five-spice powder

Peking duck has been roasted in China for centuries, and it's still a fixture in Chinese restaurants around the world. When brought into the home kitchen, it's a recipe that requires an eye for technique and a little patience. Although you probably can't pump air under the duck's skin, as is traditional in commercial kitchens, you can carefully work your fingers under the skin to separate it from the flesh. Peking duck is traditionally served with sliced cucumber and green onions, as well as pancakes and hoisin sauce, which can be purchased at an Asian market and many grocery stores.

1. In a large pot, bring 4 quarts of the water to a rolling boil over high heat.

2. While the water is heating, using your fingers and the back of a metal spoon, carefully separate the duck skin from the breasts and thigh meat, reaching in as deeply as possible while being careful not to tear the skin.

3. Working in a clean sink, rinse the duck inside and out with cold water. Then ladle the boiling water all over the outside of the duck to blanch the skin, turning the bird as necessary and trying not to pour any boiling water inside the cavity. Pat the duck dry with paper towels.

4. In a small saucepan, combine the maltose syrup, soy sauce, and the remaining ¼ cup water and heat over low heat until the mixture thins and is pourable (the consistency of maple syrup), about 5 minutes.

5. Season the duck inside and out with the salt. Then rub the cavity with the hoisin sauce and five-spice powder. Coat the outside of the duck with the maltose syrup mixture, working it evenly over all of the skin (this is sticky stuff, so it's best to don a pair of plastic gloves).

6. Place a wire rack in a baking pan and lay the duck, breast side up, on the rack. Refrigerate, uncovered, for at least 24 hours or up to 3 days. (If you have the room, it is ideal to hang the duck in the refrigerator using a metal hook or twine tied around the neck.)

7. To roast the duck, pour water to a depth of 2 inches into the bottom of a baking pan and set the pan on the bottom of your oven. Position the baking rack in the lower part of the oven. Preheat the oven to 325°F for 30 minutes.

8. Place a roasting rack in a roasting pan and place the duck, breast side up, on the rack. Working quickly so the steam doesn't escape, place the duck in the oven and roast for 30 minutes. Remove the pan from the oven, set it on the stove top, and let the duck rest for 30 minutes. Carefully remove the baking pan of water from the bottom of the oven and raise the oven temperature to 425°F.

9. Return the duck to the oven and roast until the skin is deeply browned and crisp, about 20 minutes. Let rest for 10 minutes before cutting.

Is making your own hummus worth it?

→ **EVERYBODY KNOWS THAT SUPERMARKETS,** bodegas, CVS cooler cases, and overpriced airport snack bars are flooded with a delicious chickpea spread labeled "hummus." It comes conveniently packaged in many sizes and flavors (from roasted garlic to everything bagel). Few people realize, though, that this stuff you buy in the supermarket barely resembles a traditional plate of hummus you would find throughout the Middle East and Mediterranean—in Lebanon, Israel, Egypt, Syria, and the West Bank.

Like so many consumer products, the "hummus" that is premade and packaged for the masses is a Frankenstein version, reengineered to lower production costs, increase shelf life, and appeal widely to the American palate. Are Daniel and Matt fans of Sabra? Sure, from time to time, they will scoop Sabra from that little cup with those little salty pretzel disks. Is Sabra actually hummus? You can be the judge.

In Arabic, the word *hummus* means chickpeas, and the industrialized version certainly has that going for it. Yes, there are chickpeas in there. Yet the full Arabic name of the dish is hummus bi tahini (or "chickpeas with tahini"), so the popular nickname conveniently leaves the second-most-important ingredient—tahini—out of the equation. Making hummus with little or no tahini is like making mashed potatoes without butter. You *can* make it that way, but are you really making mashed potatoes? The big issue is that many Americans think they don't like tahini. (The first time Daniel made hummus was at a French restaurant, and what he remembers most is that the recipe used a *lot* of olive oil, with chickpeas and a scant amount of tahini filling in the void.) Why is this so? Because up until recently, quality tahini made from sesame seeds that have been hulled, freshly roasted, and ground to a creamy, peanut butter–like consistency hasn't been available in the United States, and poor-quality tahini is just the worst—always bitter and sometimes even rancid.

So, if you want real-deal hummus, it's not only worth making your own but pretty imperative that you do. There's really just one catch: quality tahini can sometimes be tough to find in a local market. Unless you live close to a Middle Eastern supermarket, you'll probably have to order it online (more on that later), which brings us to the next challenge. Tahini is a perishable ingredient that relies heavily on the quality of its base and only ingredient: sesame seeds. These aren't commercially grown anywhere in the United States, meaning the tahini you find in your average supermarket is coming from overseas, and the quality and freshness varies greatly from brand to brand. That means, although some may disagree (this book's editor, Julie, included), you're likely better off with a container of Sabra hummus than gambling on an unknown source of tahini.

The best tahini is made from Ethiopian sesame seeds, which, when freshly milled, have an intensely savory and subtly sweet flavor and a silky smooth, creamy texture. This is worlds apart from the dusty and bitter canned supermarket stuff. In fact, when you've invested in good tahini, we recommend using it in many dishes: try it as a condiment for vegetables, in salad dressings, and as a flavor enhancer in sauces. Commercial hummus often substitutes oil for tahini to bump up the fat content, creating the rich, creamy texture we're familiar with. But without tahini, the product falls flat, lacking flavor.

So do yourself a favor and order a jar of good-quality tahini online. It's not overly expensive, and it will last for up to six months in the fridge. Philadelphia's Soom Foods is Daniel and Matt's favorite, with Karawan, Al Wadi, Seed + Mill, and Al Kanater all tying for a close second place. Once your tahini arrives, the fun begins. All you need to do is soak some chickpeas overnight with a little baking soda (the sodium bicarbonate raises the pH of the cooking liquid, helping break down the proteins, which will give your hummus an extra creamy texture) and get cooking. ●

friend of
FOOD IQ

YOTAM OTTOLENGHI is a London-based chef, restaurateur, columnist, and best-selling cookbook author.

Since you published the cookbook *Jerusalem* in 2012, hummus has become a monster in a great way. What is the current state of hummus?

I used to be very particular about hummus, and I had a clear idea of what it needed to be. Yet over the years, I kind of let go. Because people are going to do whatever they want to do with its name or recipe, and you've got zero control.

What about beet hummus and white bean hummus?!

So, white beans are different. If you just take white beans and puree them, you can get amazing stuff. If you add beet root to chickpeas, I don't think it's good. All that sweetness doesn't work for me, and also the color is off-putting. I like beets when they're concentrated; when they're starting to go pink, it's just wrong.

Let's talk about tahini. There are hummus recipes with a little bit of tahini, and ones with a lot. How important is tahini in the hummus recipe?

It is very important if you want to get the smoothest hummus. For beautifully aerated hummus, tahini is important. It's the best fat you can introduce to chickpea puree to get that luscious paste. In London, we have a hybrid way of mixing tahini and olive oil. You don't get that kind of level of smoothness, but it's a bit heftier; it's got a different characteristic. But I think for traditional hummus, it really kind of has to have tahini, and it also needs to be a really good tahini.

Settle the debate: Is hummus a meal, or is it a side?

You can have it both ways. You're going to say I'm diplomatic, but I love it as a side or a starter, and I also love a good lunch or late breakfast in the traditional Palestinian way, which is when you go and sit down at around ten o'clock and get warm hummus and pita bread, and often it's served with something like fava beans or egg or raw onion with olive oil drizzled on top. It's one of the best things you will ever eat.

HOMEMADE HUMMUS

Makes 1 quart

1 cup dried chickpeas

2 tablespoons baking soda

3 cloves garlic

Juice of 2 lemons

Kosher salt

¾ cup high-quality tahini

¼ cup extra-virgin olive oil

Pinch of sweet paprika

Making hummus from scratch is a cinch. It just takes a little planning. You need to soak the chickpeas for at least twelve hours in advance of cooking to ensure they cook through evenly. To simplify the process, Daniel usually just soaks them at room temperature overnight in the pot he's planning to cook them in. Once you've mastered the base, you can play with different toppings: roasted peppers, sautéed mushrooms and onions, and braised lamb with pine nuts are among Daniel and Matt's favorites.

1. In a pot, combine the chickpeas, baking soda, and water to cover generously (at least 6 cups) and let soak at room temperature overnight.

2. The next day, drain the chickpeas and return them to the pot. Add water to cover by at least 3 inches and bring to a boil over high heat. Lower the heat to a simmer and cook uncovered, skimming off the scum and skins that float to the top from time to time, until the chickpeas are extremely soft and just beginning to break apart, about 45 minutes. Remove from the heat and let the chickpeas cool completely in their cooking liquid, gently agitating them from time to time to loosen their skins and skimming off any skins that float to the top. (This step can be completed up to 24 hours in advance of making the hummus.)

3. While the chickpeas are cooling, in a food processor, combine the garlic, lemon juice, and 1 tablespoon salt and process until smooth. Let sit for 10 minutes. (The acid from the lemon stabilizes the garlic and stops it from producing any undesirable flavor. Thanks to Michael Solomonov for the technique.) Add the tahini and continue processing until smooth, light, and fluffy.

4. Once the chickpeas have cooled completely, drain them into a fine-mesh strainer and pick out and discard any skins that have separated from the peas. Add the chickpeas to the food processor and process until completely smooth, 3 to 4 minutes. Adjust the seasoning with salt and lemon juice if needed.

5. Transfer to a serving dish. Drizzle with the oil and top with the paprika for color.

Should I make my own tofu?

→ **DIY TOFU ISN'T JUST** a way to change your mind-set about the possibilities of tofu. It's also a really fun home-cooking project. Making warm, silky tofu from fresh soy milk is not all that different from making ricotta from fresh cow's milk. Like ricotta, you probably won't be making your own tofu all the time, but it's worth learning how—plus, the homemade version is unlike anything you'll find in a supermarket. Before you embark, it's important to keep in mind that you're not making the firm tofu you're used to dropping into a stir-fry (that requires a longer drying process in which the water is pressed out to form firm blocks). You're making more of a soft and creamy side dish, something to eat on its own, garnished with soy sauce, ponzu, or furikake. Homemade tofu is also great for the foundation of some of the best silken tofu dishes, including Korean soondubu jjigae or Sichuan mapo tofu.

So, should you make it? Yes! You should make it especially if you don't have access to a market or restaurant that makes it daily. Daniel ate fresh tofu growing up, sold for one dollar a block at a small Korean market around the corner from his apartment on the Upper East Side. And both Daniel and Matt, as longtime New Yorkers, came of age with tofu as a staple ingredient for all forms of cooking—bearing witness as the ingredient evolved with the rise of regional Asian cooking, bucking the hippie health-food stigma created by macrobiotic cooks at ashrams in the 1970s that was perpetuated by the macho chef culture of the early 2000s.

To make fresh tofu, you'll need fresh, unprocessed soy milk. You can find it in some health food stores or Japanese markets, but, as they say in the pharmaceutical trade, results may vary. So it's best to use the stuff you make yourself. To start, soak soybeans overnight in water, then blend and strain them to make fresh soy milk. Simmer the milk to cook out the raw, bitter flavor, then add nigari, a coagulant derived from seawater, to gather the proteins. Wait fifteen minutes, and voilà, your tofu is ready to drain. "Every time I do the coagulation step, it's like a mini miracle, and I'm fucking amazed," admits cookbook author Andrea Nguyen.

A by-product of the process is yuba, the skin that forms atop the soy milk as it cools. Yuba should be carefully pulled from the pot and reserved. It's a delicacy that can be fried, steamed, stuffed, or seared. •

friend of FOOD IQ

ANDREA NGUYEN is a James Beard Award-winning cookbook author and educator, having written definitive works about dumplings, pho, the bánh mì, and Asian tofu.

What's up with that tofu you buy in the box on the shelf of your grocery store?
I call that survival tofu. It's like apocalypse tofu. It's really weird stuff that is coagulated with glucono delta-lactone, so it's like a Jell-O and pretty devoid of flavor. But it's there, and you can chop it up and do your thing with it.

There's Asian tofu dishes and hippie tofu dishes—what's the difference?
Asian tofu allows for tofu and meat to be friends. Hippie tofu is about deprivation. It's about cooking tofu in really big cheese sauces. It's about pressing huge blocks of tofu for hours so the tofu will stay intact, because people are afraid tofu will fall apart. It's about masking the flavor of tofu and not letting it express what it is fully about.

How did you grow up eating tofu?
Deep-fried tofu with fish sauce and green onion, tofu stuffed with pork, mapo tofu, silken tofu pudding. It was all really good. So when I first ate tofu while living in Santa Cruz, I was shocked. It was covered with cheese. It was covered with crud and pretty disgusting.

FRESH SILKEN TOFU

Makes 1 pound

1 cup dried soybeans

8 cups water, plus 2 tablespoons

2 teaspoons nigari (found online and in Asian specialty markets)

Freshly made silken tofu is absolutely delicious. Many people who have only been exposed to the shelf-stable stuff found in supermarkets, or to bricks of tofu plopped into soups and stews in restaurants, think of tofu as something to add to a dish. But freshly made tofu is a dish unto itself, a delicacy worth the time and energy it takes to make it. Because making your own silken tofu is an investment of time, it's worth making a bigger batch. You can serve it warm, immediately after it coagulates, then drain whatever isn't eaten and refrigerate it, where it will last for up to two weeks.

1. The day before making your tofu, put the soybeans into a pot and rinse repeatedly with cold running water until the water runs clear. Leave the soybeans in the pot covered in water to soak overnight.

2. The next day, drain the soybeans. Line a fine-mesh strainer with cheesecloth and set over a bowl. Working in small batches, in a blender, blend the soybeans with the 8 cups water until it's a smooth texture, then strain through the prepared strainer, pressing against the solids to force out as much liquid—the soy milk—as possible. Reserve the liquid. Known as okara in Japan and kongbiji in Korea, the dry pulp in the strainer is an edible by-product of making soy milk. It will keep in an airtight container in the refrigerator for up to 1 week and can be used in stir-fries, baked goods, stews, or as a base for veggie burgers. It must be cooked before eating.

3. Heat the soy milk in a large stockpot over medium heat, stirring constantly. Skim and discard any foam that rises to the surface (soy milk has a tendency to boil over, so it's best to tend to the pot constantly during this stage). Once the liquid comes to a boil, lower the heat to a simmer and simmer for 10 minutes. Turn off the heat and let the soy milk cool to 180°F, about 10 minutes.

4. In a small bowl, combine the nigari and the remaining 2 tablespoons water and stir to dissolve. When the soy milk has cooled to 180°F, scoop off the skin that has formed on top (a delicacy called yuba that you should keep and use in stir-fries, stuffed, or simply eaten as is). Give the pot a good stir, then pour in the dissolved nigari, stir again, and let sit for 10 minutes to coagulate.

5. The tofu is now ready to be spooned out of the pot and eaten warm, or drained into a cheesecloth-lined fine-mesh strainer, transferred to a storage container, and refrigerated.

Should I brine all of my meat like I do the Thanksgiving turkey?

→ **BRINING IS THE ACT** of soaking meat in a seasoned (salty and sometimes sweet) water bath in order for the seasoning to penetrate deep into the meat. Brining is important, and in general, seasoning meat in advance of cooking is one of the basic steps toward improving your cooking. It flavors the cut, allowing the salt to migrate into the center over time, and it helps to protect it from overcooking. This is Daniel and Matt's big moment to say you should try to season all of your meat in advance. The results will honestly shock you, shock your dinner guests, and give you more confidence about cooking the cuts you may have spent $25—or even $200—on. As a rule of thumb, meat should be salted at around 1 percent by weight. So, 800 grams (around 1¾ pounds) of bone-in chicken thighs should get 8 grams (around 1½ teaspoons) kosher salt, and the seasoned meat should sit for a minimum of 4 hours per pound. The amount of salt you are holding in your palm for those four chicken thighs may feel like a lot, but resist the urge to hold back. Just resist it.

Each protein reacts differently to salt. Poultry, for instance, benefits greatly from seasoning at least twenty-four hours in advance (hello, brining the bird for that late-November food holiday), whereas a one-inch-thick beef steak tends to get a cured, "hammy" flavor and a rubbery texture when it's salted overnight. Next time you buy a whole chicken to roast, rub it down, inside and out, with kosher salt and let it sit in the fridge, uncovered, for twenty-four hours. You will taste the bite of proper seasoning, and it will be much moister. Please let this fact sink in for a second. Conventional wisdom would have you think that adding salt would *dry* out a cut of meat, but in fact, it's the opposite: the salt protects the proteins from overcooking, and overcooked meat is dry.

Brining is an effective means of seasoning, working more quickly and evenly than dry salting. Cells swap the water in the meat with the seasoned brine water through osmosis, literally pulling the salt into the center. When you dry salt a cut of meat, the exterior and the smaller bits, like the wings of a chicken or the ribs of a double-cut pork chop, tend to get oversalted before the center is seasoned. The effect is magnified with larger cuts of meat that require a greater volume of salt for longer periods of time. Wet brining, however, allows for a more even and consistent distribution of flavor, seasoning the entire cut with the same amount of saltiness.

The downside of brining is that the water tends to hydrate the skin and waterlog exterior fat, so you'll have a harder time getting that crunchy, crackling, crispy skin. And crispy, crackling skin is the holy grail of meat cookery, ya dig? In general, larger cuts, such as hams and turkeys, benefit from brining, while smaller cuts like whole chickens and pork chops should be dry salted. That said, which method you use is a matter of preference and something to be experimented with. Just remember that as long as you're seasoning in advance, you're ahead of the game. •

BOTTLED SALAD DRESSING IS THE BEST MEAT MARINADE.

Both Daniel and Matt have fond memories of steaks being marinated with bottles of grocery store salad dressing. Daniel's dad, John, was known to soak skirt steaks in Italian dressing before throwing them on the grill. Matt's grandma Gert made an amazing skirt steak that was marinated in Miracle Whip-brand French dressing and then braised in a slow oven. The sweetness of the dressing cut perfectly through the fatty meat. Why do these dressings work so well? They have the same fat, salt, and acid ratio as homemade or bottled meat marinades, including one of the most common marinades of all: barbecue sauce.

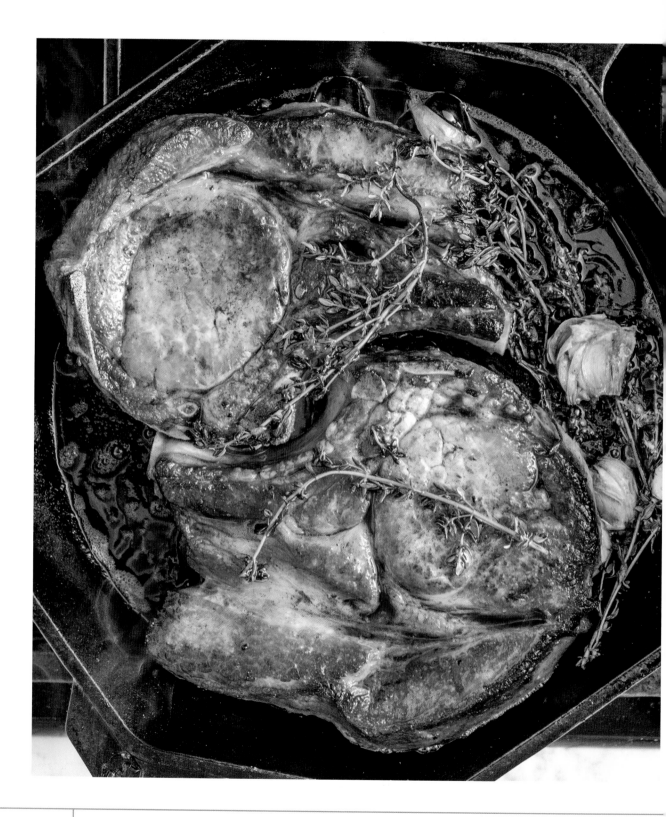

PERFECT PORK CHOPS

Makes 2 juicy pork chops

1 teaspoon black peppercorns

1 teaspoon coriander seeds

1 teaspoon juniper berries

2 bay leaves

½ cup kosher salt

½ cup light brown sugar

4 cloves garlic, smashed

6 cups water

2 thick-cut center-cut pork chops (about 1½ inches thick)

2 tablespoons vegetable oil

2 thyme sprigs

2 tablespoons unsalted butter

Rarely do you taste a home-cooked pork chop that rivals those from your favorite restaurant. The difference? It comes down to the brine. Pork chops are relatively lean–closer in fat content to a chicken breast than a steak. And by now, if you've been reading along, you know that lean meat tends to dry out when it's overcooked. Brining the chops for at least eighteen hours allows the salt and sugar to penetrate deep into the center of the meat, seasoning it and safeguarding it against overcooking. Large-scale butchery operations use specialty equipment like tumblers and injectors to speed up the process, but at home, there are no hacks or shortcuts–just good old-fashioned patience.

1. To make the brine, in a dry 4-quart stockpot, toast the peppercorns and coriander seeds over medium heat, stirring often, until they begin to darken and their fragrance makes itself apparent, about 3 minutes. Add the juniper berries, bay leaves, salt, sugar, garlic, and 3 cups of the water and bring to a simmer, stirring until the salt and sugar are completely dissolved.

2. Remove from the heat, add the remaining 3 cups water, and refrigerate the brine until completely cool.

3. Once the brine is cool, submerge the pork chops in the brine, cover, and refrigerate for at least 12 hours or up to 24 hours.

4. When ready to cook, preheat the oven to 375°F.

5. Remove the pork chops from the brine and pat dry with a paper towel. Discard the brine. Heat the oil in a cast-iron pan or a heavy-bottomed, oven-safe sauté pan over medium-high heat until just smoking. Carefully place the chops in the pan and cook for 1 minute, then transfer the pan to the oven and roast for 7 minutes.

6. To finish, return the pan to the stove top over high heat. Flip the chops, add the thyme and butter to the pan, and cook the chops, basting them with the melted butter, until sizzling and deeply browned, about 3 minutes. A quality thick-cut pork chop should be cooked to medium, not tough and well done. An instant-read thermometer inserted into the center of the chop away from bone should register 135°F, not 165°F as the FDA suggests.

7. Remove the chops from the hot pan and let them rest for 5 minutes before serving.

Should I make my own hot sauce?

→ **MAKING YOUR OWN HOT** sauce can be as simple as making a piri-piri sauce: dropping habaneros in white vinegar and letting them sit for a day. Making your own hot sauce can also involve a three-week fermentation involving fresh chiles, salt, a little bit of vinegar, and a lot of patience. Daniel has been making his own hot sauce in late summer for years and years, and early in their hanging-out-and-eating-food relationship, Daniel gifted Matt a bottle of his fermented-Fresno-chile-based, Holzman's not-so-hot sauce, which was actually pretty hot and extremely delicious, balanced and fruity and perfectly salty, opening Matt's eyes to the flexibility of the DIY pepper condiment. That fall, Matt would text Daniel about all of the ways he used the hot sauce—on scrambled eggs, drizzled on corn tortillas topped with melted cheese, atop cottage cheese.

Hot sauces are locked into every culture, from Mexico to Malaysia, and Daniel and Matt are not going to front like there aren't incredible bottled versions you can easily buy at the grocery store. With Tabasco, Crystal, Louisiana brand, and Tiger Sauce, the state of Louisiana alone is home to a murderers' row of piquant condiments. Yet there's something special, and extremely fun, about making your own. It starts with the exceedingly flavorful chile pepper, which you can source from your local farmers' market or easily buy at Whole Foods.

Chile season stretches from late summer through autumn, with different peppers ripening throughout. It's important to keep in mind that the heat level is only one of the considerations. Chiles have incredibly nuanced and varied flavor, and some lend themselves better than others to sauce making. The habanero has an intensely fruity and floral taste, the cascabel is more nutty and earthy, and Fresnos are mild and tart. You'll want to source your chiles at the height of their seasonal ripeness, which is a plug for shopping at your local farmers' market, where you can get to know the farmers and ask them to steer you in the right direction. Once the chile is selected, choose your direction. You can simply steep the peppers in salt and vinegar, roast and blend them with herbs or nuts, or ferment them.

Daniel is of eastern European descent, and he likes to say that he's not built for ingesting hot sauce that scores high on the Scoville scale. He loves hot sauce, but hot sauce doesn't always love him back. The solution of building a hot sauce from milder chiles can limit your ability to select for optimal flavor. But remember that the heat of a chile is concentrated in the seeds and surrounding white pith, so if you prefer a milder result, try removing some or all of the pith and seeds before processing the chile. ●

HOLZMAN'S NOT-SO-HOT SAUCE

Daniel developed this not-so-hot hot sauce recipe for maximum flavor with minimum spice using Fresno chiles, jalapeño's tamer red cousins that are widely available in the late summer. Feel free to use whatever chiles you prefer, customizing the heat to your liking. Making your own sauce is extremely rewarding, but the process takes time, so it's worth making a big batch. If you start during the height of early autumn chile season, your bottles will be ready just in time to be holiday stocking stuffers. For newbies, the world of fermentation can be frustrating; it's often hard to tell if anything is even happening. The key is patience. Fermentation takes time, and there's nothing to do but wait. Daniel promises: it's working.

1. Cut a slit in each chile to allow the brine to penetrate, then pack them into two 1-quart canning jars (or pasta sauce jars work well). Add the garlic, dividing the cloves evenly between the jars. **continued →**

→ continued

**Makes twelve
5-ounce jars**

500 grams Fresno
chiles, stemmed

25 grams garlic cloves
(about ½ head)

100 grams kosher
salt, plus 70 grams to
finish

2 quarts hot water

125 grams (½ cup)
distilled white vinegar,
plus 250 grams (1
cup) to finish

2. To make the fermentation brine, in a large bowl, whisk the 100 grams salt into the hot water, dissolving it completely. Add the 125 grams vinegar and whisk to combine. Ladle the brine into the jars, covering the chiles and garlic completely but leaving at least ½ inch headspace. The headspace is important, or the brine will bubble over the rim when the fermentation begins. It is also important to keep the chiles and garlic fully submerged in the brine. Otherwise, they can grow mold, which will ruin the hot sauce. Packing the chiles tightly into the jar will help hold them in place, but if they insist on floating, cut out a round from a plastic to-go soup container lid or a plastic milk bottle and wedge it into the jar to hold them down.

3. Cover the jars with their lids, but do not screw them tight. The fermentation process produces gas that will need to escape. Leave the jars out at room temperature to ferment for 5 to 7 weeks (the time needed for the process depends on the temperature and will take 5 weeks at 75°F but up to 2 months if your house is cooler). After a few days on the countertop, you will notice small bubbles forming at the surface, signifying the beginning of the fermentation process. The bubbling will continue until all of the sugars have been eaten by the yeasts. Fermentation is finished when all of the bubbling has ceased. Leaving the peppers for longer can't hurt, so err on the side of extra time, and don't worry if the garlic turns blue or a white film gathers on the surface of the brine. So long as dark, fuzzy mold doesn't grow, the fermentation process is working perfectly.

4. Once the fermentation process has ceased, drain the contents of the jars, reserving the liquid. Pack the chiles and garlic into a blender, adding back just enough of the liquid to cover them by 1 inch (discard the rest), then blend on high speed until completely pulverized and pureed, about 10 minutes. Add the remaining 70 grams kosher salt and 250 grams vinegar to the blender and blend on high speed for an additional 5 minutes.

5. Pour the pureed hot sauce back into the jars, cover loosely with the lids, and return to the countertop for a secondary fermentation. The sauce will separate overnight, and the solids will fall to the bottom of the jar. Each day, tighten the lid on each jar and shake vigorously to mix. Then loosen the lids and let rest overnight. Repeat the process of shaking the sauce daily until, after 8 to 10 days, the sauce no longer separates overnight.

6. Divide the sauce among twelve 5-ounce jars and cap tightly. The sauce is stable at room temperature for up to 2 months, but it will last for up to 3 years in the refrigerator.

What's the secret to great fried chicken?

→ **FRIED CHICKEN IS A** food that has taken on mythical energies—sometimes shrouded in secrecy, with histories furthered by tales of clandestine spice blends and techniques passed along from father to son, and sometimes taken to the grave when that father and son had a poorly timed falling out. Daniel and Matt love a good food yarn, and there's no better one than the origin story of Nashville hot chicken, which involves a cheating man, a crafty woman with revenge on her mind, an extremely hot sauce, and a chicken that has been so fully absorbed into pop culture that it has its own potato chip flavor—the real sign of a foodstuff with legs.

For Daniel, fried chicken should be analyzed in two parts: the chicken and the crust. Some places pay way more attention to the crust: the crunchy outer layer that leads to the tender, well-seasoned meat. Others seem to prioritize applying flavor to the meat through rubs and brines. The flavor of the meat, in fact, can sometimes transcend the crunch of a perfectly fried thigh. In Daniel's mind, a proper southern fried chicken is never, ever, ever dry. The meat is moist and extremely flavorful.

And the secret to moist and flavorful meat? A multiday stint in a marinade of buttermilk and salt, time enough for the enzymes in the buttermilk to tenderize and the salt to migrate to the interior. Oakland chef Kyle Itani soaks his chicken for three days, adding potato starch to the marinade, for his famous Hopscotch buttermilk fried chicken served with soba biscuits. The best fried chicken Matt ever tasted was at chef Asha Gomez's now-closed Atlanta restaurant Cardamom Hill, which was brined for a few days in a unique puree of buttermilk, ginger, serrano chiles, cilantro, mint, and twenty garlic cloves. The chicken was served with waffles and some maple syrup spiked with coriander and cumin. The key to both of these chickens, as well as Daniel's recipe, is patience and planning.

Now, there is more than one way to fry a chicken. Deep-frying and pressure frying are methods often utilized by the professionals, and there's nothing wrong with investing in a basket setup if you have the space. But the classic technique is the shallow fry, which is also the easiest to execute in a home kitchen (save the cleanup—be warned that your stove will be covered with a heavy mist of chicken grease). To shallow fry, you add enough oil to a cast-iron pan to reach halfway up the chicken parts when they're carefully lowered into the crackling hot oil. The chicken is cooked on one side first, then flipped to cook and crisp the second side. Shallow frying is a bit more difficult than deep-frying, but it requires no special equipment, and many southerners will argue that it's the only legitimate way to fry a bird. ●

FORTY-EIGHT-HOUR MARINATED BUTTERMILK FRIED CHICKEN

Serves 4

1 (3½-pound) whole chicken, cut into 8 pieces (2 thighs, 2 drumsticks, each breast halved)

Kosher salt

4 cups buttermilk

1 tablespoon sweet paprika

1 tablespoon garlic powder

3 teaspoons freshly ground black pepper

4 cups vegetable oil

2 cups all-purpose flour

½ cup cornstarch

While frying chicken, the ability to manage the heat is critical. If the oil is too hot, the flour will burn before the chicken cooks, and if it is too cool, the crust will be soggy and greasy. Maintaining the oil between 350° and 375°F vaporizes the moisture as it cooks, ensuring a long-lasting crispy crust. Using a deep-frying thermometer that clips to the side of the pot will take a lot of the guesswork out of the equation. And if you're wondering how the pros do it, they use a thermometer, too, so it's nothing to be ashamed about.

You'll want to adjust the temperature throughout cooking, raising the heat when you first add the cool chicken, then tapering it off throughout the cooking process as the oil heats back up. Remember that there's a significant lag between when you adjust the heat and when the temperature change registers on the thermometer, so be patient and make small adjustments as you go.

1. In a large bowl, season the chicken pieces with 2 tablespoons salt, cover, and refrigerate for 1 hour.

2. Add the buttermilk, paprika, garlic powder, and 1 teaspoon of the pepper and mix thoroughly. Cover and refrigerate for 48 hours, turning the chicken every 12 hours to marinate evenly (a large ziplock plastic freezer bag is ideal for this).

3. When ready to cook, set a wire rack on a sheet pan to use for draining the cooked chicken. Heat the oil in a large Dutch oven or other large, heavy-bottomed pan over high heat to 375°F. The oil should be about 2 inches deep.

4. In a large bowl, stir together the flour, cornstarch, the remaining 2 teaspoons pepper, and 1 tablespoon salt. You'll need to fry the chicken in batches to avoid crowding the pan. One at a time, lift the chicken pieces from the marinade, allowing the excess to drip off, then toss them in the flour mixture, coating completely and shaking off the excess, and carefully lower, skin side down, into the hot oil. (Adding the chicken too quickly can cause the hot oil to boil over, so work slowly and carefully, adding one piece at a time.)

5. Cook the chicken until golden brown on the skin side, about 10 minutes. Then, using tongs, flip the pieces and cook for an additional 10 minutes. Transfer the chicken pieces to the draining rack and season each piece with a pinch of salt. Repeat as necessary until all of the chicken is cooked. Serve warm.

Should I make my own jam, jelly, or marmalade?

→ **DANIEL HAS LONG BEEN** obsessed with the magical alchemy of preserving foods the old-fashioned way: canning, dehydrating, candying, pickling, and fermenting writ large. He loves it all, as you've likely noticed by now in reading the questions in this book. He views jam, jelly, and marmalade no differently. You put in the time, and the marriage of fruit, sugar, and pectin will produce something extraordinary, worth far more than the sum of their parts.

The big difference between these three forms of spreadable fruit is the inclusion or exclusion of pith, peel, and pulp. In general, jam is unstrained and includes the pulp. Jelly, on the other hand, is strained, using just the juice. Marmalade is a little more complicated. It's like jelly for grown-ups, made from citrus juice (no pulp), but with the addition of the fruit's candied rind for sharper flavors (it's sometimes spiked with Scotch whisky) and formidable texture. Marmalade has some die-hard fans, mainly across the pond in the United Kingdom, and an afternoon dive into marmalade Reddit is worth a read.

The unifying ingredient in all three is pectin, a plant-based jelling agent that thickens the fruit juice or puree and gives the spreads their, well, spreadable texture. Some fruits, like plums and quinces, have enough pectin to jell on their own, but for most, you'll need to add powdered pectin to aid in thickening. Not to overcomplicate things, but there are two types of pectin: one that works in concert with sugar and heat to thicken fruit, and another that works with calcium. Sugar-based pectin is more widely available and slightly cheaper, but it requires an exorbitant amount of sugar and must be heated to 210°F in order to fully thicken (this is why jam is often so sweet). Calcium-activated pectin (sometimes labeled "low-sugar pectin") is harder to find and a little more expensive, but it enables you to thicken jams and jellies with less sugar and minimal heat.

Whichever direction you go, one word to the wise: mix your pectin and sugar into the fruit while the fruit is cold. If you add powdered pectin to already hot fruit, it will clump into pesky little granules that are impossible to remove or dissolve, ruining your afternoon project.

Another popular option is called freezer jam. Traditionally, jam is cooked in order to break down the cells and mix the ingredients. Enough sugar and acid are added to preserve the product, then it is sealed in an airtight jar, where it sits, shelf-stable at room temperature, until duty (that is, your slice of toasted sourdough) calls. Cooking blueberries and peaches has its merits, but it also changes their color and flavor profile. Cooking fruits like watermelon, cantaloupe, and bananas is out of the question, which is why you never see these fruits in the preserves aisle of your supermarket. For freezer jam, you dissolve the sugar and pectin in your fruit juice or puree and then—as the name implies—you freeze it. Because the method is relatively fast and doesn't require any special equipment, it's easy to make small batches, plus it alleviates the food-safety concerns that accompany pressure canning.

The process for making freezer jam is simple: (1) Cut and mix your fruit and sugar in the top of a double boiler over boiling water until the sugar is completely dissolved. (2) Dissolve pectin in water and bring to a boil. (3) Mix the pectin with the macerated fruit. (4) Freeze until ready to consume. (5) Thaw and enjoy. The next time you have a pint or two of strawberries that are passing their prime, whip up a quick batch of freezer jam. You'll be happy you did. ●

APPLEJACK JELLY

**Makes twelve
6-ounce jars**

3 cups sugar

2 tablespoons
calcium-activated
pectin (Daniel prefers
Pomona's brand)

1 teaspoon calcium
powder (comes with
low-sugar pectin)

2 quarts fresh
apple cider (bottled
juice works but has
significantly less
flavor)

¾ cup Laird's
Applejack

¾ cup fresh lemon
juice

1 teaspoon kosher
salt

Sterilizing Query

Laird & Company is America's oldest distillery, and it has been producing applejack, the American version of a French apple brandy called calvados, in New Jersey for more than three hundred years. Traditionally, apple jelly is made by stewing apples, then pressing the pulp to extract the juice and pectin. But starting with the juice and then adding in pectin simplifies the process significantly. Every fall, Daniel goes apple picking and juices the fresh, tart apples to make jelly. If you're planning to juice your own apples, you'll need start with 30 percent more juice than you'll need, as fresh juice produces a lot of scum that must be skimmed from the top as it heats.

1. In a saucepan, whisk together the sugar, pectin, calcium powder, and apple cider, then bring to a simmer over medium-low heat, stirring continuously until all of the solids have dissolved.

2. Add the applejack, lemon juice, and salt to the simmering cider and cook for 6 minutes.

3. Ladle the hot cider mixture into twelve 6-ounce jars, leaving 1 inch headspace at the top of each jar. Following the manufacturer's instructions, close the jars with their lids. The jelly will be ready to serve as soon as it has cooled. If your jars have two-part lids, press against the center of the lid with a fingertip; if it remains depressed, the seal is good and the jars can be stored away in your pantry, where they will keep for up to 1 year. If the seal is not good, the jelly will keep in the refrigerator for up to 3 weeks.

Should I cure my own meat, and won't that maybe kill me?

→ **THE ORIGIN OF THIS** question isn't necessarily Daniel and Matt's love of breaking down the thrilling world of nitrates v. nitrites (spoiler: it's actually pretty cool). It's more that, from years and years of professional cooking, Daniel has witnessed many customers (and friends) question whether a sausage was fully cooked because of its pink center. The paradox is that, while all sorts of cured sausages give plenty of folks pause, rarely do people think twice about biting into a cold hot dog straight from the pack. We've all been there.

So why the rosy center on the Hebrew National? It all comes down to nitrites, called curing salts, which are used to rapidly dehydrate proteins so they can last longer. In addition to adding a very distinct pinkish color, they present a specific "hammy" flavor associated with cured meats. You likely know the flavor well, but maybe you haven't thought about it twice. Nitrates are like the _100_ of saltiness, but they also play an essential role in cooking.

When you salt-cure a piece of meat without nitrites, the technique requires a whole lot more salt, often producing an overly salty outcome. Also, the color shifts over time to an unappetizing shade of gray. But with nitrites, the meat color is locked in and stays pink over long periods of time—and the process requires only about a tenth of the salt. So the color is better, and the flavor is more palatable.

Curing salts come in two forms: nitrites straight up, and nitrites with the addition of nitrates—labeled Prague Powder #1 and #2, or Instacure #1 and #2, respectively. (When Daniel first told Matt about these substances, he thought it was spelled "Prog Powder," which was the working title for his _Yes_ tribute podcast.) Instacure #1 is mostly used for cooking applications, like hot dogs, bacon, and ham. The addition of nitrates gives Instacure #2 a head start in dehydration, and it's mainly used for raw, cured applications, like salami and coppa.

You might be thinking by now, "But aren't nitrites and nitrates super unhealthy?" Over the years, there have been links between nitrites and cancer, and some producers have sold tube steaks without nitrites (at the time of this writing, Whole Foods has a ban on selling anything containing the ingredients). But, per the authors' research, the jury is still out on whether eating nitrites in moderation is a good or a bad thing—and we suggest you form your own opinion.

For the home cook, playing around with nitrites and nitrates can be a lot of fun. (You didn't think this was possible, did you?) It can allow you to transform basic cuts of meat into your own DIY charcuterie board. Does DIY charcuterie sound dangerous? Well, isn't that half the fun of a weekend cooking project? In all seriousness, this is advanced-level stuff, and a failed project has the potential to put you in harm's way, so make sure to follow all recipes to the letter. When you cure something, you're taking the water out of it. Nitrites and nitrates advance the speed and intensity of the dehydration—drying the meat faster than harmful bacteria can proliferate. The potential downside would not only be consuming raw meat if you fail to stick the landing on the curing time but also ingesting too much of a dehydrating agent.

If you're interested in delving into the world of curing, it's best to start simple, with whole-muscle preparations like cooked ham or raw coppa. These will save you the added complication of grinding, mixing, and casing, which can be a little overwhelming and harder to monitor. In time, you can graduate to the salamis and mortadellas of the world. Just remember, working with cooked products is absolutely easier and safer than raw preparations. What follows is a recipe for Daniel's 120-hour cured ham. It's an easy entry into the world of cured meats, and you'll be shocked by how incredibly delicious the outcome is. Indeed, few things are more satisfying than frying a thick slice of your own home-cured ham.

FOOD IQ

120-HOUR HONEY-BAKED HAM

1 (6-pound) boneless ham roast

½ cup kosher salt

1 teaspoon Instacure #1

1 cup honey

1 teaspoon ground cloves

Curing meat, be it sausages, dried salumi, or country ham, takes time and patience, and there's simply no rushing the process. You see those 120 hours in the title? That is not a joke. But there's nothing like the rush of satisfaction you get from making that long-awaited first cut and confirming that the meat cured properly and is absolutely delicious. The transformation is truly astounding: a few teaspoons of Instacure and some patience completely change the color, texture, and flavor of a couple pounds of meat. However, to arrive at that end point, you must heed these warnings: Be extremely careful when working with curing salts not to taste the raw seasoning. And make sure to follow the guidelines for curing time, as eating unprocessed curing salts has serious health risks, including the distinct possibility that you will drop dead.

All warnings aside, curing your own ham is a weekend culinary project worth tackling at least once in your life as a home cook. It will result in not only an extremely delicious ham but also a greater appreciation for the ham makers around the world, from Yunnan to Youngstown.

1. Put the ham roast into a large plastic freezer bag, add the salt, Instacure, honey, and cloves, and seal the bag closed. Then massage the bag to mix and coat the roast thoroughly with the seasonings. (Warming the honey in the microwave for 30 seconds with the metal lid removed will make it easy to pour and measure.)

2. Refrigerate for 5 days, massaging and rotating daily.

3. When ready to cook, remove the ham roast from the freezer bag and rinse it under cold running water for 5 minutes.

4. Pour water to a depth of 1 inch into a baking pan, place the pan on the bottom of your oven, and then preheat the oven to 275°F.

5. Set a roasting rack in a roasting pan and place the ham on the rack. Bake until an instant-read thermometer inserted into the center of the roast registers 165°F, about 2¾ hours. Check your ham from time to time during cooking for color; if it begins to darken and burn before coming up to temperature, tent the ham with aluminum foil for the remainder of the cooking time.

How do I grow my own sprouts?

→ **ARE WE REALLY CLOSING** the first volume of *Food IQ* with a question about sprouts? You might think it's a bit anticlimactic, and more than a bit hippieish. But you should hear Daniel out on this one. Daniel pushed hard for this question, and it's great that he did. Daniel's mother was a big sprouter, and growing up, he learned about not just the health benefits but also the extremely cool ways sprouts can be worked into home cooking. Sprouts are fun. It's a gentleman-farmer vibe in the friendly confines of your refrigerator. And unlike growing your own mushrooms, which can't produce enough to compete with what you can buy in the grocery store, growing your own sprouts actually has a lot of utility to it.

Have you ever wondered why you don't see that many sprouts at the grocery store? You've got nine types of apples and seventeen types of citrus for your choosing, but only one small box of mung bean sprouts hidden in the corner. This is because sprouts have a very short shelf life—only a few days—making them a difficult product for stores to inventory and sell without suffering spoilage and loss. But just because you can't find them in your local supermarket doesn't mean you shouldn't be cooking with them.

You can pretty much sprout any seed (vegetable, legume, flower, or grain) if you have the proper growing environment. There are a number of different methods for sprouting (check out sproutpeople.org for all the latest and greatest recipes, gadgets, and lively conversation), but basically, all you have to do is soak, rinse, and wait, and the seeds will sprout on their own. One of the easiest methods requires only a small cloth sack, in which you first soak your lentils or radish seeds for twenty-four hours and then you hang over the sink.

A quick daily rinse will keep your "garden" moist and active, and within four to five days, your sack will be brimming with fresh, edible sprouts.

Sprouts vary widely in flavor and size, from crunchy three-inch mung beans to fiery, spicy, hair-fine mustard. They can be grown from pumpkin, sunflower, chive, mustard, and chia seeds (of the famous pottery that grows). In the end, growing sprouts is extremely rewarding, adding a moist crunch to a burger, a crispy punch of flavor to a salad, or a satisfying mild respite to a bowl of spicy soup. •

SPROUTED CHICKPEA FALAFEL

Makes 24 falafel

2 cups dried chickpeas

2 quarts water

1 cup packed fresh parsley leaves

½ cup packed fresh cilantro leaves

½ cup chopped fresh dill sprigs, tough stems removed

1 small onion, roughly chopped

6 cloves garlic

2 teaspoons kosher salt

1 teaspoon freshly ground black pepper

1 tablespoon ground cumin

1 tablespoon ground coriander

Vegetable oil for deep-frying

2 tablespoons sesame seeds

2 tablespoons chickpea flour

1 teaspoon baking powder

Homemade Shallot Labneh (page 287) for serving

Homemade Hummus (page 305) for serving

Warmed pita for serving

Making fresh falafel is an undertaking on its own, even without the added time and planning necessary to sprout the chickpeas in advance. But trust Daniel and Matt when they tell you that if there's one long and tedious recipe in this book that is absolutely worth the time and energy it will take, then freshly made falafel is a strong contender. Sprouting the chickpeas adds a subtle sweetness and unparalleled ethereal texture that's unattainable by simply soaking dried beans. And the addition of plenty of fresh herbs both delivers bright flavor and turns your falafel a beautiful, vibrant green.

1. Rinse the chickpeas, then place in a bowl, add the water, and soak at room temperature overnight. The next day, drain the chickpeas, transfer them to your sprouting bag, and hang them over your kitchen sink. Alternatively, put the chickpeas in a colander, set the colander in a bowl, cover the colander with a moist towel, and put the whole setup in a cool, dark place. Rinse and drain the chickpeas every 8 hours, returning them to their sprouting container until the sprouts grow a ¼-inch tail, 3 to 5 days.

2. Working in batches, combine the sprouted chickpeas with the parsley, cilantro, dill, onion, garlic, salt, pepper, cumin, and coriander in a food processor and pulse to grind and blend everything into a wet, mealy dough the texture of rough sand. As each batch is ready, transfer it to a bowl.

3. Cover the bowl and refrigerate the mixture overnight.

4. When ready to cook, pour the oil to a depth of 4 inches into a heavy 4-quart saucepan and heat over medium-high heat to 375°F on a deep-frying thermometer. Line a platter with paper towels and set it near the stove.

5. Add the sesame seeds, chickpea flour, and baking powder to the falafel mixture and mix to incorporate. Cook a small tester falafel in the hot oil, then taste and adjust the seasoning with additional salt as needed.

6. Working in batches of eight pieces, scoop heaping tablespoons of the mixture and flatten them gently. Resist the urge to roll the dough between your palms into perfect spheres. You want to retain as much of the rough and grainy natural texture of the falafel mixture as possible, which will crisp into a crunchy coating when fried. Carefully lower the falafel balls into the oil and fry until they are a deep golden brown, about 4 minutes. When the falafel are ready, using a slotted spoon or spider, transfer them to the towel-lined platter to drain.

7. Serve the falafel warm with the labneh, hummus, and pita.

EPILOGUE

→ **THE COVID PANDEMIC CHANGED** many aspects of our lives, from the way we work to how we pass the time—through endless Netflix, NBA League Pass, and maybe a Han Kang or Sally Rooney novel thrown into the mix. We've learned to communicate through boxes and black mirrors, and we've watched more CNN this year than in all previous years combined (including George W. Bush's wars, 9/11, and *Parts Unknown* every Sunday). We've also, as a society, pushed our home cooking into new territory.

Before the pandemic, the kitchen was at the back of the mind for many, far from being seen as a source of entertainment through sourdough bread baking, Dalgona coffee swirling, and shaking all sorts of interesting things atop freshly popped popcorn. In 2020, we moved to new homes, lusted over larger ovens, and bought knives, pans, grills, smokers, woks, pour-over coffee makers, sous vide machines, salad spinners, air fryers, and spices, sauces, rubs, salts, and high-quality mayonnaise—all with the goal of improving our cooking. Many of us did, in fact, get better at cooking. And while many of the same frustrations exist (limited counter space, too many recipes, too tired to care), the interest in cooking at home has never been greater. Everybody has a favorite recipe or food photo to share from their large victories and small struggles.

In 2020, cookbook sales were at their highest levels in a decade. And there's never been a better time to scan YouTube, Instagram, and TikTok for interesting cooking videos from the most unexpected places. (There was also fighting on Twitter about cast-iron pans, which got a little heated around month ten of the lockdown.)

This is all to say that we—Daniel and Matt—see you out there, and we hope that *Food IQ* is arriving to a healthier and slightly happier society—one in which restaurants are open for business (maybe you can visit Daniel at his new pizzeria in Los Angeles), but also where home cooking has gained even more momentum. And with that momentum, you've read and cooked through these one hundred questions with abandon, but you're also—Bourdain callback—hungry for more.

First, we sincerely thank you for reading. Second, we're busy working on another hundred questions, answers, and recipes, and we want to hear from you. Visit our website, thefoodiq.com, and send us an email with the question you most want answered. We'll write you back with our quick take, and possibly we'll dive into it in greater detail in the next book. Thank you again for reading. Happy cooking.

Spring 2021

ACKNOWLEDGMENTS and THANK YOUS:

→ *FOOD IQ* **COULD NOT** have been written, edited, copyedited, photographed, designed, illustrated, marketed, sold, and later creased, splattered, debated, discussed, highlighted, and splattered some more, without the support of a great many people. But that all starts with you, dear reader of this book—and the asker of so many great questions along the way. It's your deep enthusiasm for home cooking, and your thirst for food-culture knowledge, that allowed us to write a book tackling so many cool topics. This is also to say: Do you have a question? You can always reach out to us: @chefholzman and @mattrodbard. The next chapter of *Food IQ* is in the works.

Specifically, we'd like to mention a few important people. This book would not have happened without the incredible support and creativity from the team at Harper Wave. Our editor, Julie Will, is the best in the business, and she supported our vision from day one. Thanks to Emma Kupor for keeping an eye on all the fine print (there's so much fine print when writing a book!), and for the support from Leah Carlson-Stanisic, Yelena Gitlin Nesbit, and the crack marketing, publicity, and production teams.

Our designer, Lizzie Allen, is a rising star, and we feel so lucky to have collaborated with her in such a fun and vibrant way. It's pretty simple: Whatever Ed Anderson photographs looks cool and full of life and promise—even a raw cow's tongue. Thank you, Ed! Katie Watson's diligent recipe testing and photo-shoot styling really saved the day. Miguel Villalobos drew all the drawings in the book, and we love Miguel for doing that. Thank you to Amelia Ayrelan Iuvino for reading our first and second drafts (and third and fourth, in many cases). You saw things we couldn't see, and we cannot thank you enough. Thanks to Sharon Silva for putting the book through a very fine strainer.

Our agents, Eve Attermann at WME and Angela Miller at Folio Literary Management, are amazing, and they offered the best notes two hardheaded guys could have asked for. Thanks to Josh Bider at WME; Casey and Howie Kahn at FreeTime Media.

DANIEL WOULD LIKE TO THANK: All of the contributing chefs and home cooks who helped develop, test, and contribute.

MATT WOULD LIKE TO THANK: Apple Computer, Google Docs, Adobe, Zoom (for real, thank you, Zoom). Thank you, Talia Baiocchi, Tatiana Bautista, Anna Hezel, and all of my amazingly talented colleagues at *TASTE* and *PUNCH*. And thank you, Lorena Jones and Aaron Wehner at Ten Speed/Crown for the continued support and encouragement. Thank you, Neil Russo, for the incredible creative support, and my family in Michigan, New Jersey, and Virginia. Thank you, Rick and Cheryl Rodbard. You raised a very good eater. And, most of all, thank you to my wife, Tamar Anitai, for supporting, and for allowing me to crunch on crisp autumn apples and carrots in a small Brooklyn apartment with only minimal feedback. That is love.

Finally, thank you to all the experts, chefs, journalists, and passionate food folks we spoke with to help us answer these 100 questions. There are too many of you to list here, but your time and knowledge is greatly appreciated.

INDEX

ABOUT THE AUTHORS

DANIEL HOLZMAN is the founder-chef of the Meatball Shop restaurants in New York City and coauthor of *The Meatball Shop Cookbook*. A sought-after educator and recipe-writer, Daniel has been published in the *New York Times*, *Saveur*, and *TASTE* and has appeared in countless broadcast segments on shows such as *Today*, *Good Morning America*, *CBS This Morning*, *The Tonight Show*, *The Martha Stewart Show*, and *Anderson Cooper 360*.

MATT RODBARD is the founding editor in chief of the James Beard Award-winning online food magazine *TASTE* and the coauthor of *Koreatown: A Cookbook*, a *New York Times* best seller. He has been published in the *New York Times*, *Wall Street Journal*, *Bon Appétit*, *Saveur*, *GQ*, *Travel + Leisure*, and *Lucky Peach*. Matt was the host of the *TASTE* Podcast featuring interviews with thought leaders in food and media.

DANIEL HOLZMAN started his cooking career at the age of fifteen at Le Bernardin in New York City before attending the Culinary Institute of America with a full scholarship from the James Beard Foundation. In 2010, he opened The Meatball Shop on New York City's Lower East Side, which now boasts locations in Williamsburg, the West Village, Chelsea, the Upper East Side, and Hell's Kitchen, and he is the coauthor of *The Meatball Shop Cookbook*. Daniel has appeared frequently in the media, including on *Good Morning America*, the *Today* show, and *The Tonight Show with Jay Leno*, and has been featured in an array of publications, such as the *New York Times*, *Food & Wine*, *Saveur*, *People*, *Food Network Magazine*, and *GQ*. He lives in Los Angeles.

MATT RODBARD is the founding editor in chief of the James Beard Award-winning online food magazine *TASTE* and the coauthor of *Koreatown: A Cookbook*, a *New York Times* bestseller. He has been published in the *New York Times*, the *Wall Street Journal*, *Bon Appétit*, *Saveur*, *GQ*, *Travel + Leisure*, and *Lucky Peach*. Matt is the host of the *TASTE Podcast*, featuring interviews with thought leaders in food and media.